summer blonde

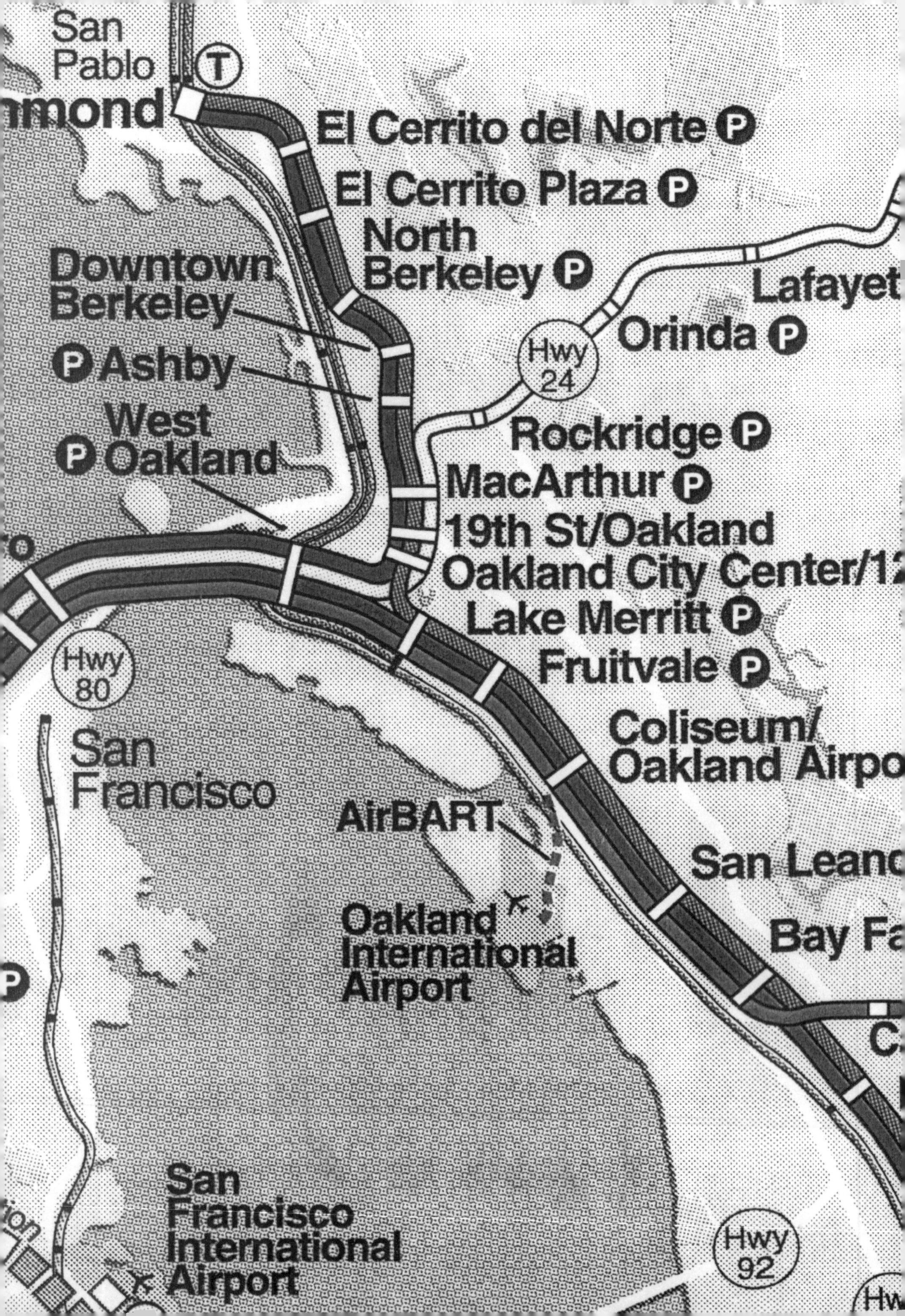
San Pablo
T
nmond
El Cerrito del Norte P
El Cerrito Plaza P
North Berkeley P
Downtown Berkeley
P Ashby
West Oakland P
Lafayet
Orinda P
Hwy 24
Rockridge P
MacArthur P
19th St/Oakland
Oakland City Center/12
Lake Merritt P
Fruitvale P
Hwy 80
Coliseum/ Oakland Airpo
San Francisco
AirBART
San Leand
Oakland International Airport
Bay Fa
P
San Francisco International Airport
Hwy 92

summer blonde

FOUR STORIES BY

ADRIAN TOMINE

DRAWN & QUARTERLY PUBLICATIONS

montreal

ALSO BY ADRIAN TOMINE

32 Stories
Sleepwalk and Other Stories

The stories presented here were originally published in issues five through eight of Adrian Tomine's comic book series *Optic Nerve*.

First Softcover Edition: June 2003
ISBN 1-896597-57-2
Printed in Hong Kong.
10 9 8 7 6 5 4 3 2 1

Drawn & Quarterly
P.O. Box 48056
Montreal, Quebec
Canada H2V 4S8
www.drawnandquarterly.com

Publisher: Chris Oliveros
Publicity: Elizabeth Walker

National Library of Canada Cataloguing in Publication Data
Tomine, Adrian, 1974-
Summer Blonde : four stories / Adrian Tomine.
ISBN 1-896597-57-2
Regular hardcover edition: ISBN 1-896597-49-1
Signed and numbered hardcover edition: ISBN 1-896597-50-5
1. American wit and humor, Pictorial. I. Title.
NC1429.T66S86 2003   741.5'973
C2003-901620-X

Distributed in the USA and abroad by
Chronicle Books
85 Second Street
San Francisco, CA 94105
(800) 722–6657

Distributed in Canada by
Raincoast Books
9050 Shaughnessy Street
Vancouver, B.C. V6P 6E5
(800) 663–5714

Original artwork available at:
www.comicartcollective.com/tomine

To
Itaru & Shizuko Ina
and
Susumu & Tomoe Tomine

CONTENTS

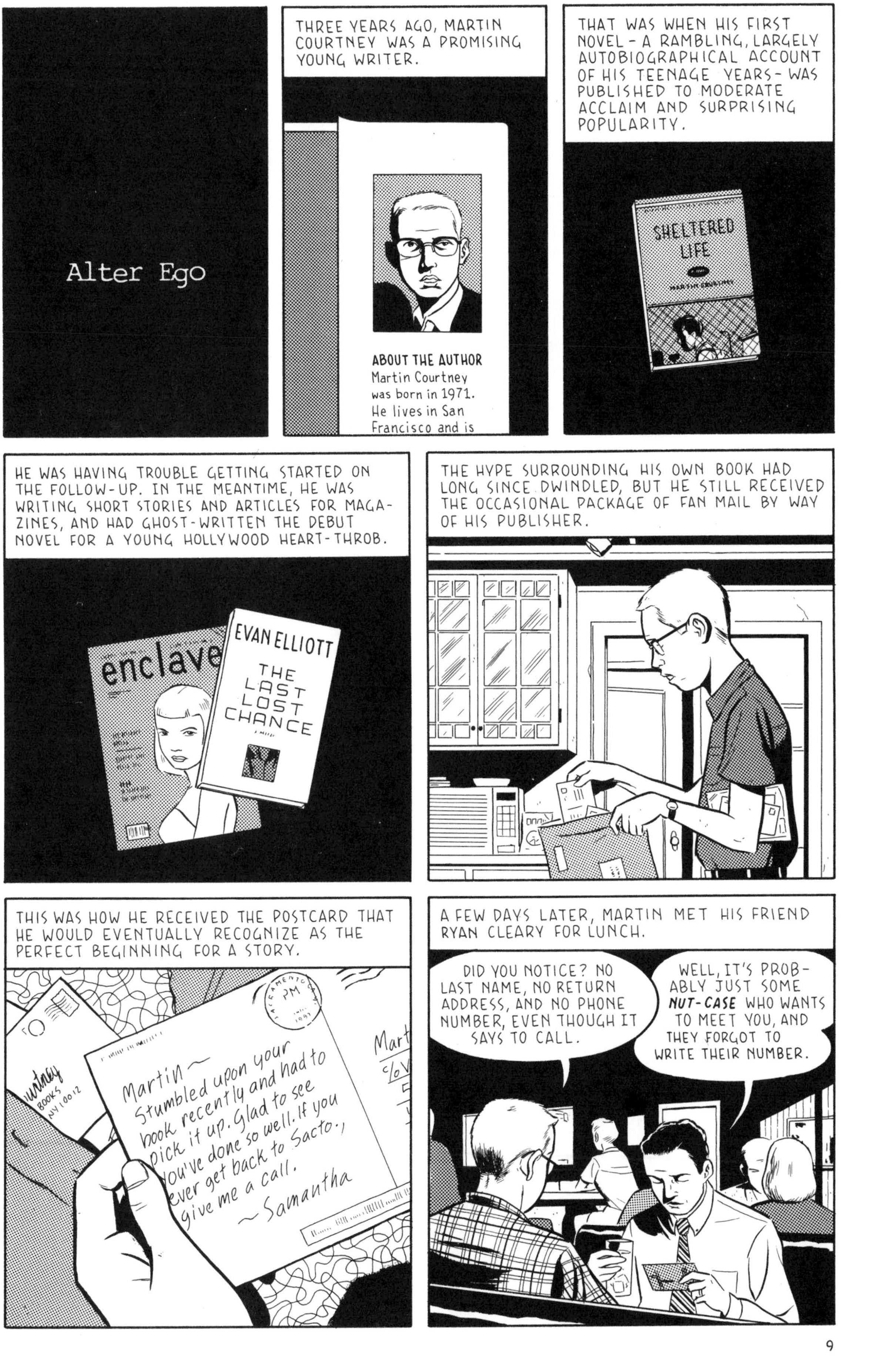
Alter Ego
THREE YEARS AGO, MARTIN COURTNEY WAS A PROMISING YOUNG WRITER.
ABOUT THE AUTHOR
Martin Courtney was born in 1971. He lives in San Francisco and is
THAT WAS WHEN HIS FIRST NOVEL - A RAMBLING, LARGELY AUTOBIOGRAPHICAL ACCOUNT OF HIS TEENAGE YEARS - WAS PUBLISHED TO MODERATE ACCLAIM AND SURPRISING POPULARITY.
SHELTERED LIFE
HE WAS HAVING TROUBLE GETTING STARTED ON THE FOLLOW-UP. IN THE MEANTIME, HE WAS WRITING SHORT STORIES AND ARTICLES FOR MAGAZINES, AND HAD GHOST-WRITTEN THE DEBUT NOVEL FOR A YOUNG HOLLYWOOD HEART-THROB.
enclave
EVAN ELLIOTT
THE LAST LOST CHANCE
THE HYPE SURROUNDING HIS OWN BOOK HAD LONG SINCE DWINDLED, BUT HE STILL RECEIVED THE OCCASIONAL PACKAGE OF FAN MAIL BY WAY OF HIS PUBLISHER.
THIS WAS HOW HE RECEIVED THE POSTCARD THAT HE WOULD EVENTUALLY RECOGNIZE AS THE PERFECT BEGINNING FOR A STORY.
Martin ~ Stumbled upon your book recently and had to pick it up. Glad to see you've done so well. If you ever get back to Sacto., give me a call. ~ Samantha
A FEW DAYS LATER, MARTIN MET HIS FRIEND RYAN CLEARY FOR LUNCH.
DID YOU NOTICE? NO LAST NAME, NO RETURN ADDRESS, AND NO PHONE NUMBER, EVEN THOUGH IT SAYS TO CALL.
WELL, IT'S PROBABLY JUST SOME NUT-CASE WHO WANTS TO MEET YOU, AND THEY FORGOT TO WRITE THEIR NUMBER.

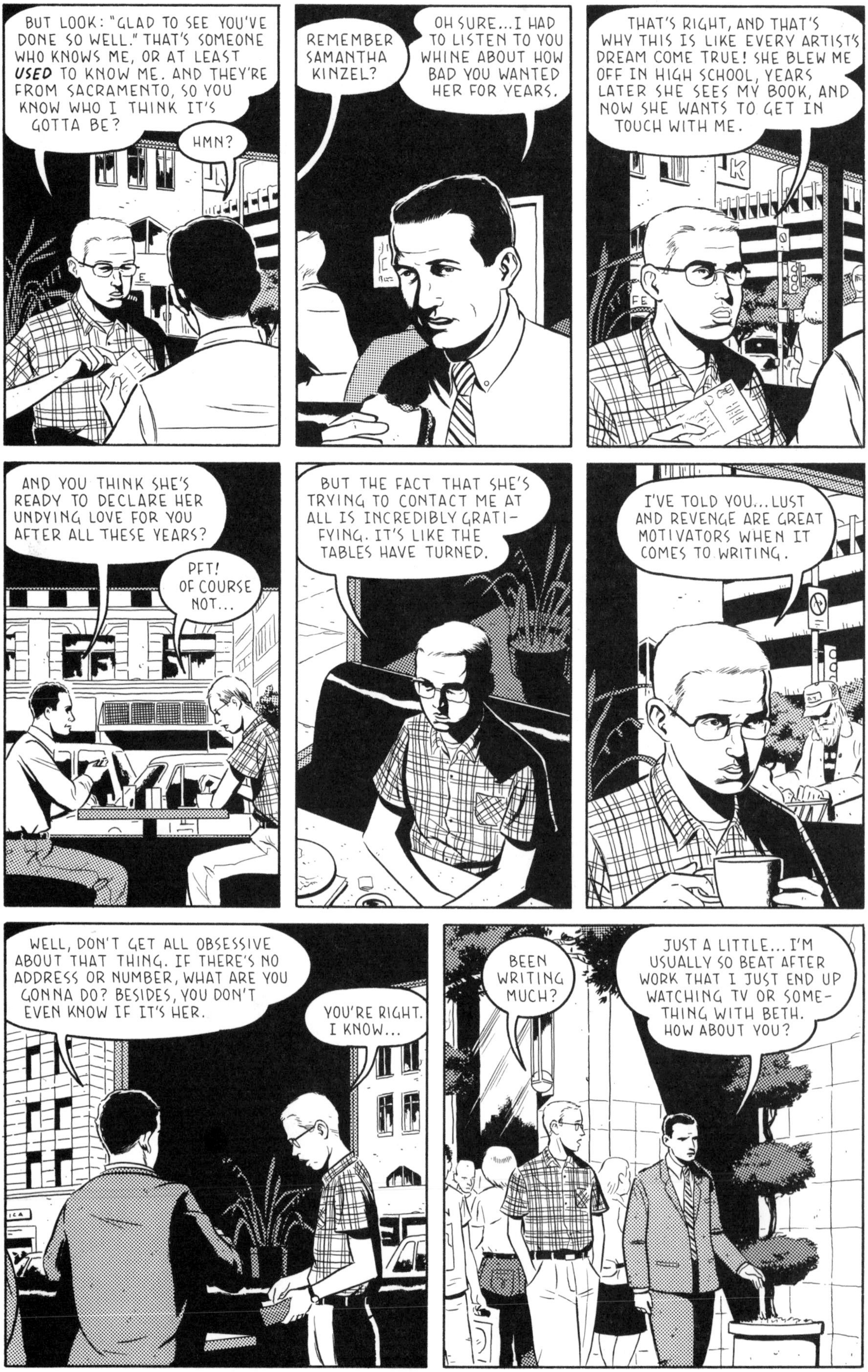
BUT LOOK: "GLAD TO SEE YOU'VE DONE SO WELL." THAT'S SOMEONE WHO KNOWS ME, OR AT LEAST *USED* TO KNOW ME. AND THEY'RE FROM SACRAMENTO, SO YOU KNOW WHO I THINK IT'S GOTTA BE?
HMN?
REMEMBER SAMANTHA KINZEL?
OH SURE... I HAD TO LISTEN TO YOU WHINE ABOUT HOW BAD YOU WANTED HER FOR YEARS.
THAT'S RIGHT, AND THAT'S WHY THIS IS LIKE EVERY ARTIST'S DREAM COME TRUE! SHE BLEW ME OFF IN HIGH SCHOOL, YEARS LATER SHE SEES MY BOOK, AND NOW SHE WANTS TO GET IN TOUCH WITH ME.
AND YOU THINK SHE'S READY TO DECLARE HER UNDYING LOVE FOR YOU AFTER ALL THESE YEARS?
PFT! OF COURSE NOT...
BUT THE FACT THAT SHE'S TRYING TO CONTACT ME AT ALL IS INCREDIBLY GRATIFYING. IT'S LIKE THE TABLES HAVE TURNED.
I'VE TOLD YOU... LUST AND REVENGE ARE GREAT MOTIVATORS WHEN IT COMES TO WRITING.
WELL, DON'T GET ALL OBSESSIVE ABOUT THAT THING. IF THERE'S NO ADDRESS OR NUMBER, WHAT ARE YOU GONNA DO? BESIDES, YOU DON'T EVEN KNOW IF IT'S HER.
YOU'RE RIGHT. I KNOW...
BEEN WRITING MUCH?
JUST A LITTLE... I'M USUALLY SO BEAT AFTER WORK THAT I JUST END UP WATCHING TV OR SOMETHING WITH BETH. HOW ABOUT YOU?

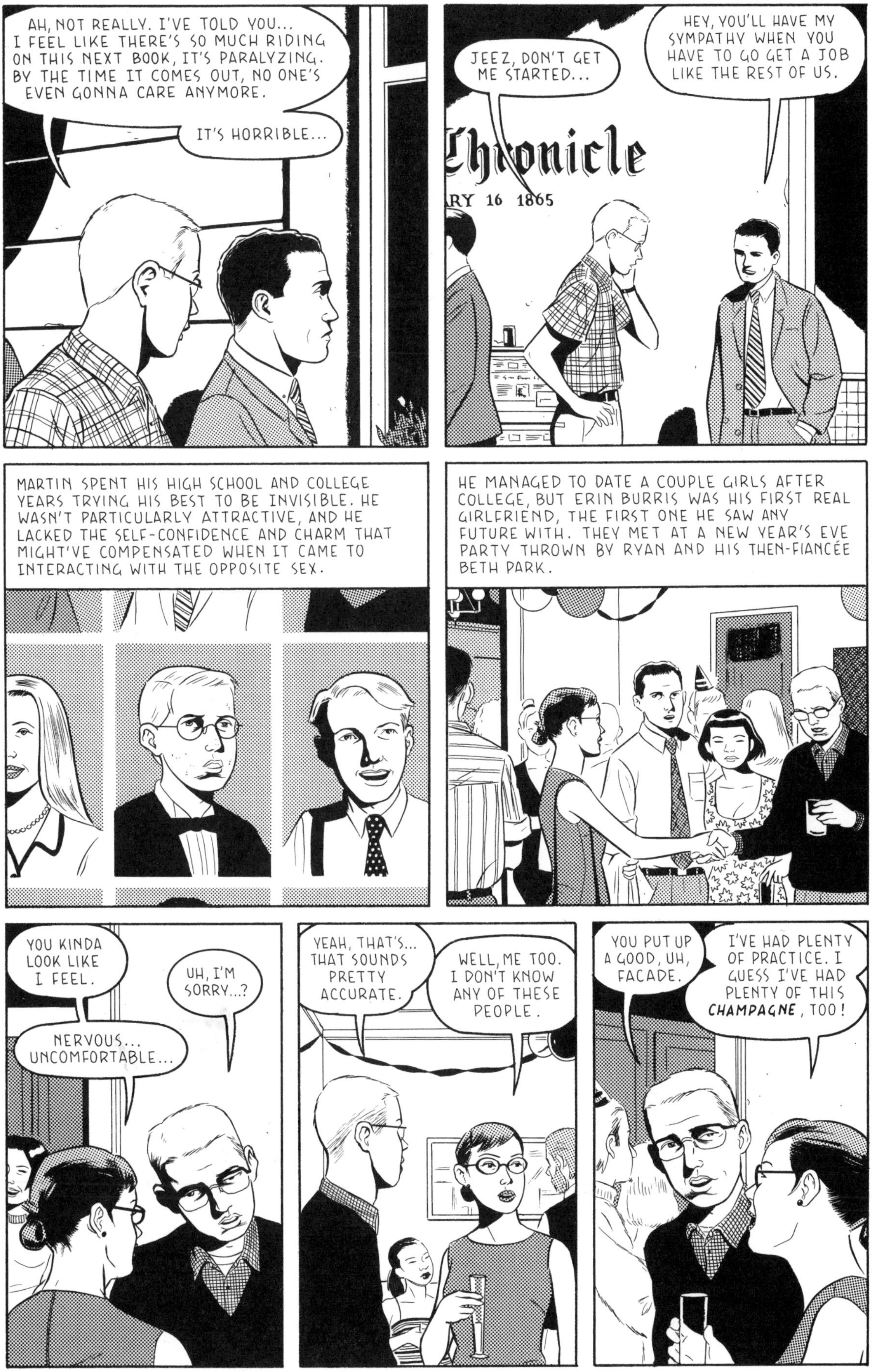

AH, NOT REALLY. I'VE TOLD YOU... I FEEL LIKE THERE'S SO MUCH RIDING ON THIS NEXT BOOK, IT'S PARALYZING. BY THE TIME IT COMES OUT, NO ONE'S EVEN GONNA CARE ANYMORE.
IT'S HORRIBLE...
Chronicle
RY 16 1865
JEEZ, DON'T GET ME STARTED...
HEY, YOU'LL HAVE MY SYMPATHY WHEN YOU HAVE TO GO GET A JOB LIKE THE REST OF US.
MARTIN SPENT HIS HIGH SCHOOL AND COLLEGE YEARS TRYING HIS BEST TO BE INVISIBLE. HE WASN'T PARTICULARLY ATTRACTIVE, AND HE LACKED THE SELF-CONFIDENCE AND CHARM THAT MIGHT'VE COMPENSATED WHEN IT CAME TO INTERACTING WITH THE OPPOSITE SEX.
HE MANAGED TO DATE A COUPLE GIRLS AFTER COLLEGE, BUT ERIN BURRIS WAS HIS FIRST REAL GIRLFRIEND, THE FIRST ONE HE SAW ANY FUTURE WITH. THEY MET AT A NEW YEAR'S EVE PARTY THROWN BY RYAN AND HIS THEN-FIANCÉE BETH PARK.
YOU KINDA LOOK LIKE I FEEL.
UH, I'M SORRY...?
NERVOUS... UNCOMFORTABLE...
YEAH, THAT'S... THAT SOUNDS PRETTY ACCURATE.
WELL, ME TOO. I DON'T KNOW ANY OF THESE PEOPLE.
YOU PUT UP A GOOD, UH, FACADE.
I'VE HAD PLENTY OF PRACTICE. I GUESS I'VE HAD PLENTY OF THIS CHAMPAGNE, TOO!

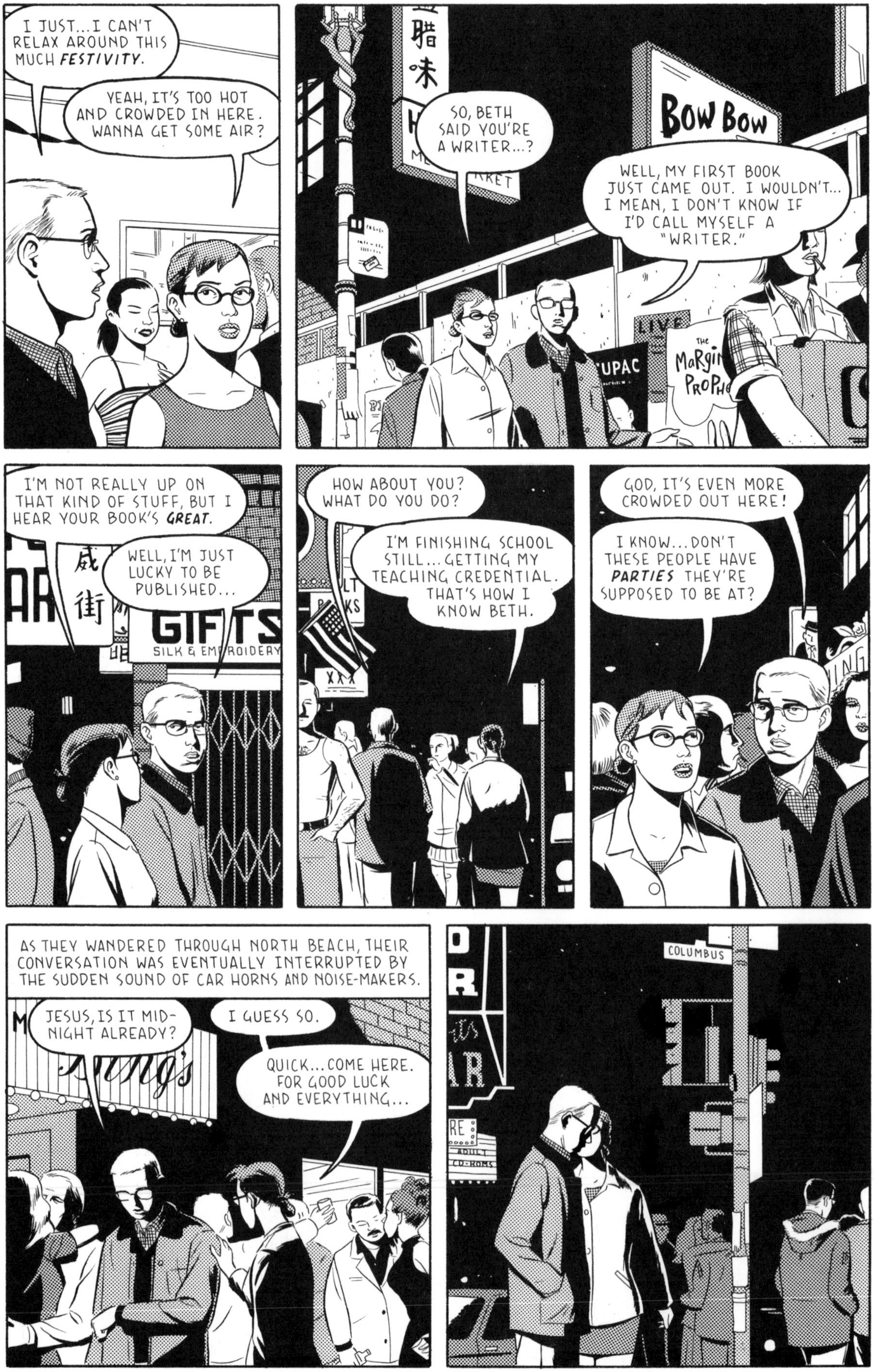
I JUST... I CAN'T RELAX AROUND THIS MUCH *FESTIVITY*.
YEAH, IT'S TOO HOT AND CROWDED IN HERE. WANNA GET SOME AIR?
BOW BOW
SO, BETH SAID YOU'RE A WRITER...?
WELL, MY FIRST BOOK JUST CAME OUT. I WOULDN'T... I MEAN, I DON'T KNOW IF I'D CALL MYSELF A "WRITER."
I'M NOT REALLY UP ON THAT KIND OF STUFF, BUT I HEAR YOUR BOOK'S *GREAT*.
WELL, I'M JUST LUCKY TO BE PUBLISHED...
GIFTS
SILK & EMBROIDERY
HOW ABOUT YOU? WHAT DO YOU DO?
I'M FINISHING SCHOOL STILL... GETTING MY TEACHING CREDENTIAL. THAT'S HOW I KNOW BETH.
GOD, IT'S EVEN MORE CROWDED OUT HERE!
I KNOW... DON'T THESE PEOPLE HAVE *PARTIES* THEY'RE SUPPOSED TO BE AT?
AS THEY WANDERED THROUGH NORTH BEACH, THEIR CONVERSATION WAS EVENTUALLY INTERRUPTED BY THE SUDDEN SOUND OF CAR HORNS AND NOISE-MAKERS.
JESUS, IS IT MIDNIGHT ALREADY?
I GUESS SO.
QUICK... COME HERE. FOR GOOD LUCK AND EVERYTHING...
COLUMBUS
ADULT CD-ROMS

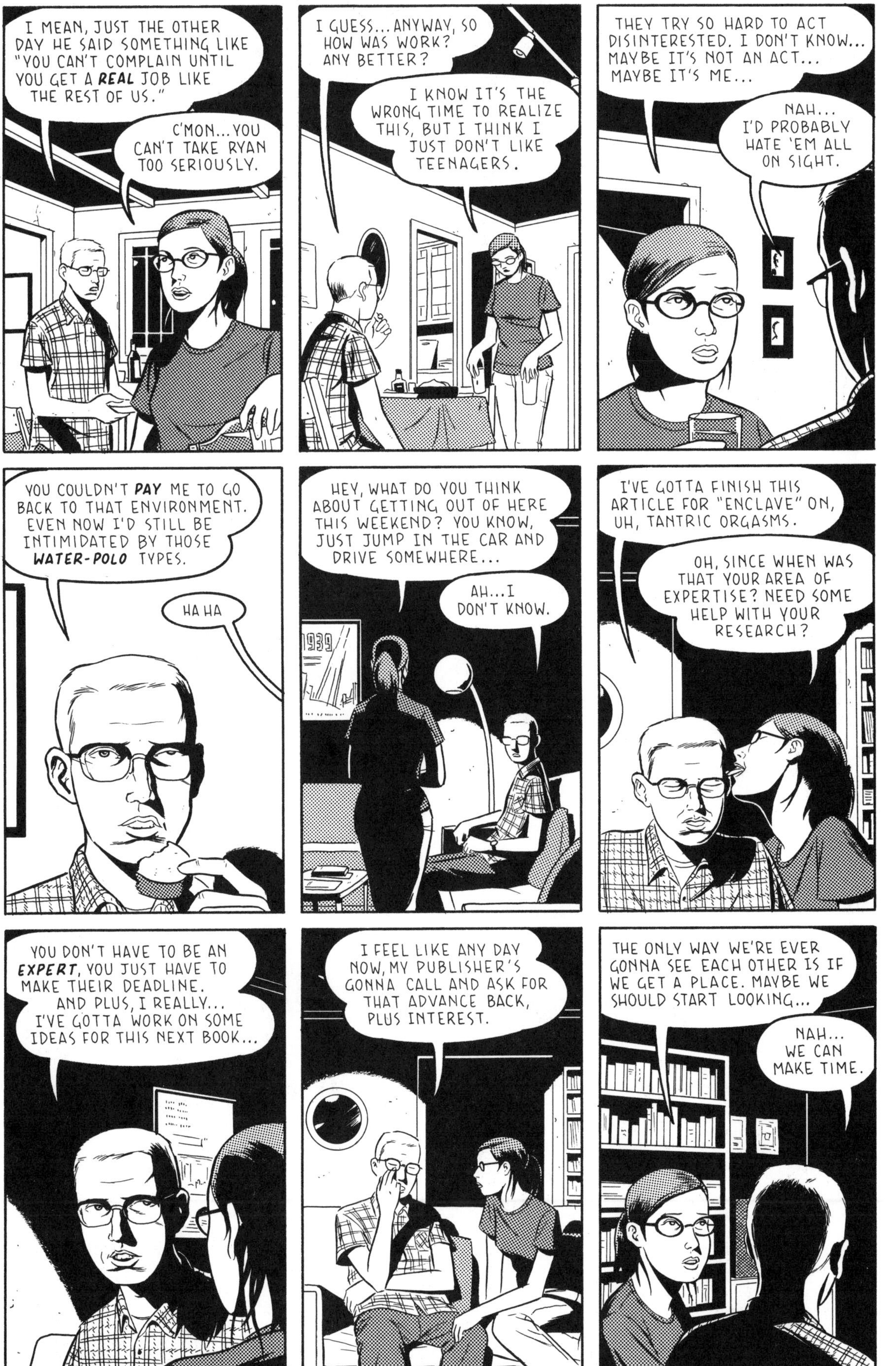

I MEAN, JUST THE OTHER DAY HE SAID SOMETHING LIKE "YOU CAN'T COMPLAIN UNTIL YOU GET A **REAL** JOB LIKE THE REST OF US."
C'MON...YOU CAN'T TAKE RYAN TOO SERIOUSLY.
I GUESS...ANYWAY, SO HOW WAS WORK? ANY BETTER?
I KNOW IT'S THE WRONG TIME TO REALIZE THIS, BUT I THINK I JUST DON'T LIKE TEENAGERS.
THEY TRY SO HARD TO ACT DISINTERESTED. I DON'T KNOW... MAYBE IT'S NOT AN ACT... MAYBE IT'S ME...
NAH... I'D PROBABLY HATE 'EM ALL ON SIGHT.
YOU COULDN'T **PAY** ME TO GO BACK TO THAT ENVIRONMENT. EVEN NOW I'D STILL BE INTIMIDATED BY THOSE **WATER-POLO** TYPES.
HA HA
HEY, WHAT DO YOU THINK ABOUT GETTING OUT OF HERE THIS WEEKEND? YOU KNOW, JUST JUMP IN THE CAR AND DRIVE SOMEWHERE...
AH...I DON'T KNOW.
1939
I'VE GOTTA FINISH THIS ARTICLE FOR "ENCLAVE" ON, UH, TANTRIC ORGASMS.
OH, SINCE WHEN WAS THAT YOUR AREA OF EXPERTISE? NEED SOME HELP WITH YOUR RESEARCH?
YOU DON'T HAVE TO BE AN **EXPERT**, YOU JUST HAVE TO MAKE THEIR DEADLINE.
AND PLUS, I REALLY... I'VE GOTTA WORK ON SOME IDEAS FOR THIS NEXT BOOK...
I FEEL LIKE ANY DAY NOW, MY PUBLISHER'S GONNA CALL AND ASK FOR THAT ADVANCE BACK, PLUS INTEREST.
THE ONLY WAY WE'RE EVER GONNA SEE EACH OTHER IS IF WE GET A PLACE. MAYBE WE SHOULD START LOOKING...
NAH... WE CAN MAKE TIME.

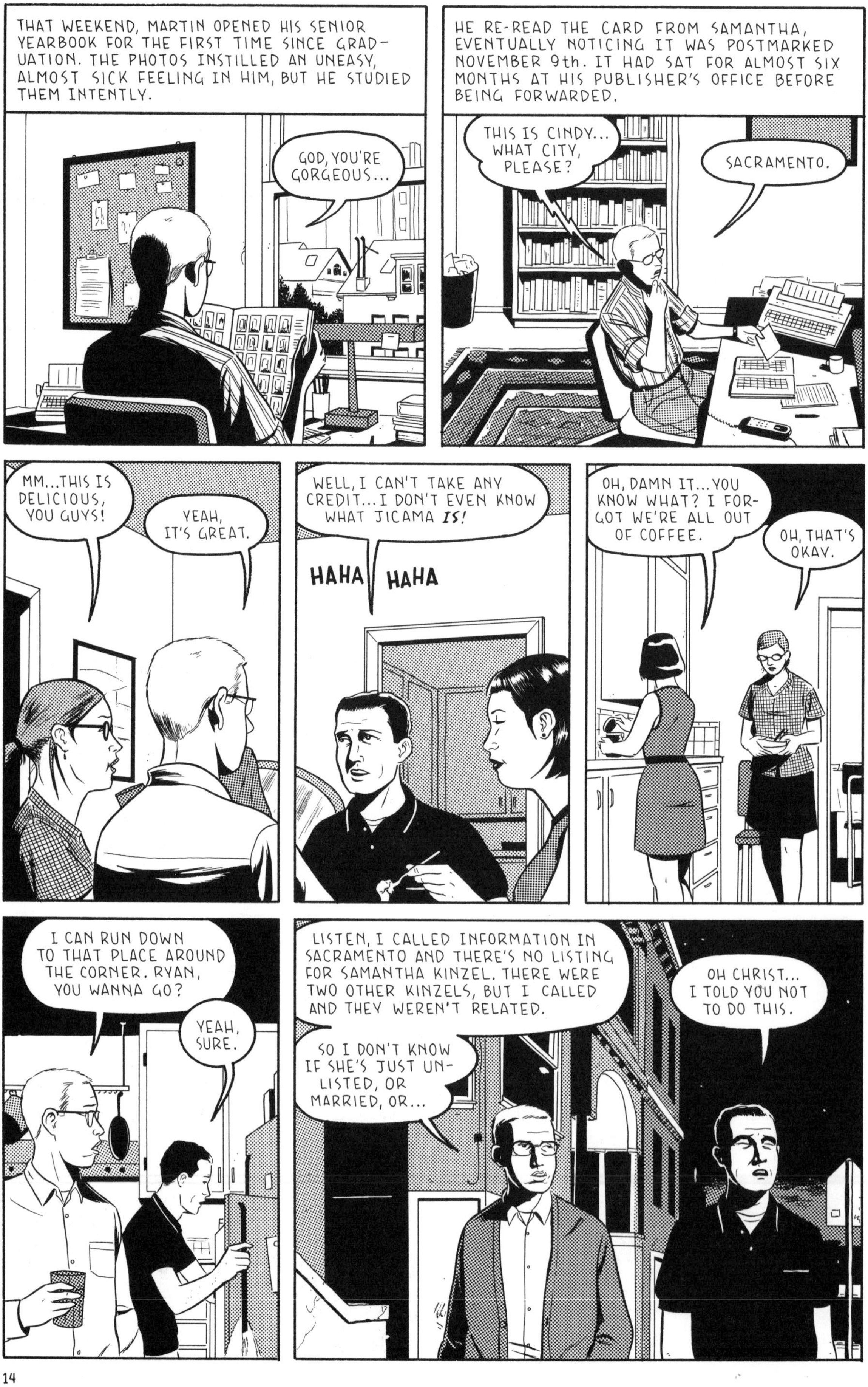
THAT WEEKEND, MARTIN OPENED HIS SENIOR YEARBOOK FOR THE FIRST TIME SINCE GRADUATION. THE PHOTOS INSTILLED AN UNEASY, ALMOST SICK FEELING IN HIM, BUT HE STUDIED THEM INTENTLY.
GOD, YOU'RE GORGEOUS...
HE RE-READ THE CARD FROM SAMANTHA, EVENTUALLY NOTICING IT WAS POSTMARKED NOVEMBER 9th. IT HAD SAT FOR ALMOST SIX MONTHS AT HIS PUBLISHER'S OFFICE BEFORE BEING FORWARDED.
THIS IS CINDY... WHAT CITY, PLEASE?
SACRAMENTO.
MM...THIS IS DELICIOUS, YOU GUYS!
YEAH, IT'S GREAT.
WELL, I CAN'T TAKE ANY CREDIT...I DON'T EVEN KNOW WHAT JICAMA *IS!*
HAHA HAHA
OH, DAMN IT...YOU KNOW WHAT? I FORGOT WE'RE ALL OUT OF COFFEE.
OH, THAT'S OKAY.
I CAN RUN DOWN TO THAT PLACE AROUND THE CORNER. RYAN, YOU WANNA GO?
YEAH, SURE.
LISTEN, I CALLED INFORMATION IN SACRAMENTO AND THERE'S NO LISTING FOR SAMANTHA KINZEL. THERE WERE TWO OTHER KINZELS, BUT I CALLED AND THEY WEREN'T RELATED.
SO I DON'T KNOW IF SHE'S JUST UNLISTED, OR MARRIED, OR...
OH CHRIST... I TOLD YOU NOT TO DO THIS.

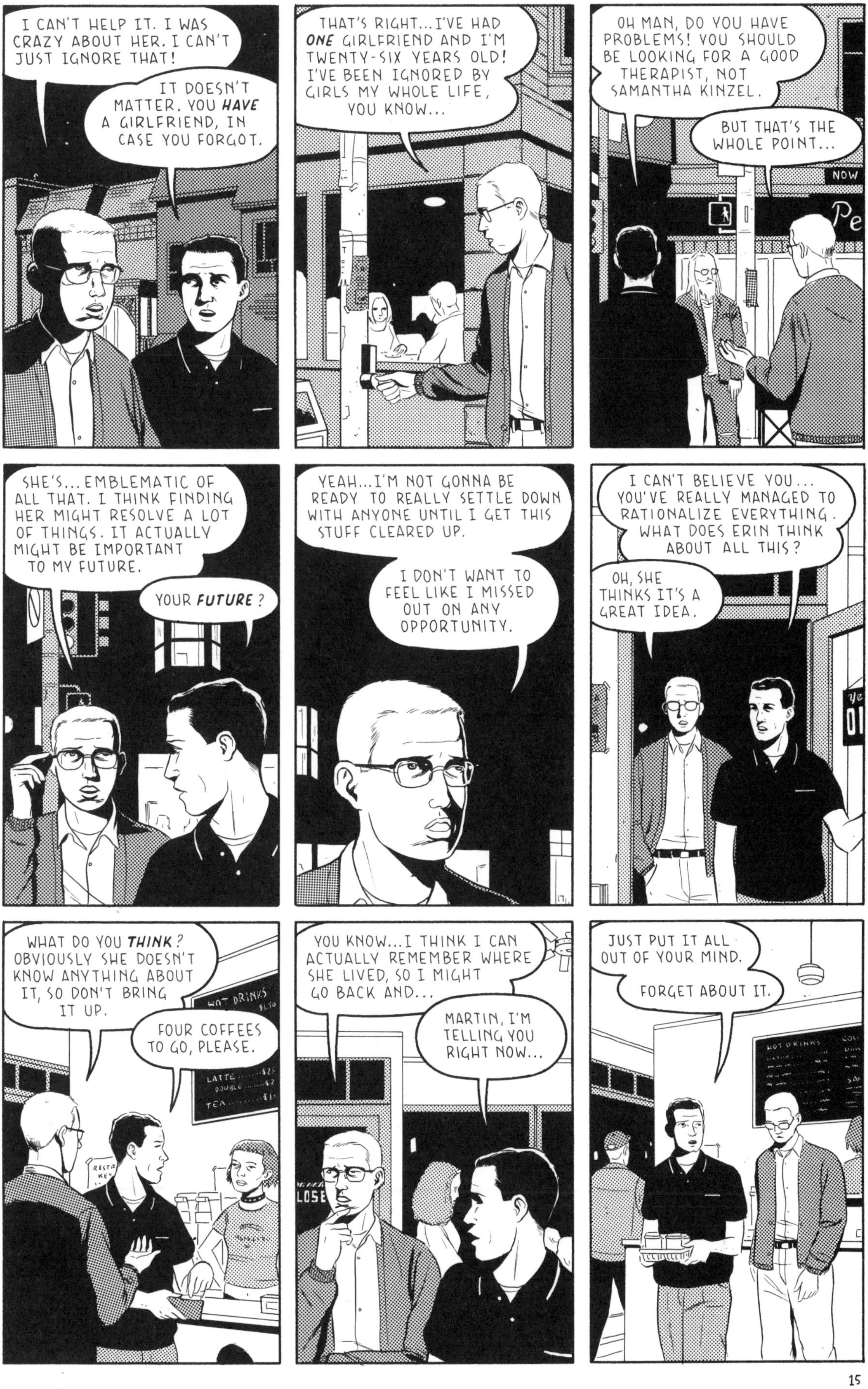
I CAN'T HELP IT. I WAS CRAZY ABOUT HER. I CAN'T JUST IGNORE THAT!
IT DOESN'T MATTER. YOU HAVE A GIRLFRIEND, IN CASE YOU FORGOT.
THAT'S RIGHT... I'VE HAD ONE GIRLFRIEND AND I'M TWENTY-SIX YEARS OLD! I'VE BEEN IGNORED BY GIRLS MY WHOLE LIFE, YOU KNOW...
OH MAN, DO YOU HAVE PROBLEMS! YOU SHOULD BE LOOKING FOR A GOOD THERAPIST, NOT SAMANTHA KINZEL.
BUT THAT'S THE WHOLE POINT...
NOW
SHE'S... EMBLEMATIC OF ALL THAT. I THINK FINDING HER MIGHT RESOLVE A LOT OF THINGS. IT ACTUALLY MIGHT BE IMPORTANT TO MY FUTURE.
YOUR FUTURE?
YEAH... I'M NOT GONNA BE READY TO REALLY SETTLE DOWN WITH ANYONE UNTIL I GET THIS STUFF CLEARED UP.
I DON'T WANT TO FEEL LIKE I MISSED OUT ON ANY OPPORTUNITY.
I CAN'T BELIEVE YOU... YOU'VE REALLY MANAGED TO RATIONALIZE EVERYTHING. WHAT DOES ERIN THINK ABOUT ALL THIS?
OH, SHE THINKS IT'S A GREAT IDEA.
WHAT DO YOU THINK? OBVIOUSLY SHE DOESN'T KNOW ANYTHING ABOUT IT, SO DON'T BRING IT UP.
FOUR COFFEES TO GO, PLEASE.
HOT DRINKS
YOU KNOW... I THINK I CAN ACTUALLY REMEMBER WHERE SHE LIVED, SO I MIGHT GO BACK AND...
MARTIN, I'M TELLING YOU RIGHT NOW...
JUST PUT IT ALL OUT OF YOUR MIND.
FORGET ABOUT IT.
HOT DRINKS

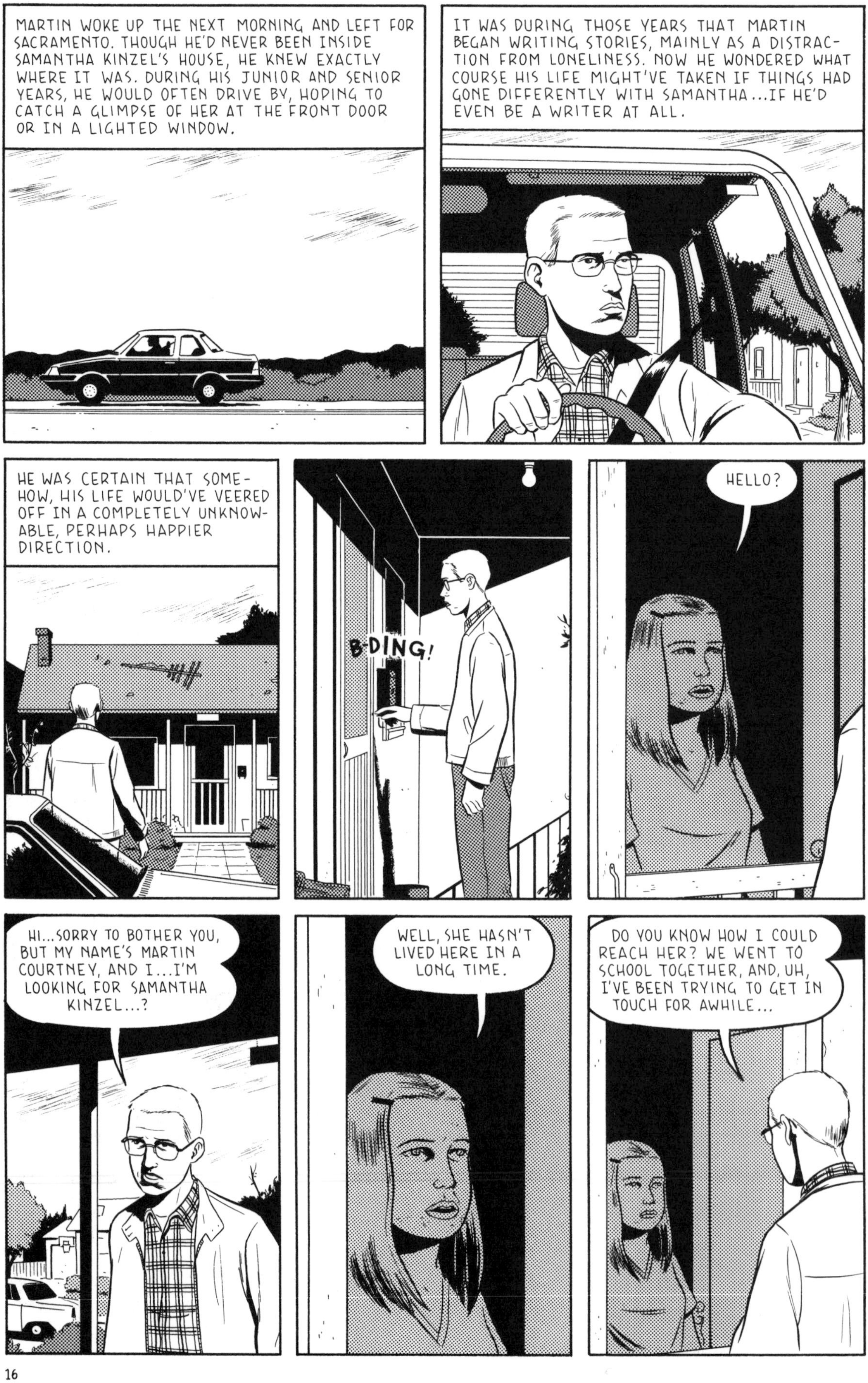
MARTIN WOKE UP THE NEXT MORNING AND LEFT FOR SACRAMENTO. THOUGH HE'D NEVER BEEN INSIDE SAMANTHA KINZEL'S HOUSE, HE KNEW EXACTLY WHERE IT WAS. DURING HIS JUNIOR AND SENIOR YEARS, HE WOULD OFTEN DRIVE BY, HOPING TO CATCH A GLIMPSE OF HER AT THE FRONT DOOR OR IN A LIGHTED WINDOW.
IT WAS DURING THOSE YEARS THAT MARTIN BEGAN WRITING STORIES, MAINLY AS A DISTRACTION FROM LONELINESS. NOW HE WONDERED WHAT COURSE HIS LIFE MIGHT'VE TAKEN IF THINGS HAD GONE DIFFERENTLY WITH SAMANTHA...IF HE'D EVEN BE A WRITER AT ALL.
HE WAS CERTAIN THAT SOMEHOW, HIS LIFE WOULD'VE VEERED OFF IN A COMPLETELY UNKNOWABLE, PERHAPS HAPPIER DIRECTION.
B-DING!
HELLO?
HI...SORRY TO BOTHER YOU, BUT MY NAME'S MARTIN COURTNEY, AND I...I'M LOOKING FOR SAMANTHA KINZEL...?
WELL, SHE HASN'T LIVED HERE IN A LONG TIME.
DO YOU KNOW HOW I COULD REACH HER? WE WENT TO SCHOOL TOGETHER, AND, UH, I'VE BEEN TRYING TO GET IN TOUCH FOR AWHILE...

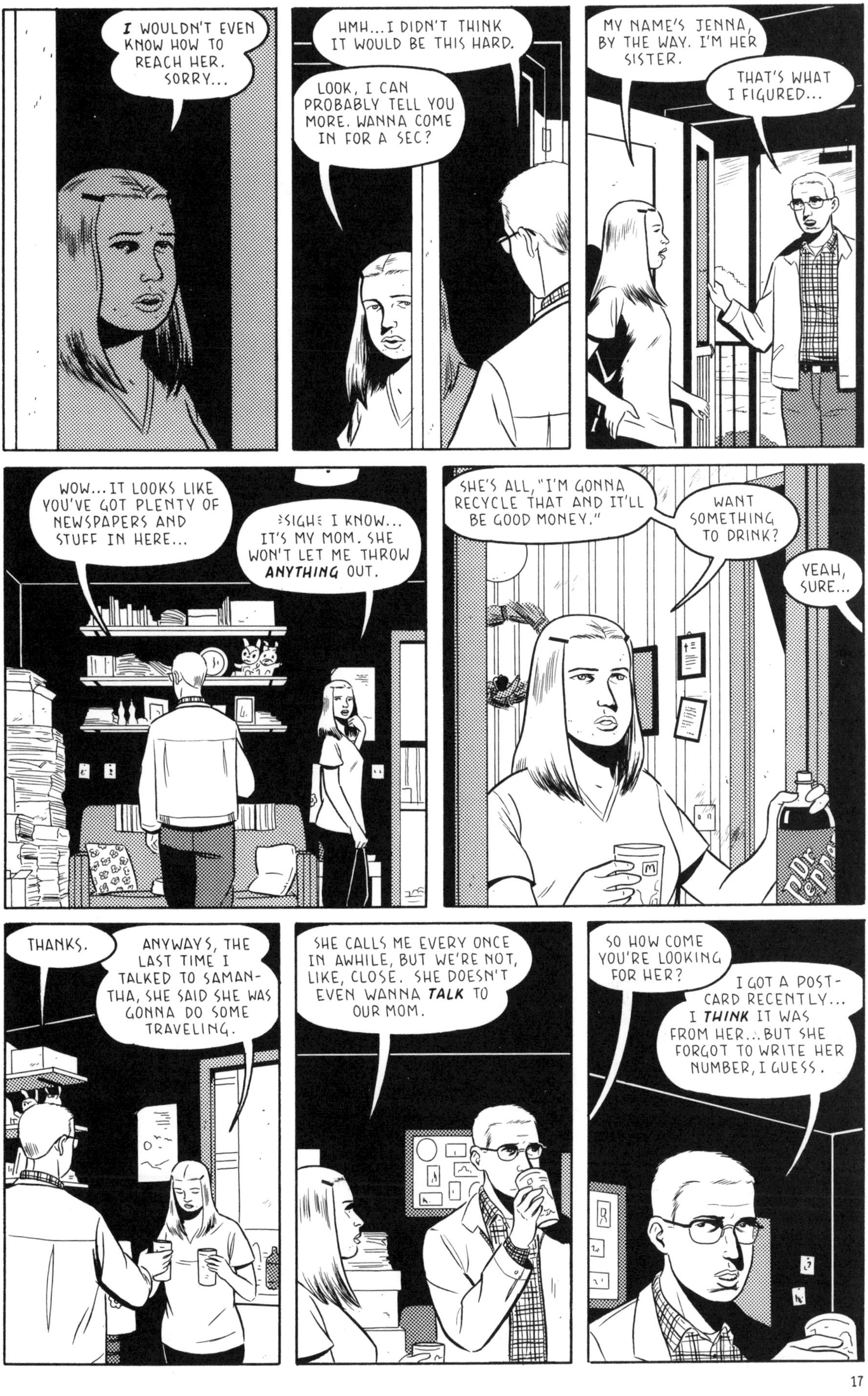
I WOULDN'T EVEN KNOW HOW TO REACH HER. SORRY...
HMH... I DIDN'T THINK IT WOULD BE THIS HARD.
LOOK, I CAN PROBABLY TELL YOU MORE. WANNA COME IN FOR A SEC?
MY NAME'S JENNA, BY THE WAY. I'M HER SISTER.
THAT'S WHAT I FIGURED...
WOW... IT LOOKS LIKE YOU'VE GOT PLENTY OF NEWSPAPERS AND STUFF IN HERE...
SIGH I KNOW... IT'S MY MOM. SHE WON'T LET ME THROW ANYTHING OUT.
SHE'S ALL, "I'M GONNA RECYCLE THAT AND IT'LL BE GOOD MONEY."
WANT SOMETHING TO DRINK?
YEAH, SURE...
THANKS.
ANYWAYS, THE LAST TIME I TALKED TO SAMANTHA, SHE SAID SHE WAS GONNA DO SOME TRAVELING.
SHE CALLS ME EVERY ONCE IN AWHILE, BUT WE'RE NOT, LIKE, CLOSE. SHE DOESN'T EVEN WANNA TALK TO OUR MOM.
SO HOW COME YOU'RE LOOKING FOR HER?
I GOT A POSTCARD RECENTLY... I THINK IT WAS FROM HER... BUT SHE FORGOT TO WRITE HER NUMBER, I GUESS.

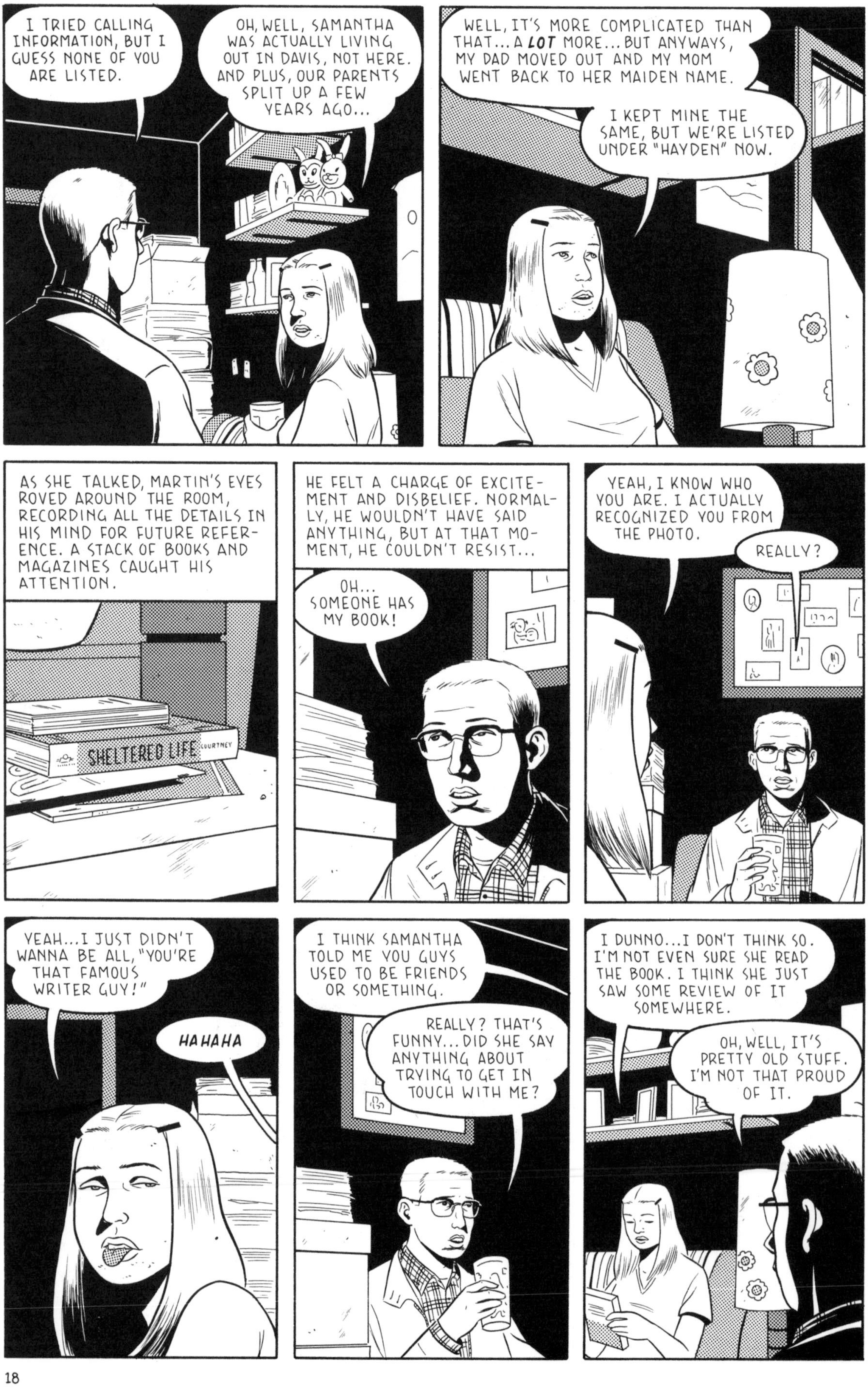

I TRIED CALLING INFORMATION, BUT I GUESS NONE OF YOU ARE LISTED.
OH, WELL, SAMANTHA WAS ACTUALLY LIVING OUT IN DAVIS, NOT HERE. AND PLUS, OUR PARENTS SPLIT UP A FEW YEARS AGO...
WELL, IT'S MORE COMPLICATED THAN THAT... A **LOT** MORE... BUT ANYWAYS, MY DAD MOVED OUT AND MY MOM WENT BACK TO HER MAIDEN NAME.
I KEPT MINE THE SAME, BUT WE'RE LISTED UNDER "HAYDEN" NOW.
AS SHE TALKED, MARTIN'S EYES ROVED AROUND THE ROOM, RECORDING ALL THE DETAILS IN HIS MIND FOR FUTURE REFERENCE. A STACK OF BOOKS AND MAGAZINES CAUGHT HIS ATTENTION.
SHELTERED LIFE
COURTNEY
HE FELT A CHARGE OF EXCITEMENT AND DISBELIEF. NORMALLY, HE WOULDN'T HAVE SAID ANYTHING, BUT AT THAT MOMENT, HE COULDN'T RESIST...
OH... SOMEONE HAS MY BOOK!
YEAH, I KNOW WHO YOU ARE. I ACTUALLY RECOGNIZED YOU FROM THE PHOTO.
REALLY?
YEAH...I JUST DIDN'T WANNA BE ALL, "YOU'RE THAT FAMOUS WRITER GUY!"
HAHAHA
I THINK SAMANTHA TOLD ME YOU GUYS USED TO BE FRIENDS OR SOMETHING.
REALLY? THAT'S FUNNY... DID SHE SAY ANYTHING ABOUT TRYING TO GET IN TOUCH WITH ME?
I DUNNO...I DON'T THINK SO. I'M NOT EVEN SURE SHE READ THE BOOK. I THINK SHE JUST SAW SOME REVIEW OF IT SOMEWHERE.
OH, WELL, IT'S PRETTY OLD STUFF. I'M NOT THAT PROUD OF IT.

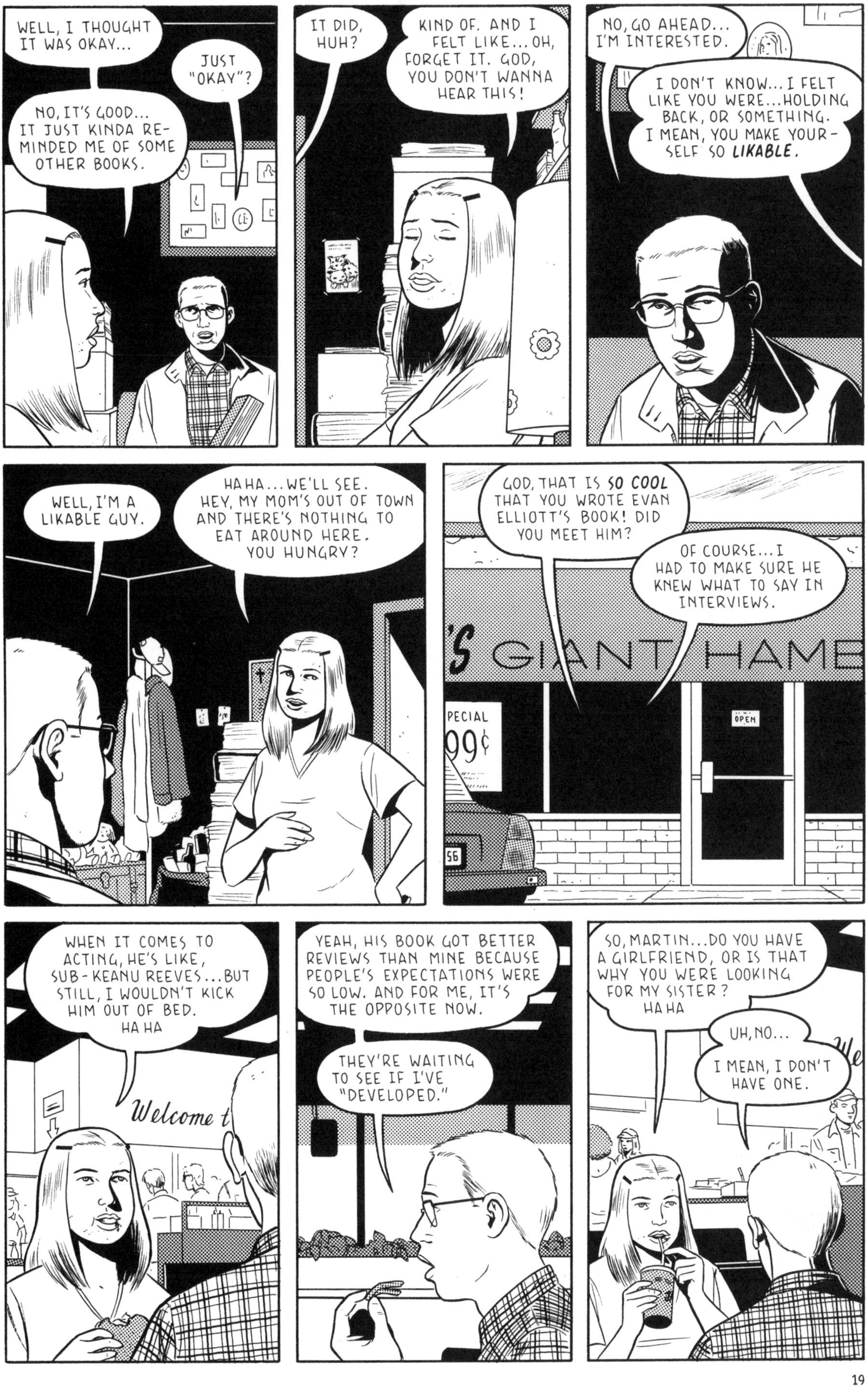
WELL, I THOUGHT IT WAS OKAY...
JUST "OKAY"?
NO, IT'S GOOD... IT JUST KINDA RE-MINDED ME OF SOME OTHER BOOKS.
IT DID, HUH?
KIND OF. AND I FELT LIKE... OH, FORGET IT. GOD, YOU DON'T WANNA HEAR THIS!
NO, GO AHEAD... I'M INTERESTED.
I DON'T KNOW... I FELT LIKE YOU WERE... HOLDING BACK, OR SOMETHING. I MEAN, YOU MAKE YOUR-SELF SO **LIKABLE.**
WELL, I'M A LIKABLE GUY.
HA HA... WE'LL SEE. HEY, MY MOM'S OUT OF TOWN AND THERE'S NOTHING TO EAT AROUND HERE. YOU HUNGRY?
GOD, THAT IS **SO COOL** THAT YOU WROTE EVAN ELLIOTT'S BOOK! DID YOU MEET HIM?
OF COURSE... I HAD TO MAKE SURE HE KNEW WHAT TO SAY IN INTERVIEWS.
'S GIANT HAMB
PECIAL
99¢
OPEN
WHEN IT COMES TO ACTING, HE'S LIKE, SUB-KEANU REEVES... BUT STILL, I WOULDN'T KICK HIM OUT OF BED. HA HA
Welcome t
YEAH, HIS BOOK GOT BETTER REVIEWS THAN MINE BECAUSE PEOPLE'S EXPECTATIONS WERE SO LOW. AND FOR ME, IT'S THE OPPOSITE NOW.
THEY'RE WAITING TO SEE IF I'VE "DEVELOPED."
SO, MARTIN... DO YOU HAVE A GIRLFRIEND, OR IS THAT WHY YOU WERE LOOKING FOR MY SISTER? HA HA
UH, NO...
I MEAN, I DON'T HAVE ONE.

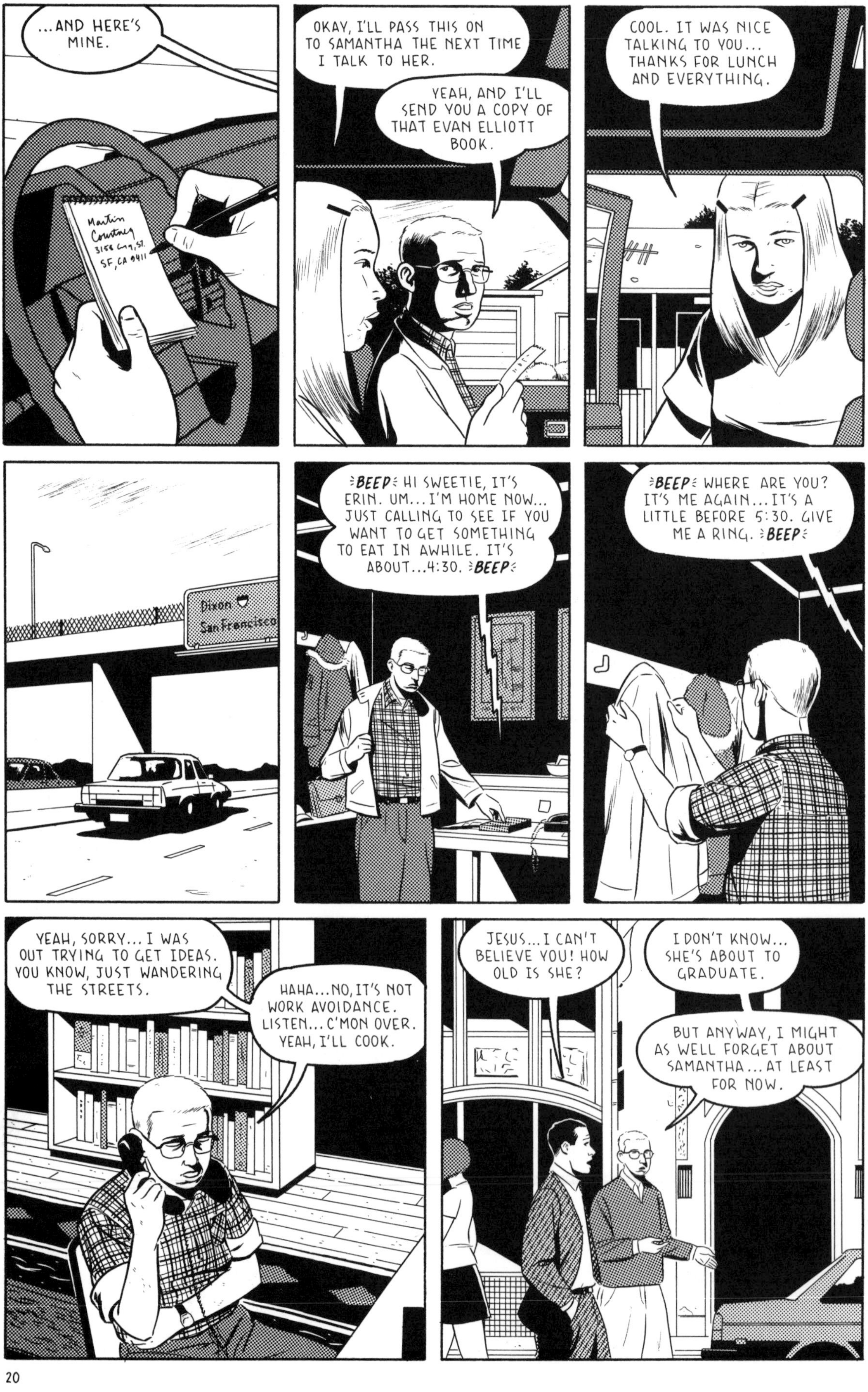
...AND HERE'S MINE.
Martin Courtney 3158 ... St. SF, CA 9411
OKAY, I'LL PASS THIS ON TO SAMANTHA THE NEXT TIME I TALK TO HER.
YEAH, AND I'LL SEND YOU A COPY OF THAT EVAN ELLIOTT BOOK.
COOL. IT WAS NICE TALKING TO YOU... THANKS FOR LUNCH AND EVERYTHING.
Dixon
San Francisco
BEEP HI SWEETIE, IT'S ERIN. UM...I'M HOME NOW... JUST CALLING TO SEE IF YOU WANT TO GET SOMETHING TO EAT IN AWHILE. IT'S ABOUT...4:30. BEEP
BEEP WHERE ARE YOU? IT'S ME AGAIN...IT'S A LITTLE BEFORE 5:30. GIVE ME A RING. BEEP
YEAH, SORRY... I WAS OUT TRYING TO GET IDEAS. YOU KNOW, JUST WANDERING THE STREETS.
HAHA...NO, IT'S NOT WORK AVOIDANCE. LISTEN... C'MON OVER. YEAH, I'LL COOK.
JESUS...I CAN'T BELIEVE YOU! HOW OLD IS SHE?
I DON'T KNOW... SHE'S ABOUT TO GRADUATE.
BUT ANYWAY, I MIGHT AS WELL FORGET ABOUT SAMANTHA... AT LEAST FOR NOW.

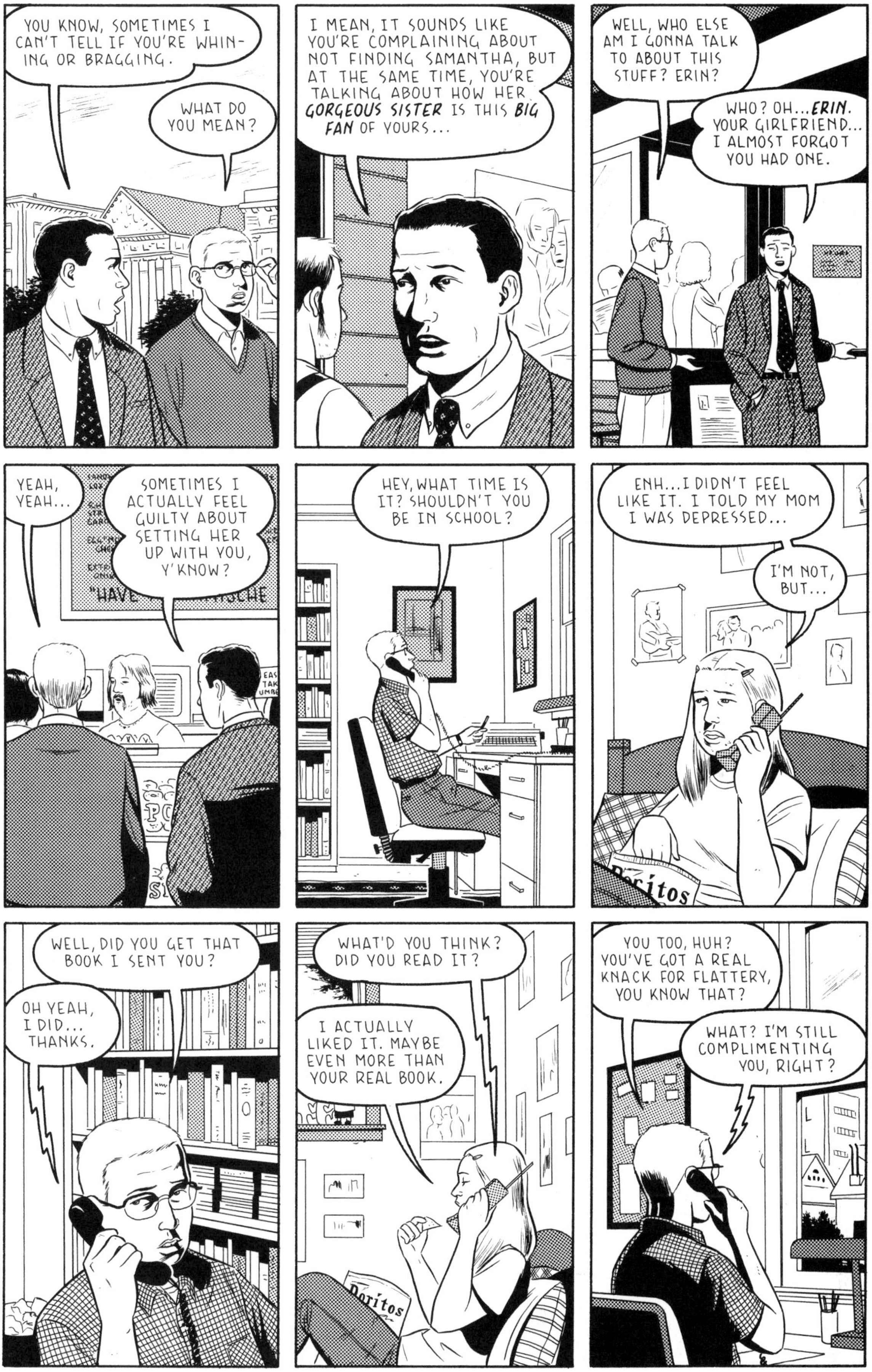
YOU KNOW, SOMETIMES I CAN'T TELL IF YOU'RE WHIN-ING OR BRAGGING.
WHAT DO YOU MEAN?
I MEAN, IT SOUNDS LIKE YOU'RE COMPLAINING ABOUT NOT FINDING SAMANTHA, BUT AT THE SAME TIME, YOU'RE TALKING ABOUT HOW HER **GORGEOUS SISTER** IS THIS **BIG FAN** OF YOURS...
WELL, WHO ELSE AM I GONNA TALK TO ABOUT THIS STUFF? ERIN?
WHO? OH...**ERIN**. YOUR GIRLFRIEND... I ALMOST FORGOT YOU HAD ONE.
YEAH, YEAH...
SOMETIMES I ACTUALLY FEEL GUILTY ABOUT SETTING HER UP WITH YOU, Y'KNOW?
HEY, WHAT TIME IS IT? SHOULDN'T YOU BE IN SCHOOL?
ENH...I DIDN'T FEEL LIKE IT. I TOLD MY MOM I WAS DEPRESSED...
I'M NOT, BUT...
Doritos
WELL, DID YOU GET THAT BOOK I SENT YOU?
OH YEAH, I DID... THANKS.
WHAT'D YOU THINK? DID YOU READ IT?
I ACTUALLY LIKED IT. MAYBE EVEN MORE THAN YOUR REAL BOOK.
Doritos
YOU TOO, HUH? YOU'VE GOT A REAL KNACK FOR FLATTERY, YOU KNOW THAT?
WHAT? I'M STILL COMPLIMENTING YOU, RIGHT?

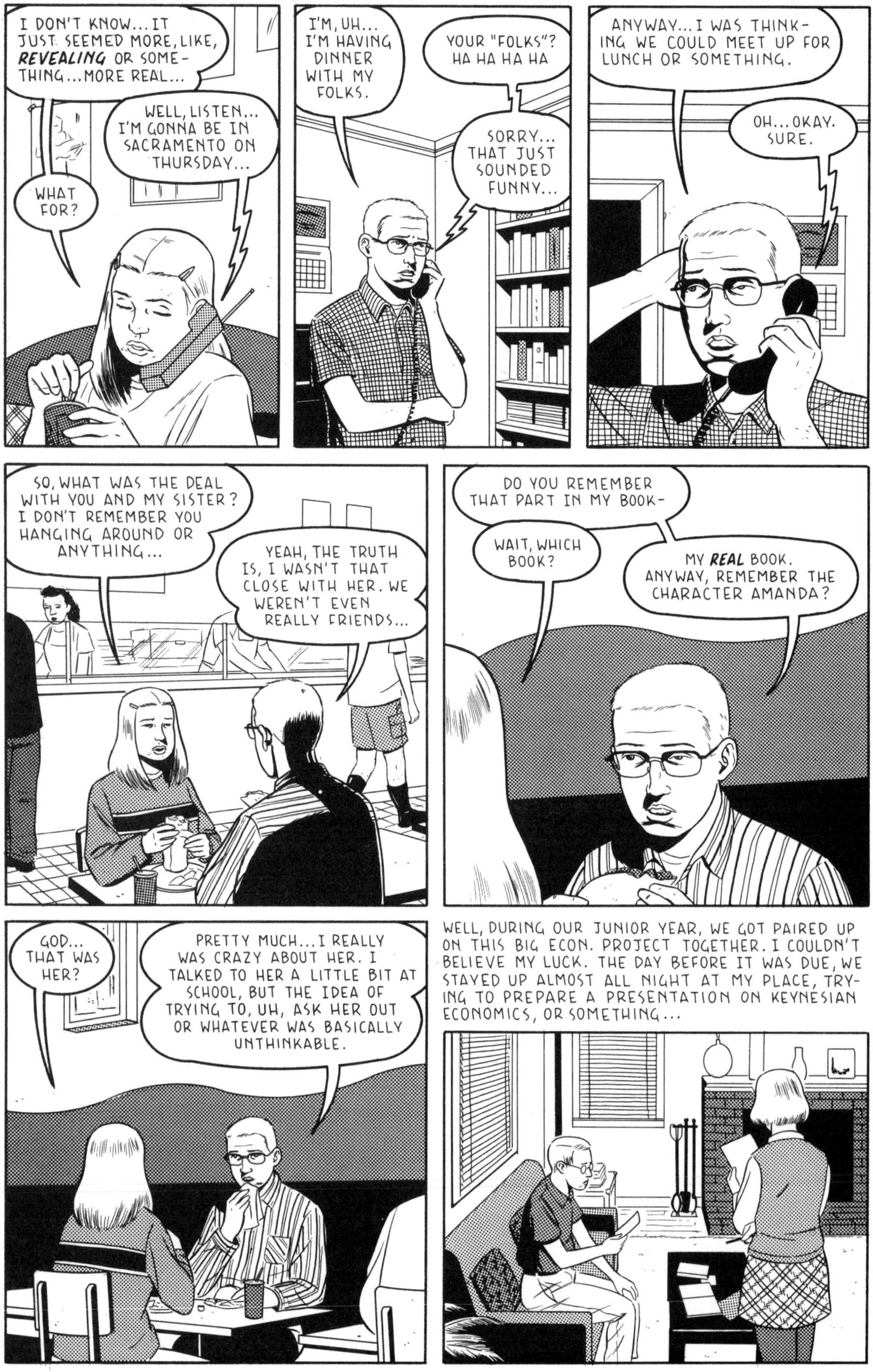
I DON'T KNOW... IT JUST SEEMED MORE, LIKE, **REVEALING** OR SOME-THING... MORE REAL...
WELL, LISTEN... I'M GONNA BE IN SACRAMENTO ON THURSDAY...
WHAT FOR?
I'M, UH... I'M HAVING DINNER WITH MY FOLKS.
YOUR "FOLKS"? HA HA HA HA
SORRY... THAT JUST SOUNDED FUNNY...
ANYWAY... I WAS THINK-ING WE COULD MEET UP FOR LUNCH OR SOMETHING.
OH... OKAY. SURE.
SO, WHAT WAS THE DEAL WITH YOU AND MY SISTER? I DON'T REMEMBER YOU HANGING AROUND OR ANYTHING...
YEAH, THE TRUTH IS, I WASN'T THAT CLOSE WITH HER. WE WEREN'T EVEN REALLY FRIENDS...
DO YOU REMEMBER THAT PART IN MY BOOK-
WAIT, WHICH BOOK?
MY **REAL** BOOK. ANYWAY, REMEMBER THE CHARACTER AMANDA?
GOD... THAT WAS HER?
PRETTY MUCH... I REALLY WAS CRAZY ABOUT HER. I TALKED TO HER A LITTLE BIT AT SCHOOL, BUT THE IDEA OF TRYING TO, UH, ASK HER OUT OR WHATEVER WAS BASICALLY UNTHINKABLE.
WELL, DURING OUR JUNIOR YEAR, WE GOT PAIRED UP ON THIS BIG ECON. PROJECT TOGETHER. I COULDN'T BELIEVE MY LUCK. THE DAY BEFORE IT WAS DUE, WE STAYED UP ALMOST ALL NIGHT AT MY PLACE, TRY-ING TO PREPARE A PRESENTATION ON KEYNESIAN ECONOMICS, OR SOMETHING...

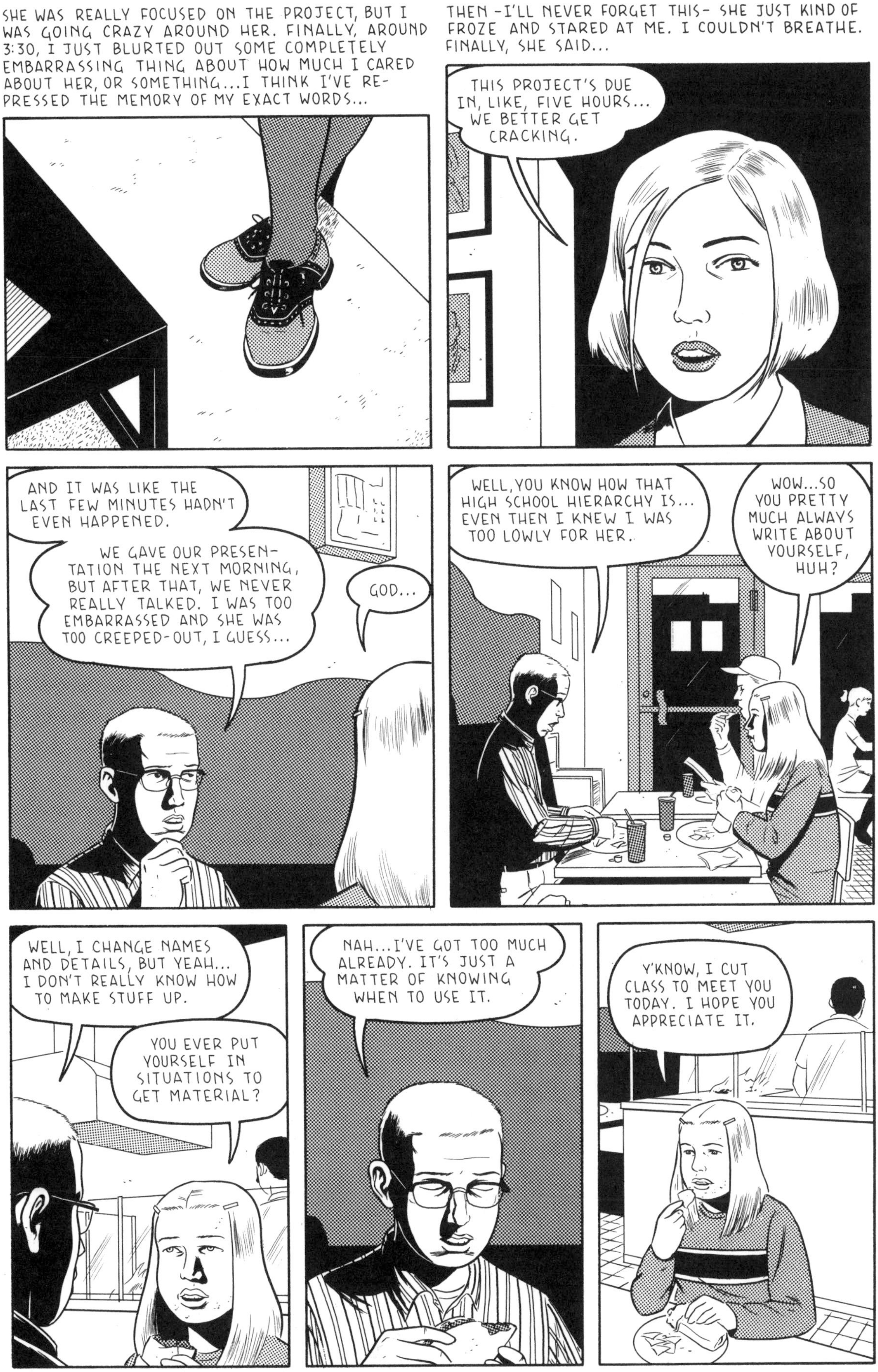
SHE WAS REALLY FOCUSED ON THE PROJECT, BUT I WAS GOING CRAZY AROUND HER. FINALLY, AROUND 3:30, I JUST BLURTED OUT SOME COMPLETELY EMBARRASSING THING ABOUT HOW MUCH I CARED ABOUT HER, OR SOMETHING...I THINK I'VE REPRESSED THE MEMORY OF MY EXACT WORDS...
THEN -I'LL NEVER FORGET THIS- SHE JUST KIND OF FROZE AND STARED AT ME. I COULDN'T BREATHE. FINALLY, SHE SAID...
THIS PROJECT'S DUE IN, LIKE, FIVE HOURS... WE BETTER GET CRACKING.
AND IT WAS LIKE THE LAST FEW MINUTES HADN'T EVEN HAPPENED.
WE GAVE OUR PRESENTATION THE NEXT MORNING, BUT AFTER THAT, WE NEVER REALLY TALKED. I WAS TOO EMBARRASSED AND SHE WAS TOO CREEPED-OUT, I GUESS...
GOD...
WELL, YOU KNOW HOW THAT HIGH SCHOOL HIERARCHY IS... EVEN THEN I KNEW I WAS TOO LOWLY FOR HER.
WOW...SO YOU PRETTY MUCH ALWAYS WRITE ABOUT YOURSELF, HUH?
WELL, I CHANGE NAMES AND DETAILS, BUT YEAH... I DON'T REALLY KNOW HOW TO MAKE STUFF UP.
YOU EVER PUT YOURSELF IN SITUATIONS TO GET MATERIAL?
NAH...I'VE GOT TOO MUCH ALREADY. IT'S JUST A MATTER OF KNOWING WHEN TO USE IT.
Y'KNOW, I CUT CLASS TO MEET YOU TODAY. I HOPE YOU APPRECIATE IT.

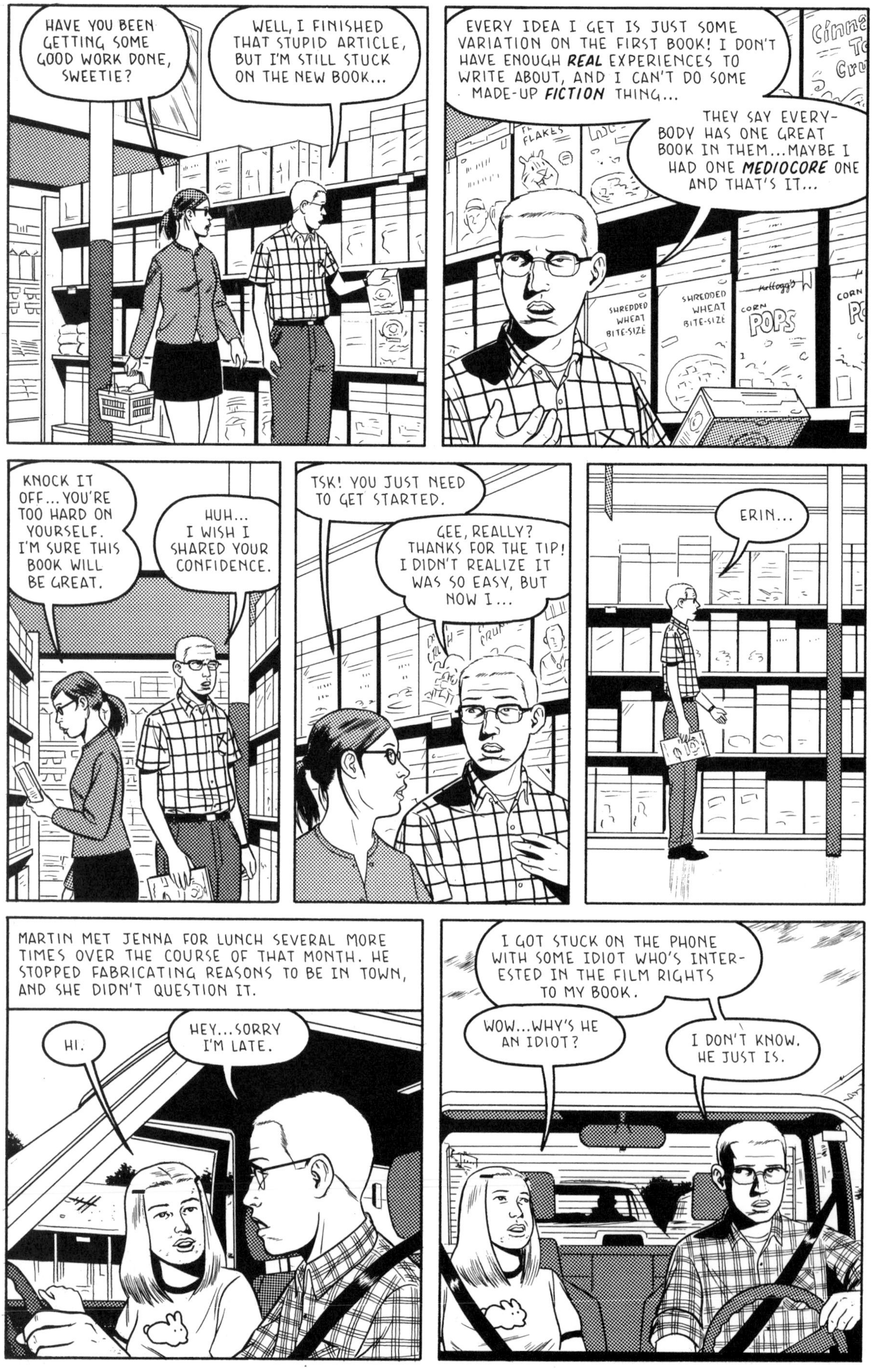
HAVE YOU BEEN GETTING SOME GOOD WORK DONE, SWEETIE?
WELL, I FINISHED THAT STUPID ARTICLE, BUT I'M STILL STUCK ON THE NEW BOOK...
EVERY IDEA I GET IS JUST SOME VARIATION ON THE FIRST BOOK! I DON'T HAVE ENOUGH **REAL** EXPERIENCES TO WRITE ABOUT, AND I CAN'T DO SOME MADE-UP **FICTION** THING...
THEY SAY EVERYBODY HAS ONE GREAT BOOK IN THEM...MAYBE I HAD ONE **MEDIOCORE** ONE AND THAT'S IT...
SHREDDED WHEAT BITE-SIZE
SHREDDED WHEAT BITE-SIZE
CORN POPS
KNOCK IT OFF... YOU'RE TOO HARD ON YOURSELF. I'M SURE THIS BOOK WILL BE GREAT.
HUH... I WISH I SHARED YOUR CONFIDENCE.
TSK! YOU JUST NEED TO GET STARTED.
GEE, REALLY? THANKS FOR THE TIP! I DIDN'T REALIZE IT WAS SO EASY, BUT NOW I...
ERIN...
MARTIN MET JENNA FOR LUNCH SEVERAL MORE TIMES OVER THE COURSE OF THAT MONTH. HE STOPPED FABRICATING REASONS TO BE IN TOWN, AND SHE DIDN'T QUESTION IT.
HI.
HEY...SORRY I'M LATE.
I GOT STUCK ON THE PHONE WITH SOME IDIOT WHO'S INTERESTED IN THE FILM RIGHTS TO MY BOOK.
WOW...WHY'S HE AN IDIOT?
I DON'T KNOW. HE JUST IS.

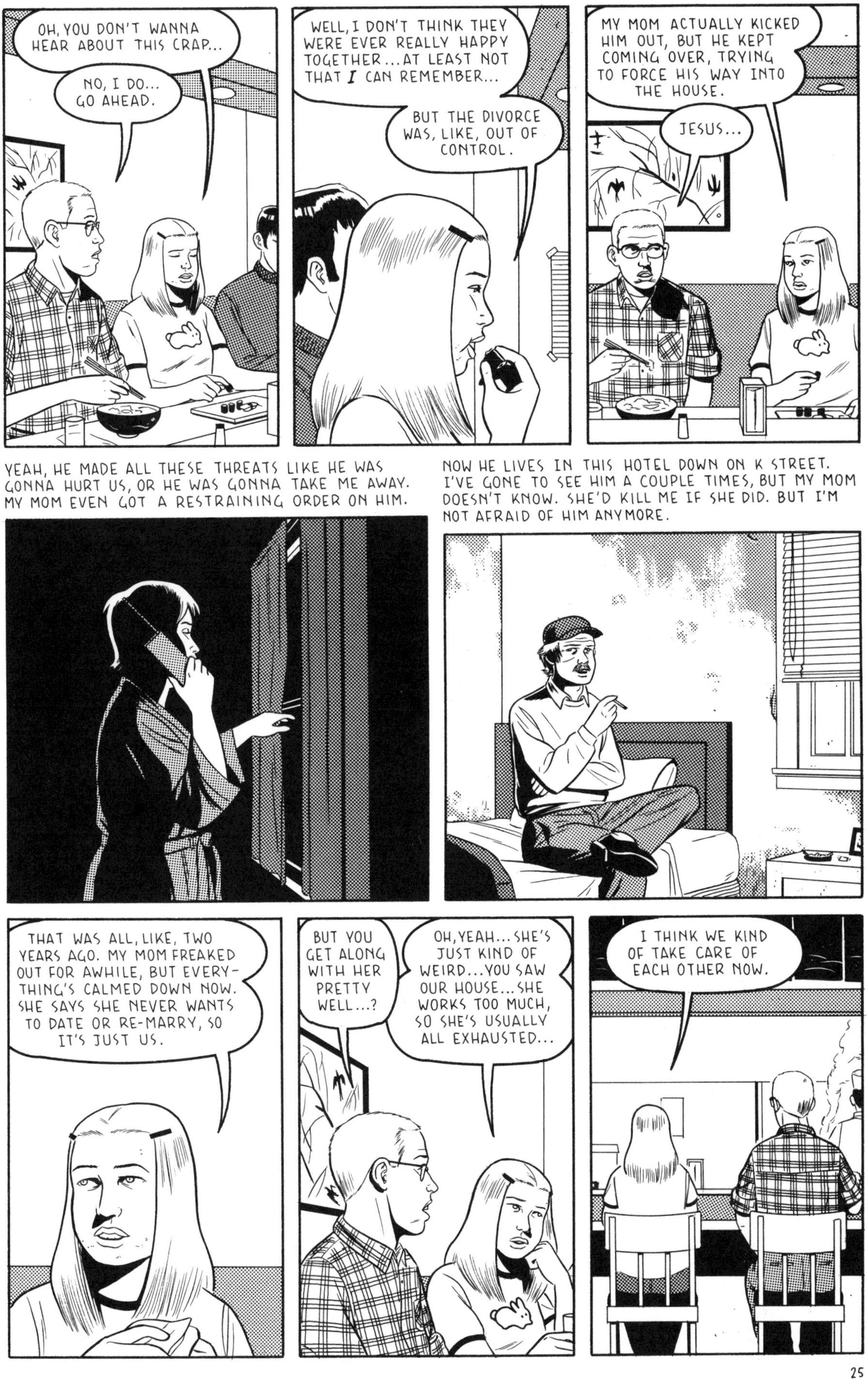
OH, YOU DON'T WANNA HEAR ABOUT THIS CRAP...
NO, I DO... GO AHEAD.
WELL, I DON'T THINK THEY WERE EVER REALLY HAPPY TOGETHER...AT LEAST NOT THAT *I* CAN REMEMBER...
BUT THE DIVORCE WAS, LIKE, OUT OF CONTROL.
MY MOM ACTUALLY KICKED HIM OUT, BUT HE KEPT COMING OVER, TRYING TO FORCE HIS WAY INTO THE HOUSE.
JESUS...
YEAH, HE MADE ALL THESE THREATS LIKE HE WAS GONNA HURT US, OR HE WAS GONNA TAKE ME AWAY. MY MOM EVEN GOT A RESTRAINING ORDER ON HIM.
NOW HE LIVES IN THIS HOTEL DOWN ON K STREET. I'VE GONE TO SEE HIM A COUPLE TIMES, BUT MY MOM DOESN'T KNOW. SHE'D KILL ME IF SHE DID. BUT I'M NOT AFRAID OF HIM ANYMORE.
THAT WAS ALL, LIKE, TWO YEARS AGO. MY MOM FREAKED OUT FOR AWHILE, BUT EVERYTHING'S CALMED DOWN NOW. SHE SAYS SHE NEVER WANTS TO DATE OR RE-MARRY, SO IT'S JUST US.
BUT YOU GET ALONG WITH HER PRETTY WELL...?
OH, YEAH... SHE'S JUST KIND OF WEIRD... YOU SAW OUR HOUSE... SHE WORKS TOO MUCH, SO SHE'S USUALLY ALL EXHAUSTED...
I THINK WE KIND OF TAKE CARE OF EACH OTHER NOW.

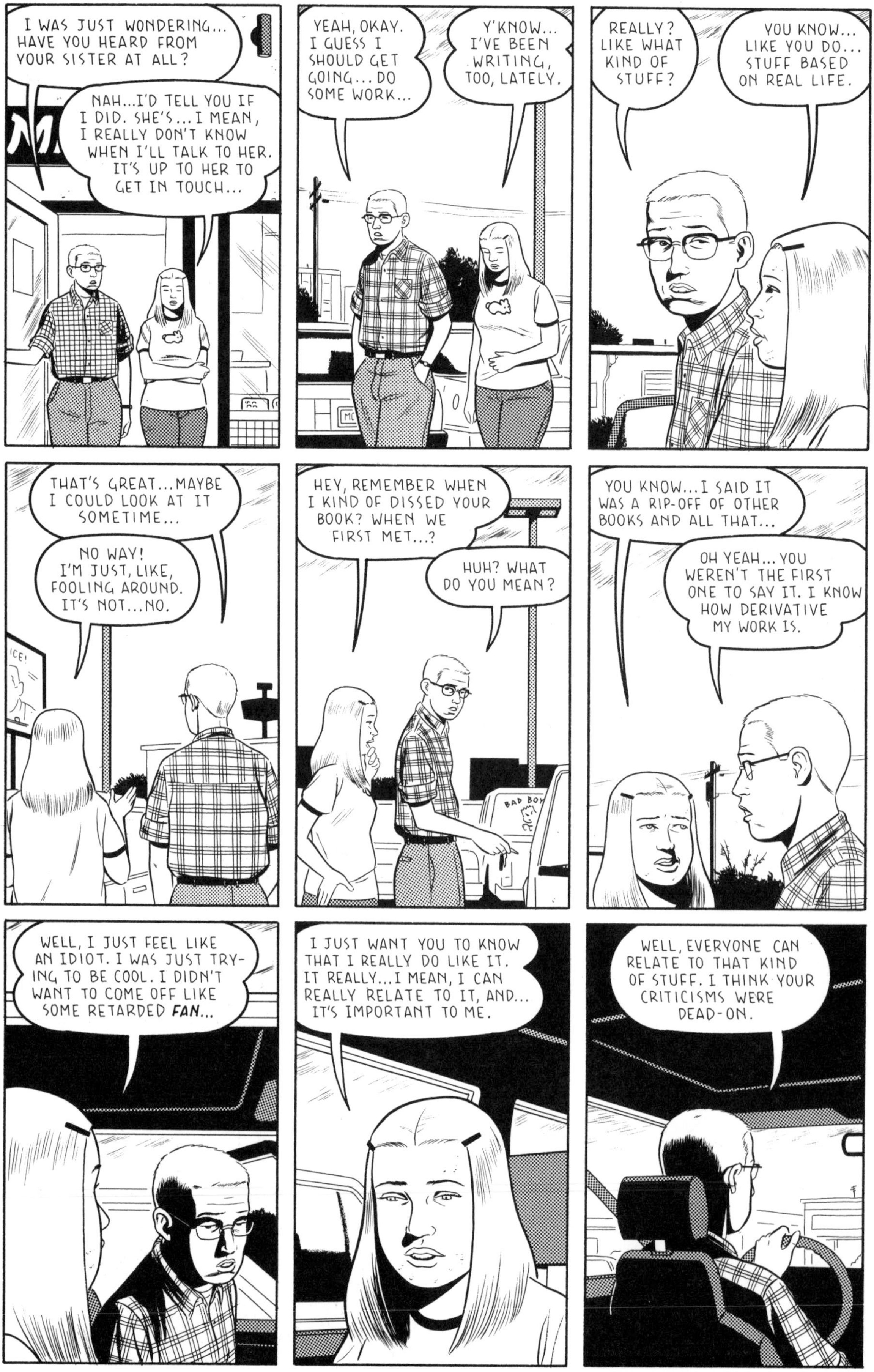
I WAS JUST WONDERING... HAVE YOU HEARD FROM YOUR SISTER AT ALL?
NAH...I'D TELL YOU IF I DID. SHE'S... I MEAN, I REALLY DON'T KNOW WHEN I'LL TALK TO HER. IT'S UP TO HER TO GET IN TOUCH...
YEAH, OKAY. I GUESS I SHOULD GET GOING... DO SOME WORK...
Y'KNOW... I'VE BEEN WRITING, TOO, LATELY.
REALLY? LIKE WHAT KIND OF STUFF?
YOU KNOW... LIKE YOU DO... STUFF BASED ON REAL LIFE.
THAT'S GREAT...MAYBE I COULD LOOK AT IT SOMETIME...
NO WAY! I'M JUST, LIKE, FOOLING AROUND. IT'S NOT...NO.
HEY, REMEMBER WHEN I KIND OF DISSED YOUR BOOK? WHEN WE FIRST MET...?
HUH? WHAT DO YOU MEAN?
BAD BOY
YOU KNOW...I SAID IT WAS A RIP-OFF OF OTHER BOOKS AND ALL THAT...
OH YEAH... YOU WEREN'T THE FIRST ONE TO SAY IT. I KNOW HOW DERIVATIVE MY WORK IS.
WELL, I JUST FEEL LIKE AN IDIOT. I WAS JUST TRYING TO BE COOL. I DIDN'T WANT TO COME OFF LIKE SOME RETARDED **FAN**...
I JUST WANT YOU TO KNOW THAT I REALLY DO LIKE IT. IT REALLY...I MEAN, I CAN REALLY RELATE TO IT, AND... IT'S IMPORTANT TO ME.
WELL, EVERYONE CAN RELATE TO THAT KIND OF STUFF. I THINK YOUR CRITICISMS WERE DEAD-ON.

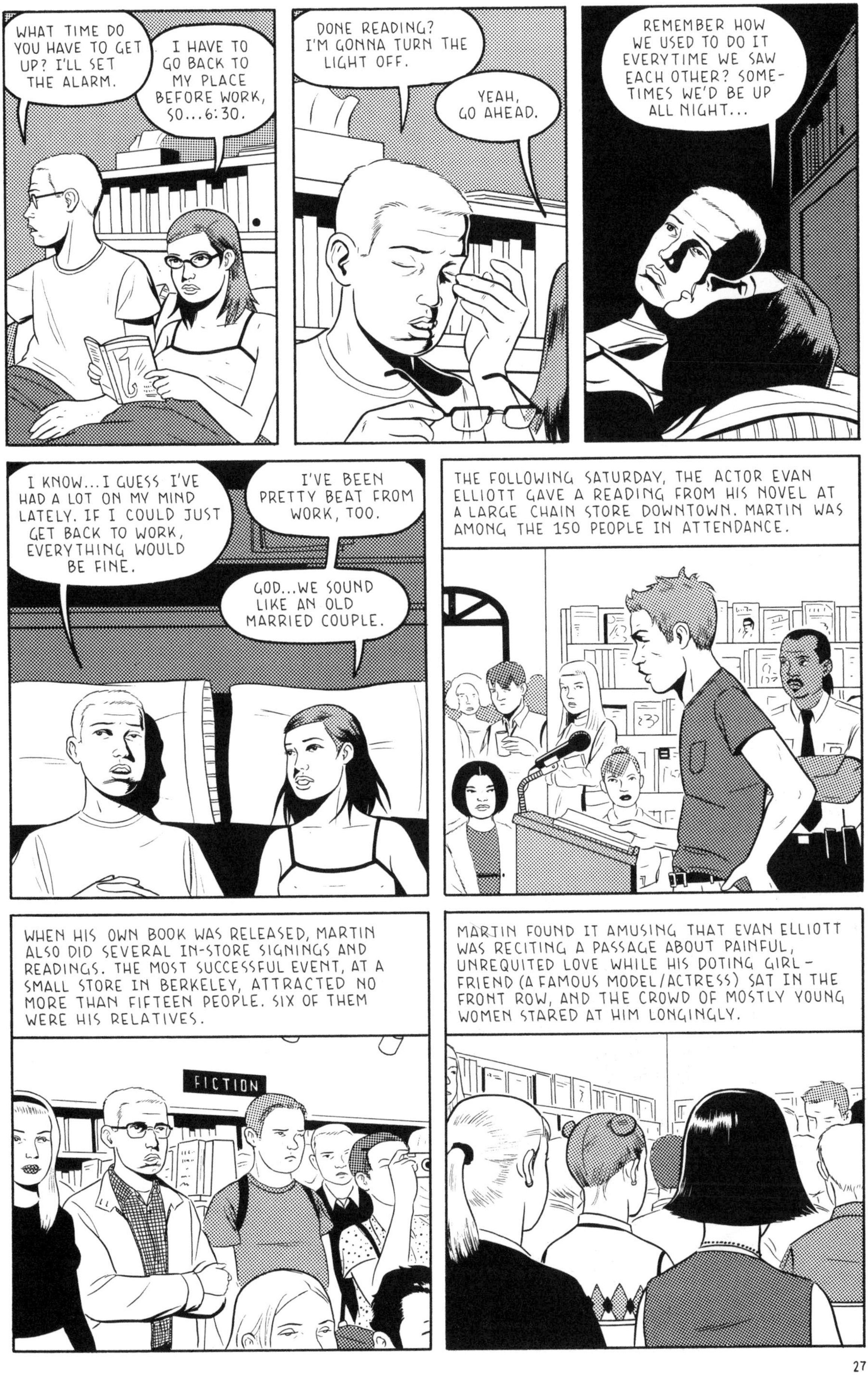
WHAT TIME DO YOU HAVE TO GET UP? I'LL SET THE ALARM.
I HAVE TO GO BACK TO MY PLACE BEFORE WORK, SO...6:30.
DONE READING? I'M GONNA TURN THE LIGHT OFF.
YEAH, GO AHEAD.
REMEMBER HOW WE USED TO DO IT EVERYTIME WE SAW EACH OTHER? SOMETIMES WE'D BE UP ALL NIGHT...
I KNOW...I GUESS I'VE HAD A LOT ON MY MIND LATELY. IF I COULD JUST GET BACK TO WORK, EVERYTHING WOULD BE FINE.
I'VE BEEN PRETTY BEAT FROM WORK, TOO.
GOD...WE SOUND LIKE AN OLD MARRIED COUPLE.
THE FOLLOWING SATURDAY, THE ACTOR EVAN ELLIOTT GAVE A READING FROM HIS NOVEL AT A LARGE CHAIN STORE DOWNTOWN. MARTIN WAS AMONG THE 150 PEOPLE IN ATTENDANCE.
WHEN HIS OWN BOOK WAS RELEASED, MARTIN ALSO DID SEVERAL IN-STORE SIGNINGS AND READINGS. THE MOST SUCCESSFUL EVENT, AT A SMALL STORE IN BERKELEY, ATTRACTED NO MORE THAN FIFTEEN PEOPLE. SIX OF THEM WERE HIS RELATIVES.
FICTION
MARTIN FOUND IT AMUSING THAT EVAN ELLIOTT WAS RECITING A PASSAGE ABOUT PAINFUL, UNREQUITED LOVE WHILE HIS DOTING GIRLFRIEND (A FAMOUS MODEL/ACTRESS) SAT IN THE FRONT ROW, AND THE CROWD OF MOSTLY YOUNG WOMEN STARED AT HIM LONGINGLY.

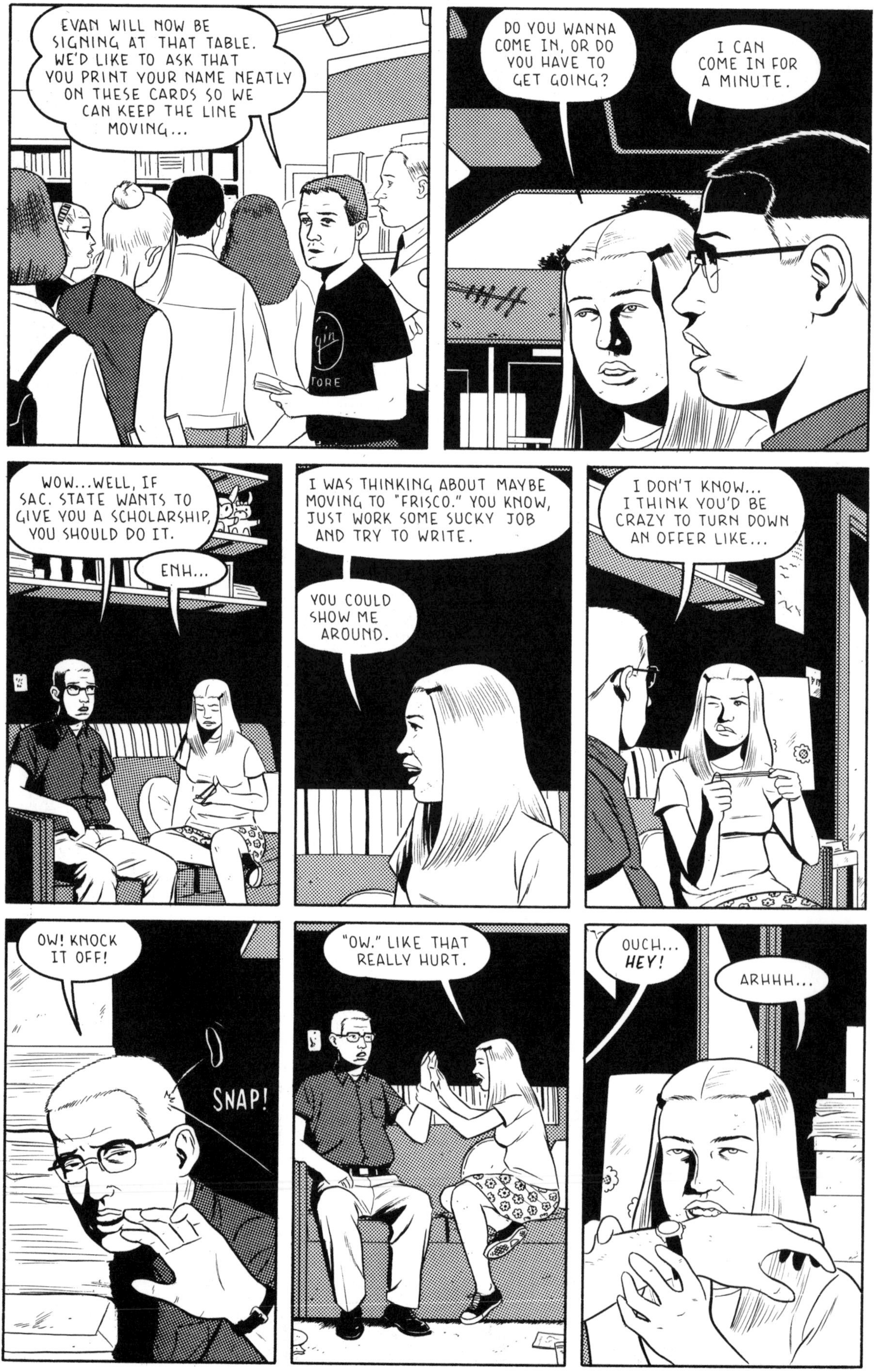
EVAN WILL NOW BE SIGNING AT THAT TABLE. WE'D LIKE TO ASK THAT YOU PRINT YOUR NAME NEATLY ON THESE CARDS SO WE CAN KEEP THE LINE MOVING...
DO YOU WANNA COME IN, OR DO YOU HAVE TO GET GOING?
I CAN COME IN FOR A MINUTE.
WOW...WELL, IF SAC. STATE WANTS TO GIVE YOU A SCHOLARSHIP, YOU SHOULD DO IT.
ENH...
I WAS THINKING ABOUT MAYBE MOVING TO "FRISCO." YOU KNOW, JUST WORK SOME SUCKY JOB AND TRY TO WRITE.
YOU COULD SHOW ME AROUND.
I DON'T KNOW... I THINK YOU'D BE CRAZY TO TURN DOWN AN OFFER LIKE...
OW! KNOCK IT OFF!
SNAP!
"OW." LIKE THAT REALLY HURT.
OUCH... HEY!
ARHHH...

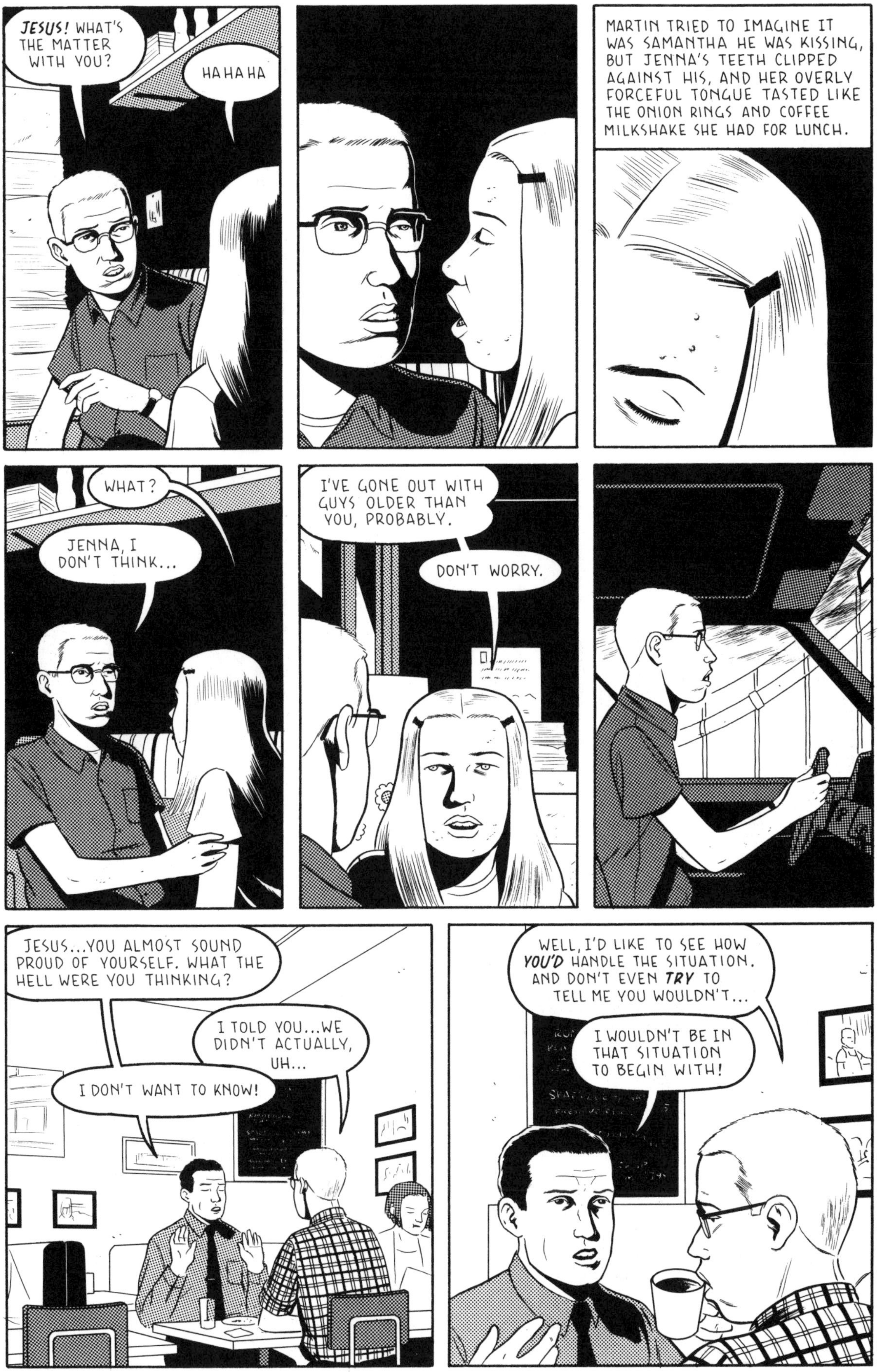
JESUS! WHAT'S THE MATTER WITH YOU?
HA HA HA
MARTIN TRIED TO IMAGINE IT WAS SAMANTHA HE WAS KISSING, BUT JENNA'S TEETH CLIPPED AGAINST HIS, AND HER OVERLY FORCEFUL TONGUE TASTED LIKE THE ONION RINGS AND COFFEE MILKSHAKE SHE HAD FOR LUNCH.
WHAT?
JENNA, I DON'T THINK...
I'VE GONE OUT WITH GUYS OLDER THAN YOU, PROBABLY.
DON'T WORRY.
JESUS...YOU ALMOST SOUND PROUD OF YOURSELF. WHAT THE HELL WERE YOU THINKING?
I TOLD YOU...WE DIDN'T ACTUALLY, UH...
I DON'T WANT TO KNOW!
WELL, I'D LIKE TO SEE HOW *YOU'D* HANDLE THE SITUATION. AND DON'T EVEN *TRY* TO TELL ME YOU WOULDN'T...
I WOULDN'T BE IN THAT SITUATION TO BEGIN WITH!

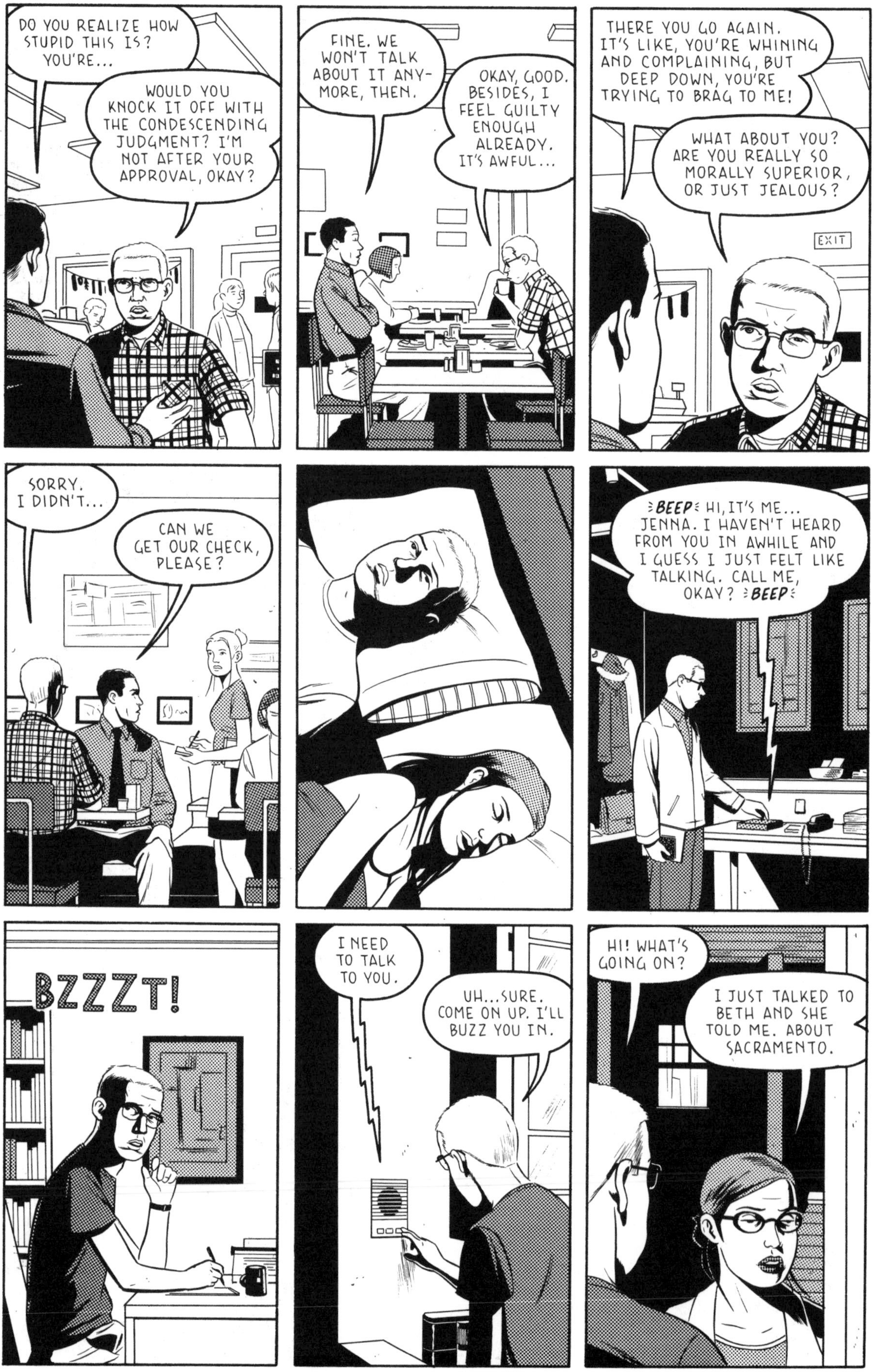
DO YOU REALIZE HOW STUPID THIS IS? YOU'RE...
WOULD YOU KNOCK IT OFF WITH THE CONDESCENDING JUDGMENT? I'M NOT AFTER YOUR APPROVAL, OKAY?
FINE. WE WON'T TALK ABOUT IT ANYMORE, THEN.
OKAY, GOOD. BESIDES, I FEEL GUILTY ENOUGH ALREADY. IT'S AWFUL...
THERE YOU GO AGAIN. IT'S LIKE, YOU'RE WHINING AND COMPLAINING, BUT DEEP DOWN, YOU'RE TRYING TO BRAG TO ME!
WHAT ABOUT YOU? ARE YOU REALLY SO MORALLY SUPERIOR, OR JUST JEALOUS?
EXIT
SORRY. I DIDN'T...
CAN WE GET OUR CHECK, PLEASE?
BEEP HI, IT'S ME... JENNA. I HAVEN'T HEARD FROM YOU IN AWHILE AND I GUESS I JUST FELT LIKE TALKING. CALL ME, OKAY? BEEP
BZZZT!
I NEED TO TALK TO YOU.
UH...SURE. COME ON UP. I'LL BUZZ YOU IN.
HI! WHAT'S GOING ON?
I JUST TALKED TO BETH AND SHE TOLD ME. ABOUT SACRAMENTO.

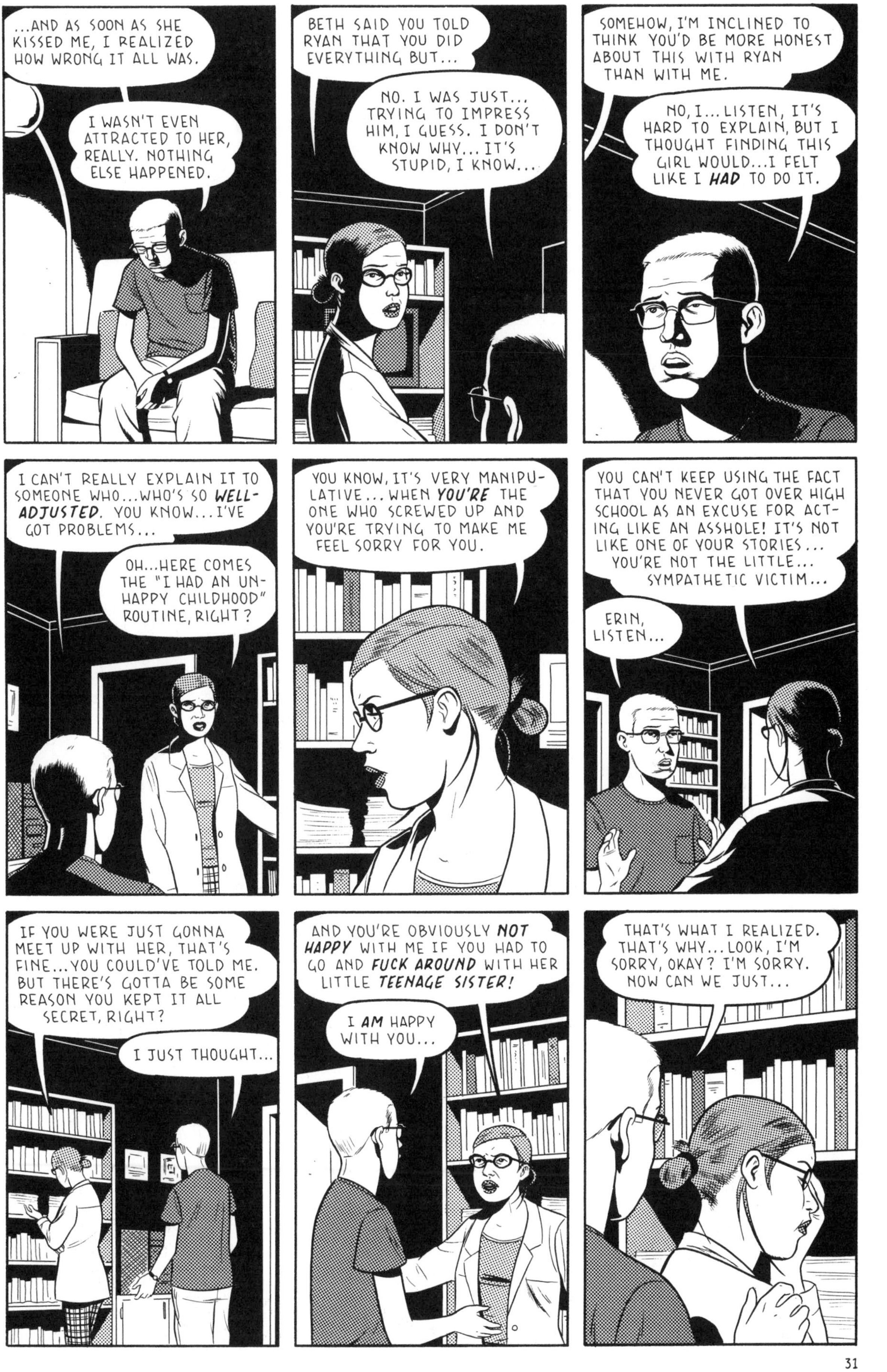
...AND AS SOON AS SHE KISSED ME, I REALIZED HOW WRONG IT ALL WAS.
I WASN'T EVEN ATTRACTED TO HER, REALLY. NOTHING ELSE HAPPENED.
BETH SAID YOU TOLD RYAN THAT YOU DID EVERYTHING BUT...
NO. I WAS JUST... TRYING TO IMPRESS HIM, I GUESS. I DON'T KNOW WHY... IT'S STUPID, I KNOW...
SOMEHOW, I'M INCLINED TO THINK YOU'D BE MORE HONEST ABOUT THIS WITH RYAN THAN WITH ME.
NO, I... LISTEN, IT'S HARD TO EXPLAIN, BUT I THOUGHT FINDING THIS GIRL WOULD...I FELT LIKE I **HAD** TO DO IT.
I CAN'T REALLY EXPLAIN IT TO SOMEONE WHO...WHO'S SO **WELL-ADJUSTED**. YOU KNOW...I'VE GOT PROBLEMS...
OH...HERE COMES THE "I HAD AN UNHAPPY CHILDHOOD" ROUTINE, RIGHT?
YOU KNOW, IT'S VERY MANIPULATIVE... WHEN **YOU'RE** THE ONE WHO SCREWED UP AND YOU'RE TRYING TO MAKE ME FEEL SORRY FOR YOU.
YOU CAN'T KEEP USING THE FACT THAT YOU NEVER GOT OVER HIGH SCHOOL AS AN EXCUSE FOR ACTING LIKE AN ASSHOLE! IT'S NOT LIKE ONE OF YOUR STORIES... YOU'RE NOT THE LITTLE... SYMPATHETIC VICTIM...
ERIN, LISTEN...
IF YOU WERE JUST GONNA MEET UP WITH HER, THAT'S FINE...YOU COULD'VE TOLD ME. BUT THERE'S GOTTA BE SOME REASON YOU KEPT IT ALL SECRET, RIGHT?
I JUST THOUGHT...
AND YOU'RE OBVIOUSLY **NOT HAPPY** WITH ME IF YOU HAD TO GO AND **FUCK AROUND** WITH HER LITTLE **TEENAGE SISTER!**
I **AM** HAPPY WITH YOU...
THAT'S WHAT I REALIZED. THAT'S WHY... LOOK, I'M SORRY, OKAY? I'M SORRY. NOW CAN WE JUST...

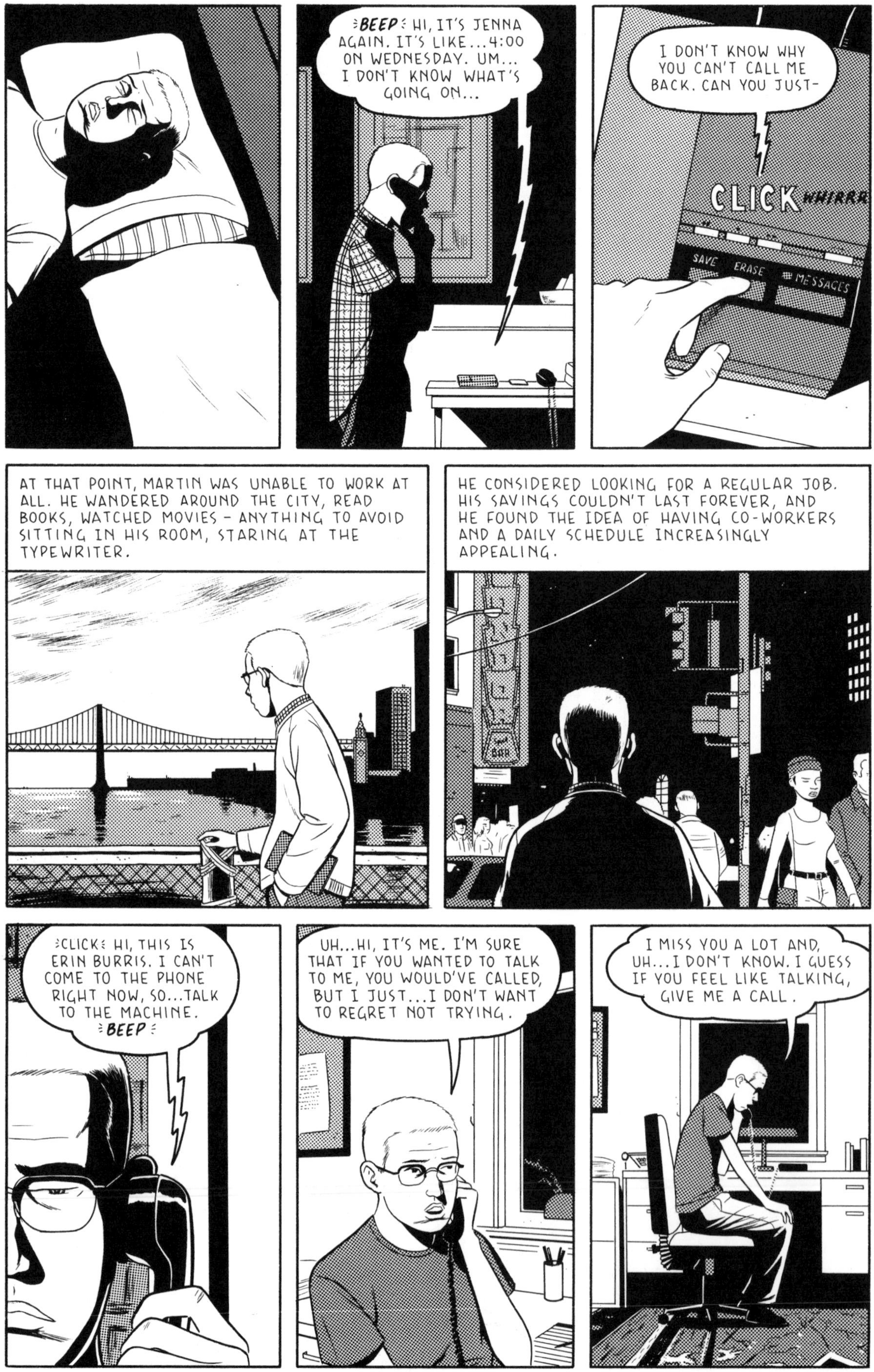

⸗BEEP⸗ HI, IT'S JENNA AGAIN. IT'S LIKE...4:00 ON WEDNESDAY. UM... I DON'T KNOW WHAT'S GOING ON...
I DON'T KNOW WHY YOU CAN'T CALL ME BACK. CAN YOU JUST-
CLICK
SAVE
ERASE
MESSAGES
AT THAT POINT, MARTIN WAS UNABLE TO WORK AT ALL. HE WANDERED AROUND THE CITY, READ BOOKS, WATCHED MOVIES – ANYTHING TO AVOID SITTING IN HIS ROOM, STARING AT THE TYPEWRITER.
HE CONSIDERED LOOKING FOR A REGULAR JOB. HIS SAVINGS COULDN'T LAST FOREVER, AND HE FOUND THE IDEA OF HAVING CO-WORKERS AND A DAILY SCHEDULE INCREASINGLY APPEALING.
⸗CLICK⸗ HI, THIS IS ERIN BURRIS. I CAN'T COME TO THE PHONE RIGHT NOW, SO...TALK TO THE MACHINE. ⸗BEEP⸗
UH...HI, IT'S ME. I'M SURE THAT IF YOU WANTED TO TALK TO ME, YOU WOULD'VE CALLED, BUT I JUST...I DON'T WANT TO REGRET NOT TRYING.
I MISS YOU A LOT AND, UH...I DON'T KNOW. I GUESS IF YOU FEEL LIKE TALKING, GIVE ME A CALL.

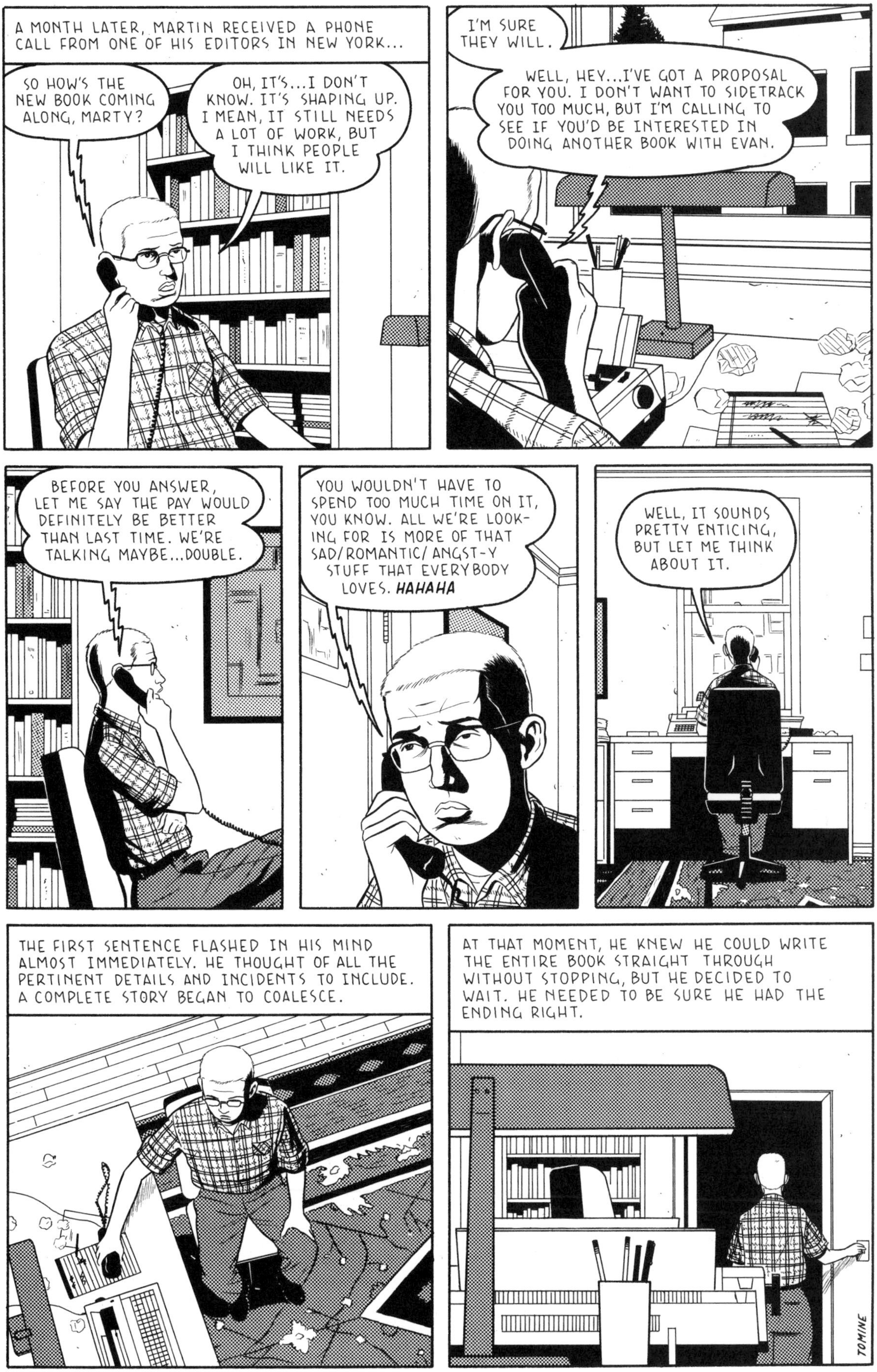
A MONTH LATER, MARTIN RECEIVED A PHONE CALL FROM ONE OF HIS EDITORS IN NEW YORK...
SO HOW'S THE NEW BOOK COMING ALONG, MARTY?
OH, IT'S...I DON'T KNOW. IT'S SHAPING UP. I MEAN, IT STILL NEEDS A LOT OF WORK, BUT I THINK PEOPLE WILL LIKE IT.
I'M SURE THEY WILL.
WELL, HEY...I'VE GOT A PROPOSAL FOR YOU. I DON'T WANT TO SIDETRACK YOU TOO MUCH, BUT I'M CALLING TO SEE IF YOU'D BE INTERESTED IN DOING ANOTHER BOOK WITH EVAN.
BEFORE YOU ANSWER, LET ME SAY THE PAY WOULD DEFINITELY BE BETTER THAN LAST TIME. WE'RE TALKING MAYBE...DOUBLE.
YOU WOULDN'T HAVE TO SPEND TOO MUCH TIME ON IT, YOU KNOW. ALL WE'RE LOOKING FOR IS MORE OF THAT SAD/ROMANTIC/ANGST-Y STUFF THAT EVERYBODY LOVES. HAHAHA
WELL, IT SOUNDS PRETTY ENTICING, BUT LET ME THINK ABOUT IT.
THE FIRST SENTENCE FLASHED IN HIS MIND ALMOST IMMEDIATELY. HE THOUGHT OF ALL THE PERTINENT DETAILS AND INCIDENTS TO INCLUDE. A COMPLETE STORY BEGAN TO COALESCE.
AT THAT MOMENT, HE KNEW HE COULD WRITE THE ENTIRE BOOK STRAIGHT THROUGH WITHOUT STOPPING, BUT HE DECIDED TO WAIT. HE NEEDED TO BE SURE HE HAD THE ENDING RIGHT.
TOMINE

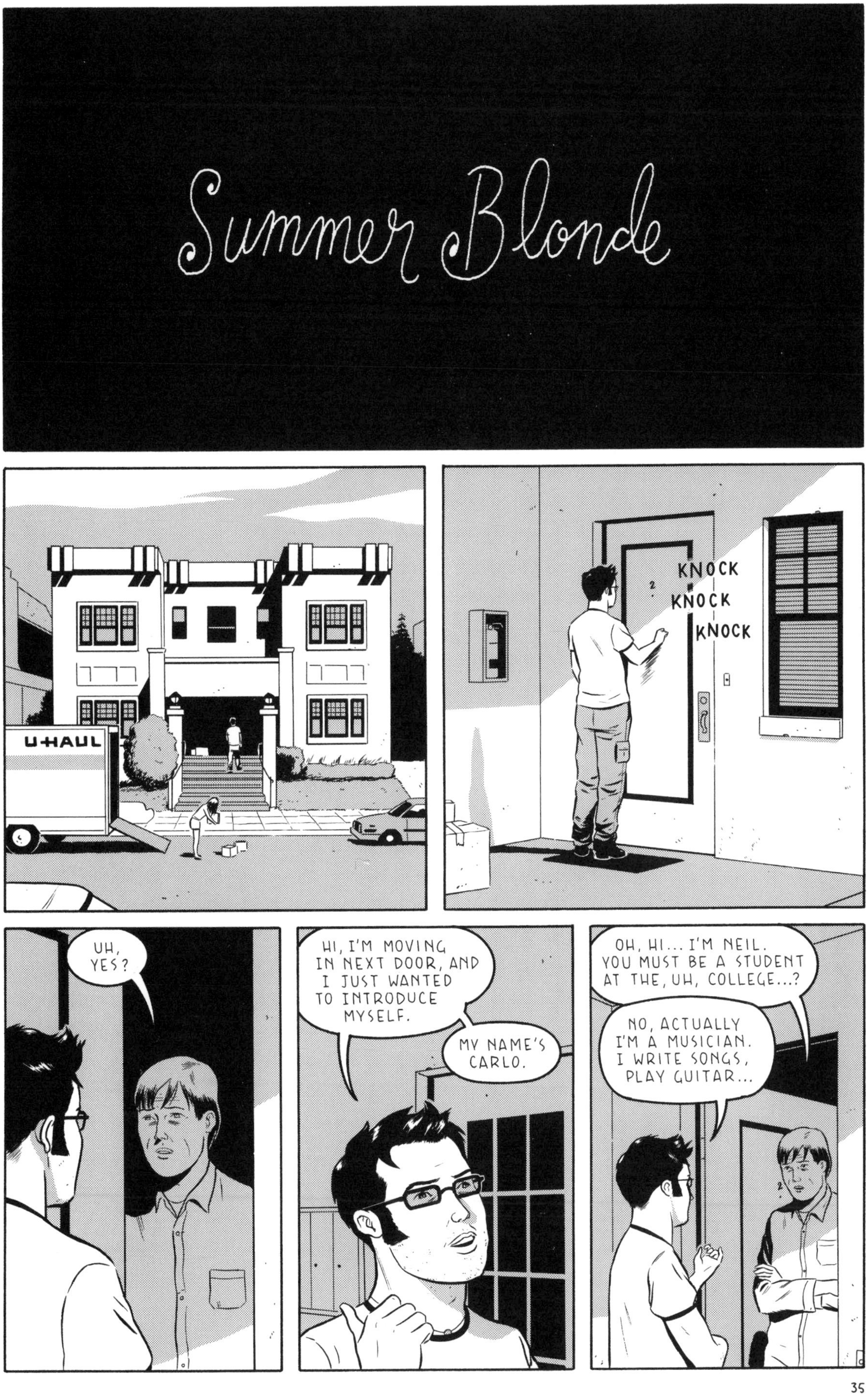
Summer Blonde
U-HAUL
KNOCK
KNOCK
KNOCK
UH, YES?
HI, I'M MOVING IN NEXT DOOR, AND I JUST WANTED TO INTRODUCE MYSELF.
MY NAME'S CARLO.
OH, HI... I'M NEIL. YOU MUST BE A STUDENT AT THE, UH, COLLEGE...?
NO, ACTUALLY I'M A MUSICIAN. I WRITE SONGS, PLAY GUITAR...

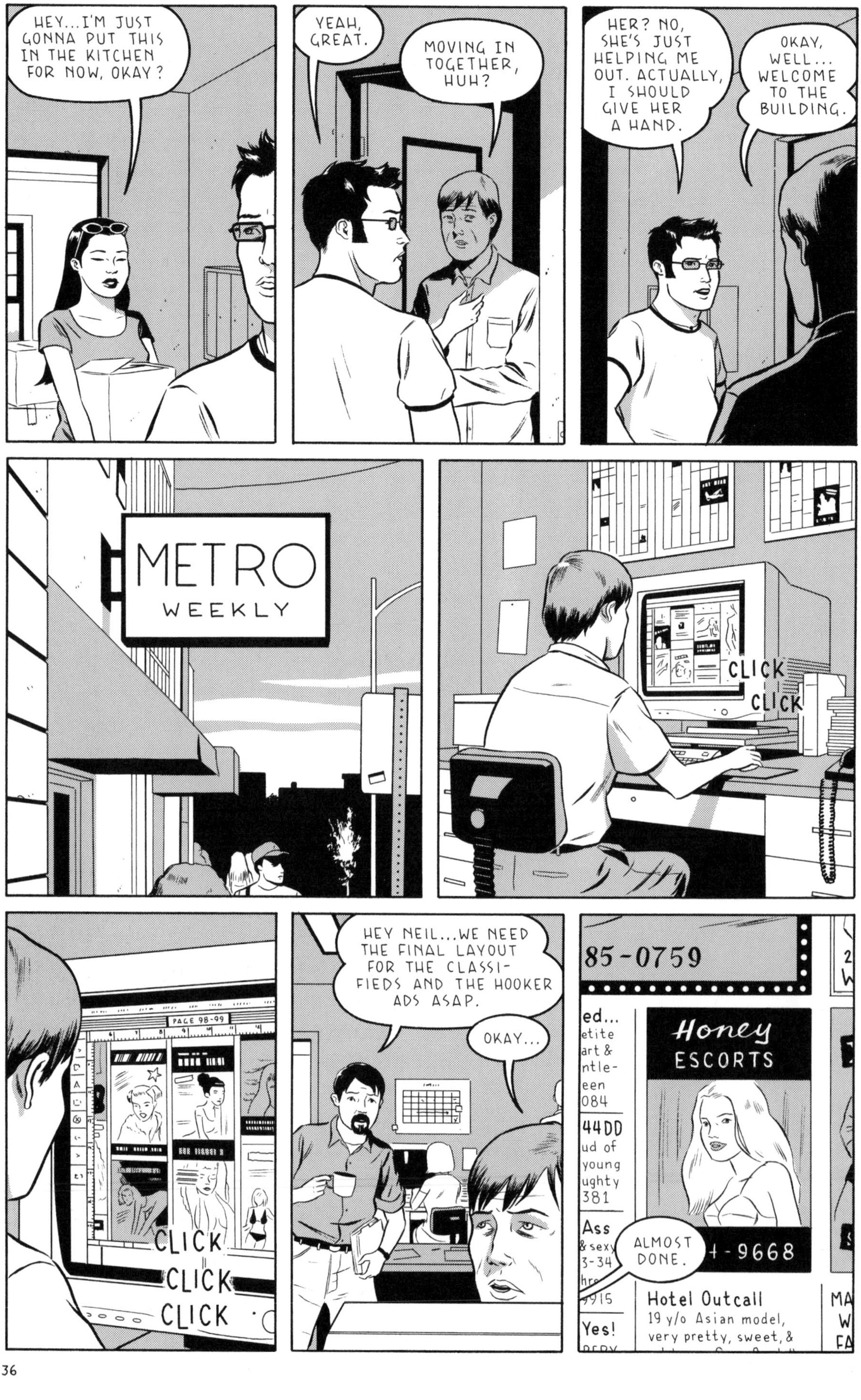
HEY...I'M JUST GONNA PUT THIS IN THE KITCHEN FOR NOW, OKAY?
YEAH, GREAT.
MOVING IN TOGETHER, HUH?
HER? NO, SHE'S JUST HELPING ME OUT. ACTUALLY, I SHOULD GIVE HER A HAND.
OKAY, WELL... WELCOME TO THE BUILDING.
METRO WEEKLY
CLICK
CLICK
PAGE 98-99
CLICK
CLICK
CLICK
HEY NEIL...WE NEED THE FINAL LAYOUT FOR THE CLASSIFIEDS AND THE HOOKER ADS ASAP.
OKAY...
85-0759
Honey
ESCORTS
ALMOST DONE.
-9668
Hotel Outcall
19 y/o Asian model,
very pretty, sweet, &
44DD
Yes!

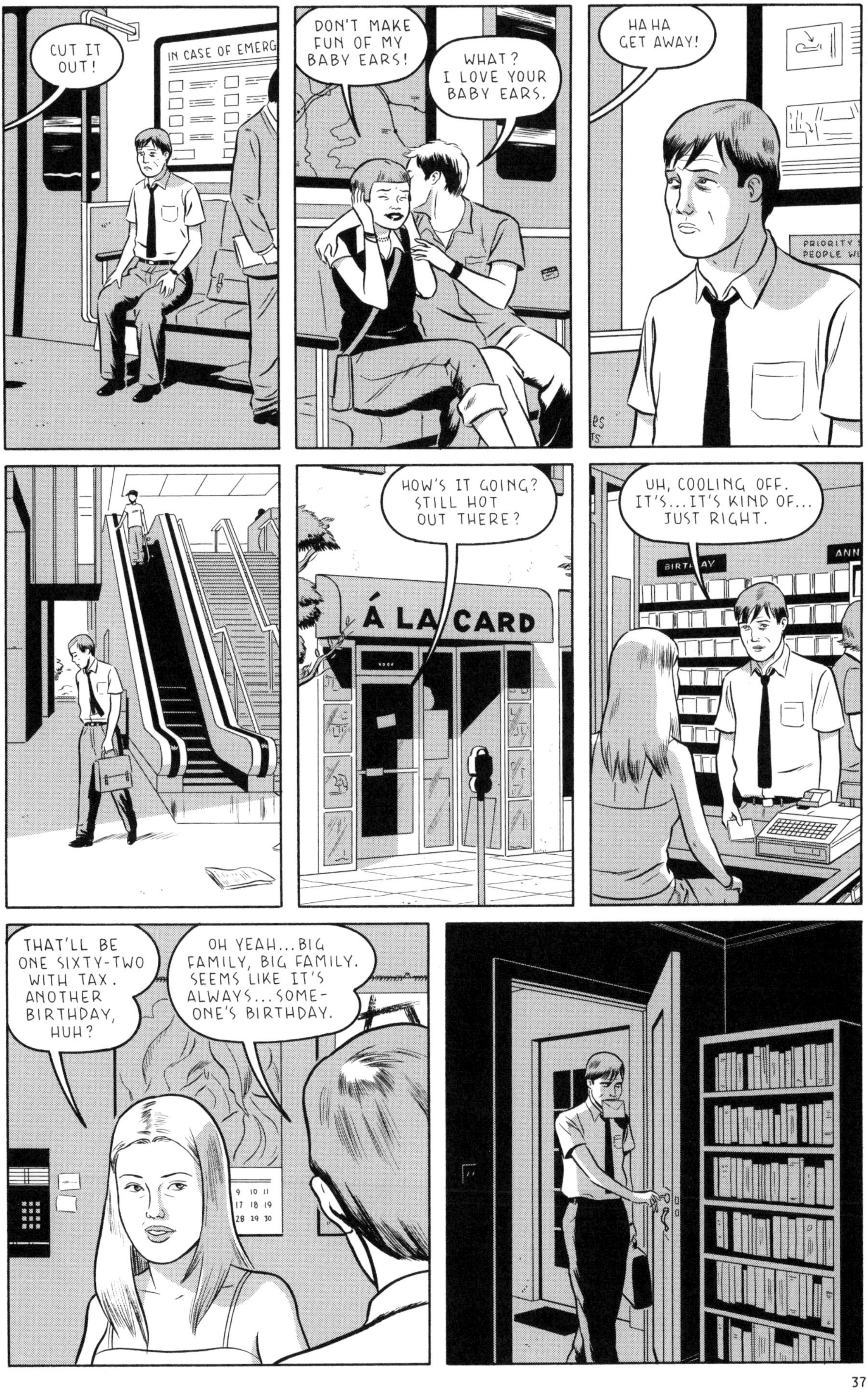
IN CASE OF EMERG
CUT IT OUT!
DON'T MAKE FUN OF MY BABY EARS!
WHAT? I LOVE YOUR BABY EARS.
HA HA GET AWAY!
PRIORITY S
PEOPLE WI
HOW'S IT GOING? STILL HOT OUT THERE?
Á LA CARD
UH, COOLING OFF. IT'S...IT'S KIND OF... JUST RIGHT.
BIRTHDAY
ANN
THAT'LL BE ONE SIXTY-TWO WITH TAX. ANOTHER BIRTHDAY, HUH?
OH YEAH...BIG FAMILY, BIG FAMILY. SEEMS LIKE IT'S ALWAYS...SOME-ONE'S BIRTHDAY.

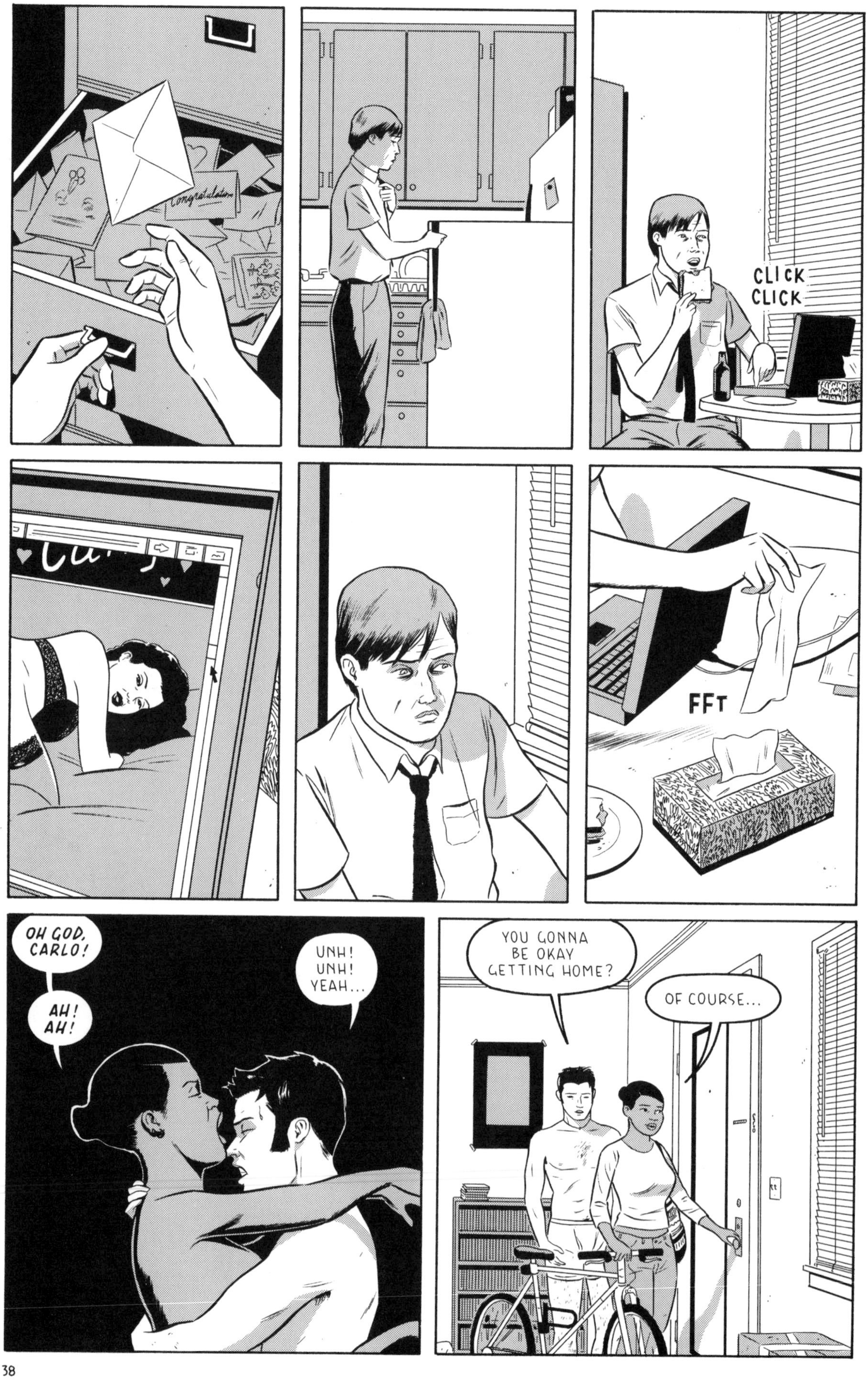
Congratulations
CLICK
CLICK
FFT
OH GOD, CARLO!
AH! AH!
UNH! UNH! YEAH...
YOU GONNA BE OKAY GETTING HOME?
OF COURSE...

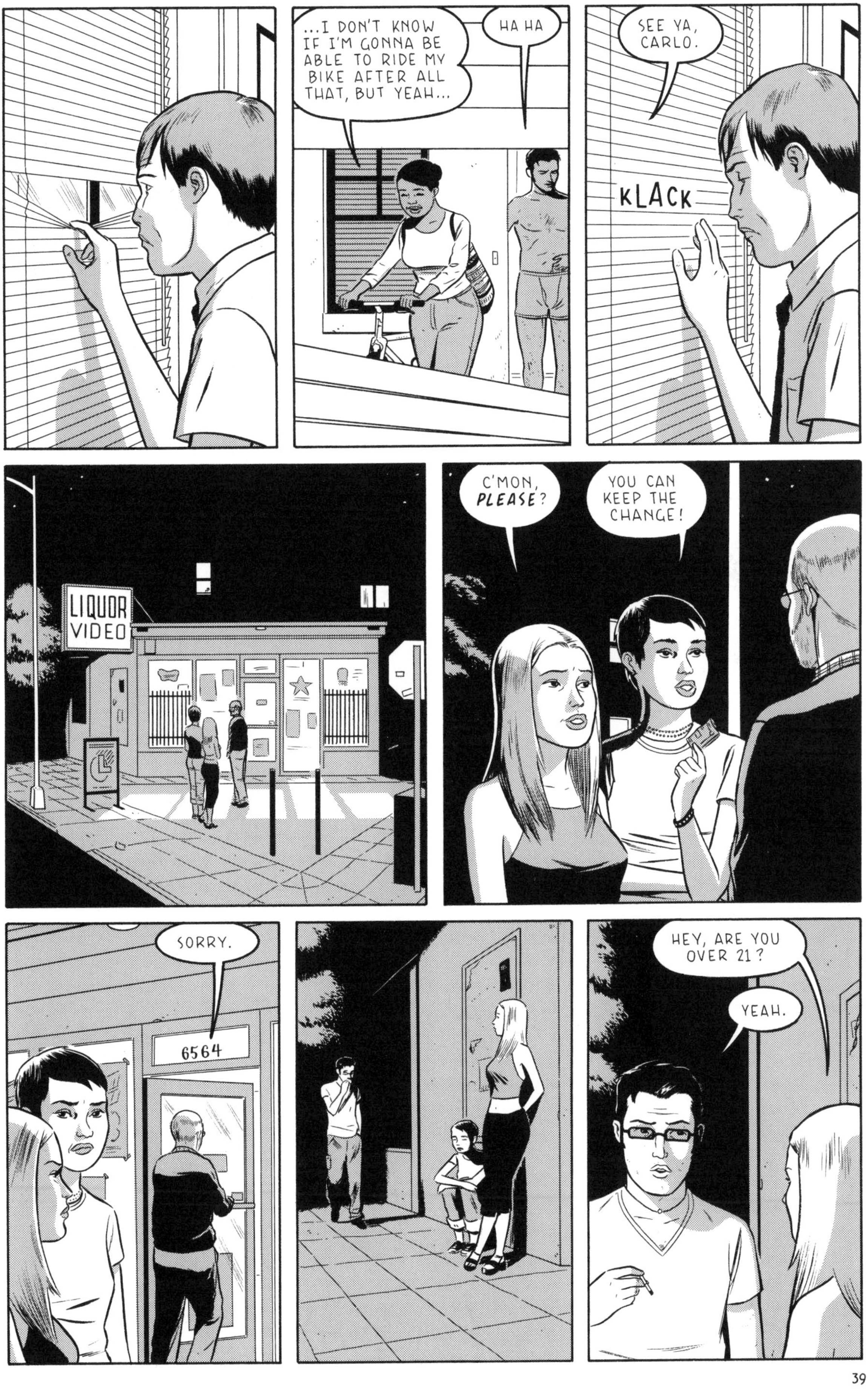
...I DON'T KNOW IF I'M GONNA BE ABLE TO RIDE MY BIKE AFTER ALL THAT, BUT YEAH...
HA HA
SEE YA, CARLO.
KLACK
LIQUOR
VIDEO
C'MON, PLEASE?
YOU CAN KEEP THE CHANGE!
SORRY.
6564
HEY, ARE YOU OVER 21?
YEAH.

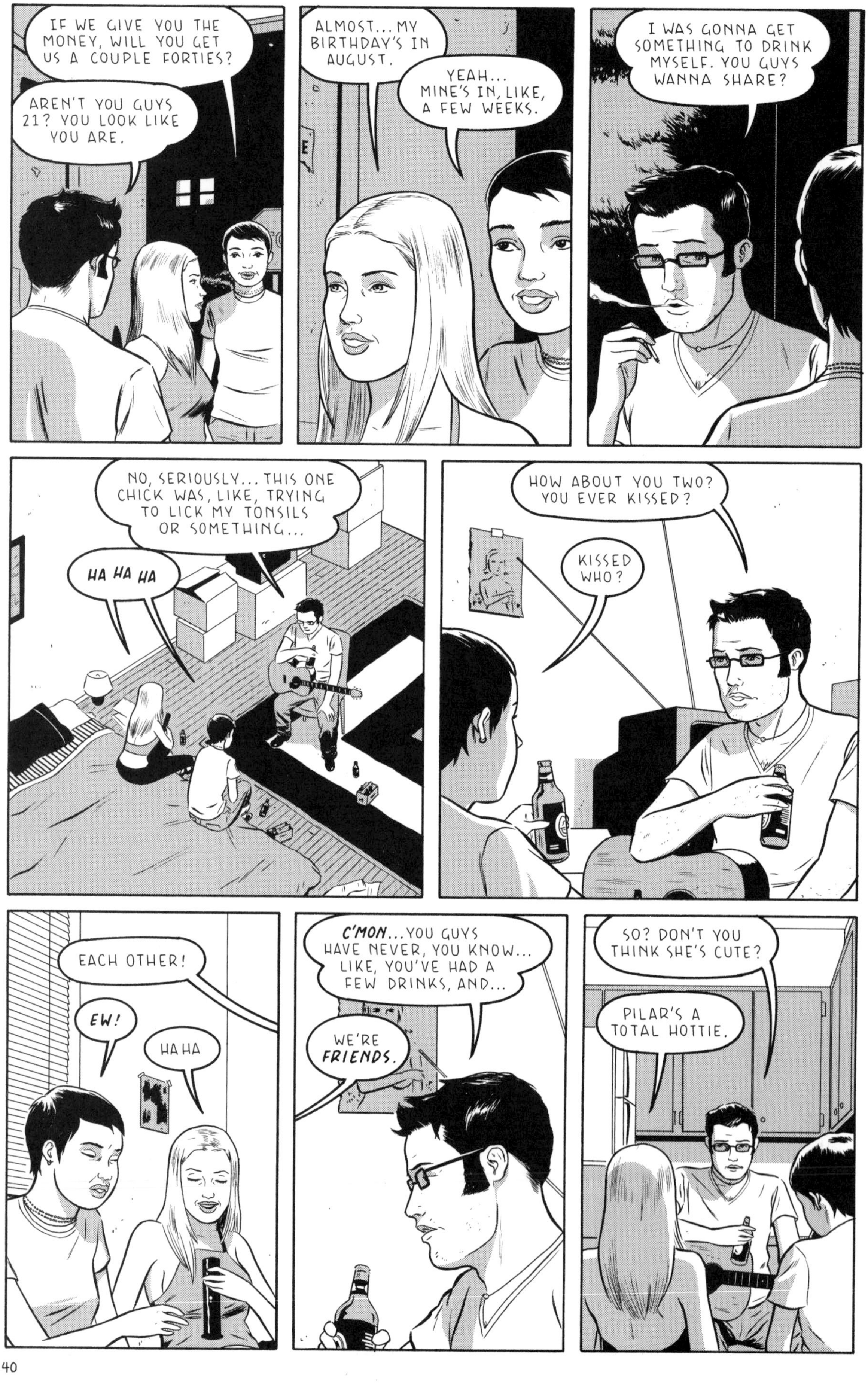
IF WE GIVE YOU THE MONEY, WILL YOU GET US A COUPLE FORTIES?
AREN'T YOU GUYS 21? YOU LOOK LIKE YOU ARE.
ALMOST... MY BIRTHDAY'S IN AUGUST.
YEAH... MINE'S IN, LIKE, A FEW WEEKS.
I WAS GONNA GET SOMETHING TO DRINK MYSELF. YOU GUYS WANNA SHARE?
NO, SERIOUSLY... THIS ONE CHICK WAS, LIKE, TRYING TO LICK MY TONSILS OR SOMETHING...
HA HA HA
HOW ABOUT YOU TWO? YOU EVER KISSED?
KISSED WHO?
EACH OTHER!
EW!
HA HA
C'MON... YOU GUYS HAVE NEVER, YOU KNOW... LIKE, YOU'VE HAD A FEW DRINKS, AND...
WE'RE FRIENDS.
SO? DON'T YOU THINK SHE'S CUTE?
PILAR'S A TOTAL HOTTIE.

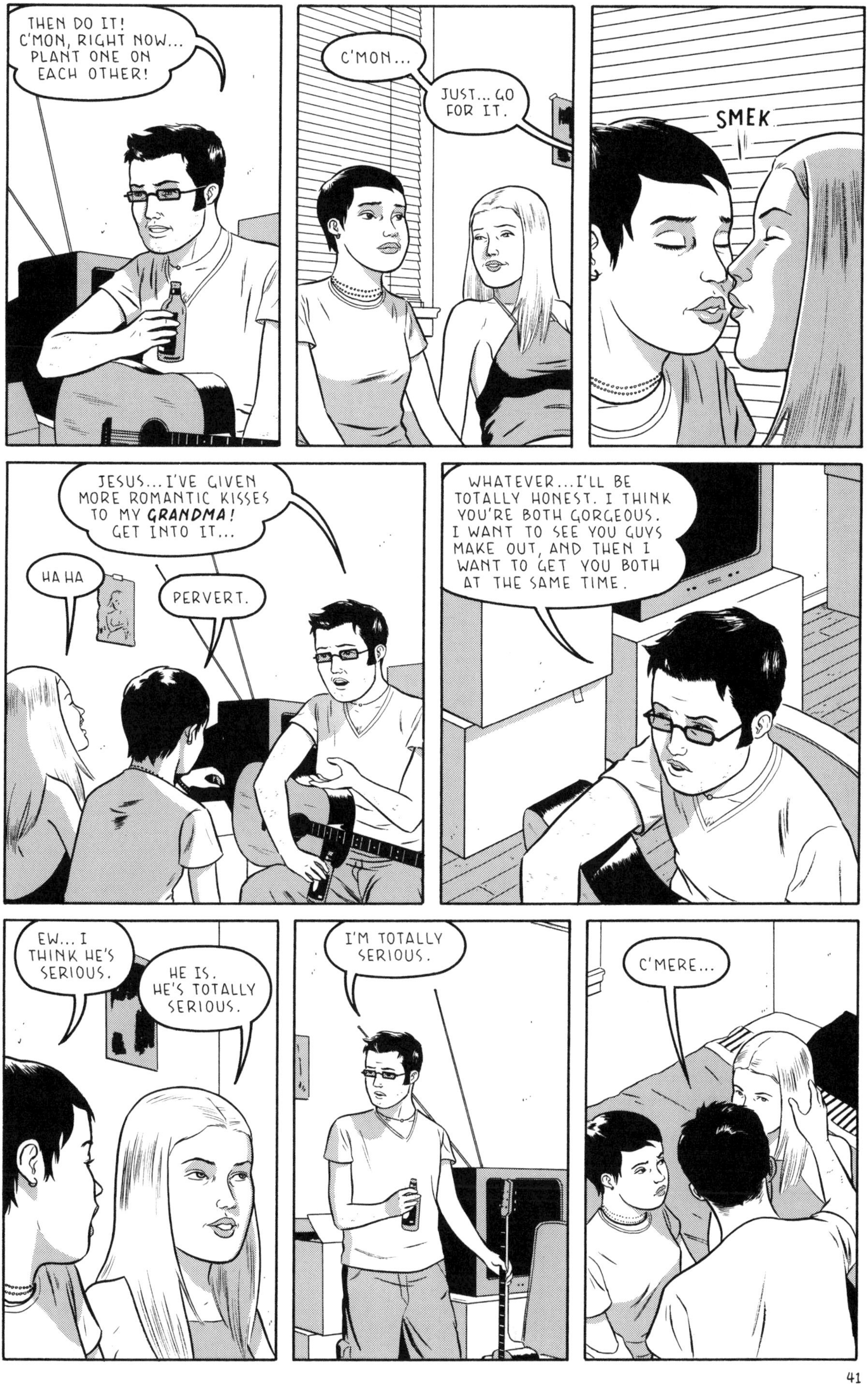
THEN DO IT! C'MON, RIGHT NOW... PLANT ONE ON EACH OTHER!
C'MON...
JUST... GO FOR IT.
SMEK
JESUS... I'VE GIVEN MORE ROMANTIC KISSES TO MY **GRANDMA!** GET INTO IT...
HA HA
PERVERT.
WHATEVER... I'LL BE TOTALLY HONEST. I THINK YOU'RE BOTH GORGEOUS. I WANT TO SEE YOU GUYS MAKE OUT, AND THEN I WANT TO GET YOU BOTH AT THE SAME TIME.
EW... I THINK HE'S SERIOUS.
HE IS. HE'S TOTALLY SERIOUS.
I'M TOTALLY SERIOUS.
C'MERE...

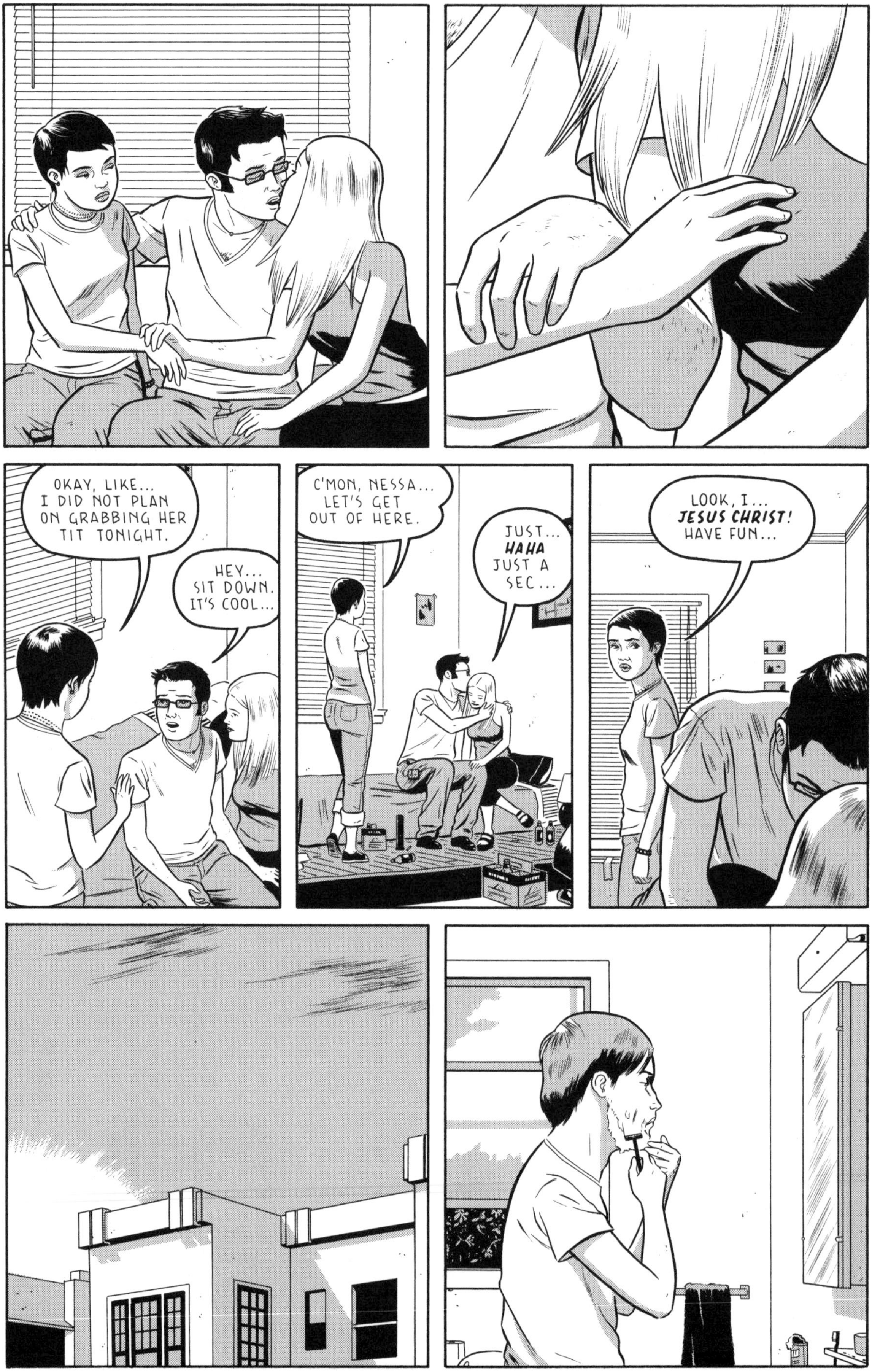
OKAY, LIKE... I DID NOT PLAN ON GRABBING HER TIT TONIGHT.
HEY... SIT DOWN. IT'S COOL...
C'MON, NESSA... LET'S GET OUT OF HERE.
JUST... **HAHA** JUST A SEC...
LOOK, I... **JESUS CHRIST!** HAVE FUN...

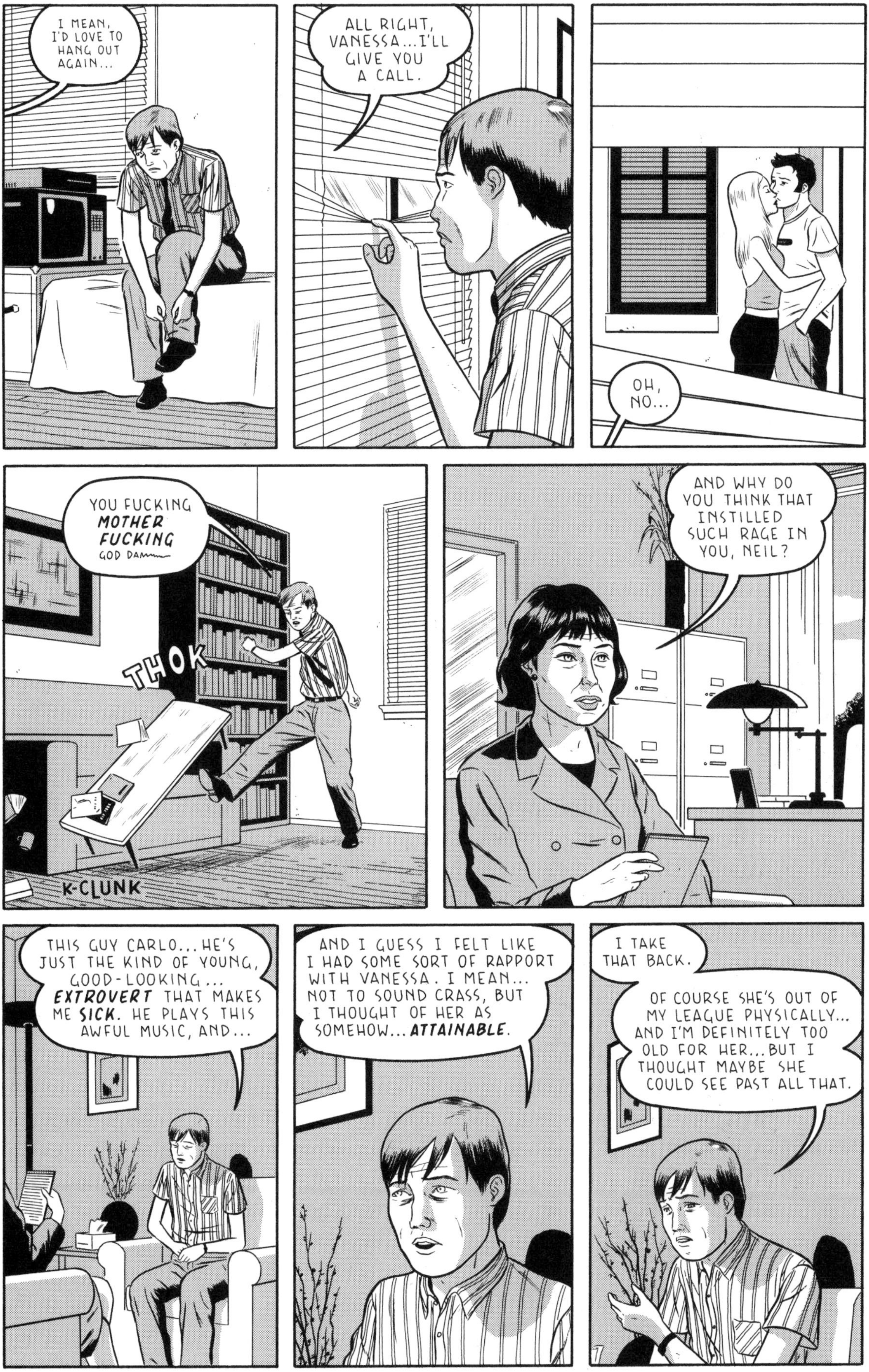
I MEAN, I'D LOVE TO HANG OUT AGAIN...
ALL RIGHT, VANESSA... I'LL GIVE YOU A CALL.
OH, NO...
YOU FUCKING **MOTHER FUCKING** GOD DAM—
THOK
K-CLUNK
AND WHY DO YOU THINK THAT INSTILLED SUCH RAGE IN YOU, NEIL?
THIS GUY CARLO... HE'S JUST THE KIND OF YOUNG, GOOD-LOOKING... **EXTROVERT** THAT MAKES ME **SICK**. HE PLAYS THIS AWFUL MUSIC, AND...
AND I GUESS I FELT LIKE I HAD SOME SORT OF RAPPORT WITH VANESSA. I MEAN... NOT TO SOUND CRASS, BUT I THOUGHT OF HER AS SOMEHOW... **ATTAINABLE**.
I TAKE THAT BACK.
OF COURSE SHE'S OUT OF MY LEAGUE PHYSICALLY... AND I'M DEFINITELY TOO OLD FOR HER... BUT I THOUGHT MAYBE SHE COULD SEE PAST ALL THAT.

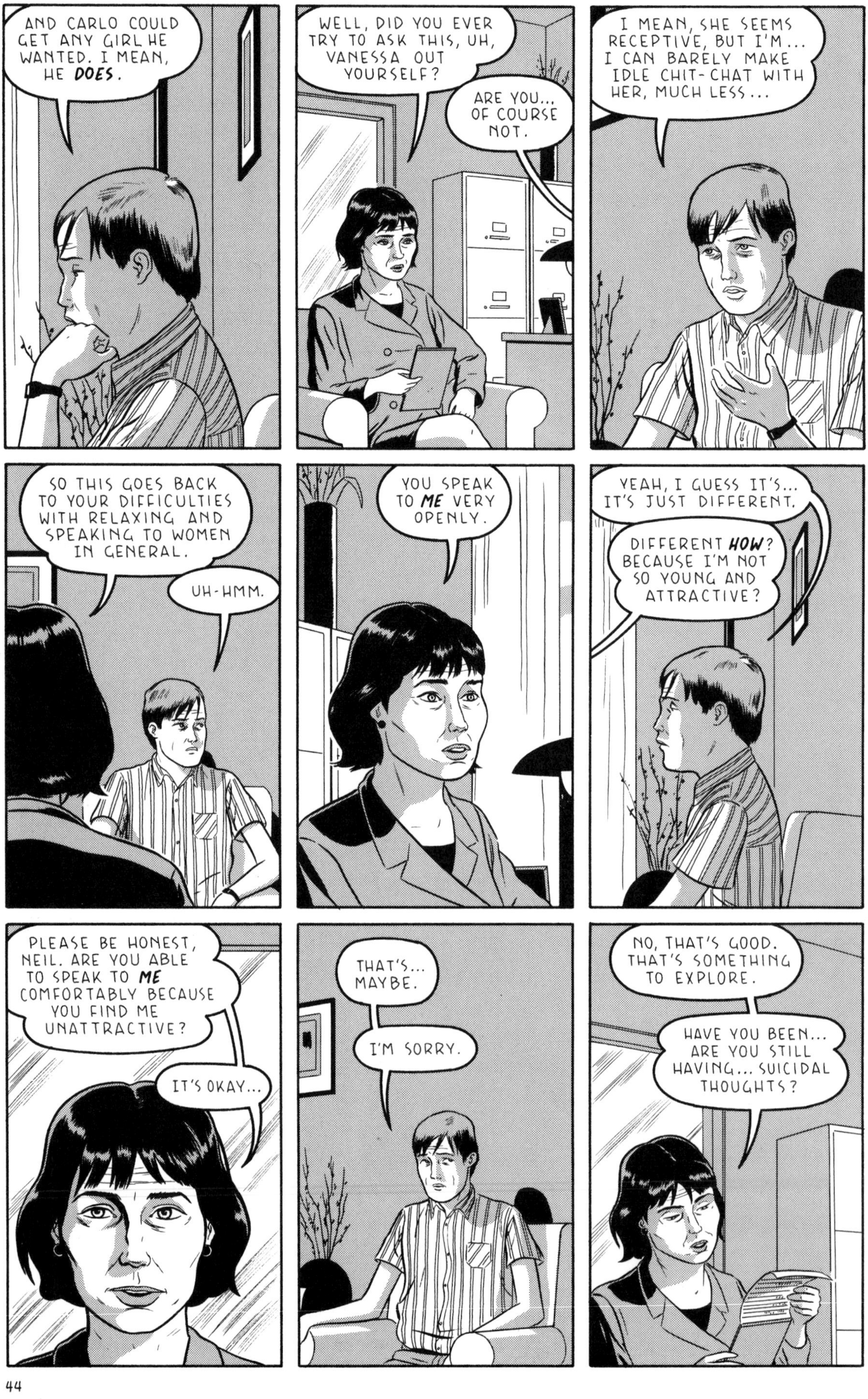
AND CARLO COULD GET ANY GIRL HE WANTED. I MEAN, HE **DOES**.
WELL, DID YOU EVER TRY TO ASK THIS, UH, VANESSA OUT YOURSELF?
ARE YOU... OF COURSE NOT.
I MEAN, SHE SEEMS RECEPTIVE, BUT I'M... I CAN BARELY MAKE IDLE CHIT-CHAT WITH HER, MUCH LESS...
SO THIS GOES BACK TO YOUR DIFFICULTIES WITH RELAXING AND SPEAKING TO WOMEN IN GENERAL.
UH-HMM.
YOU SPEAK TO **ME** VERY OPENLY.
YEAH, I GUESS IT'S... IT'S JUST DIFFERENT.
DIFFERENT **HOW**? BECAUSE I'M NOT SO YOUNG AND ATTRACTIVE?
PLEASE BE HONEST, NEIL. ARE YOU ABLE TO SPEAK TO **ME** COMFORTABLY BECAUSE YOU FIND ME UNATTRACTIVE?
IT'S OKAY...
THAT'S... MAYBE.
I'M SORRY.
NO, THAT'S GOOD. THAT'S SOMETHING TO EXPLORE.
HAVE YOU BEEN... ARE YOU STILL HAVING... SUICIDAL THOUGHTS?

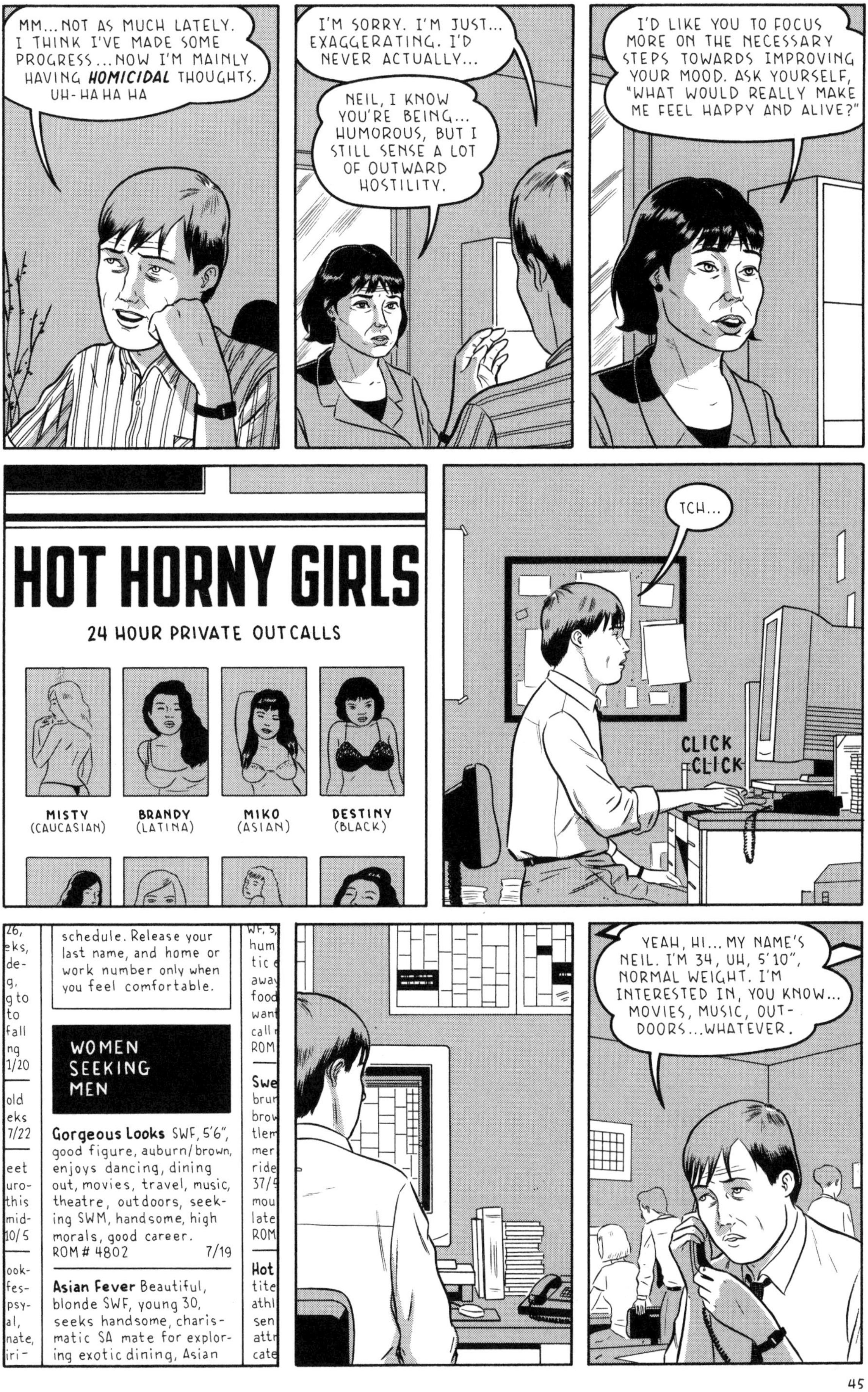
MM... NOT AS MUCH LATELY. I THINK I'VE MADE SOME PROGRESS... NOW I'M MAINLY HAVING ***HOMICIDAL*** THOUGHTS. UH-HA HA HA
I'M SORRY. I'M JUST... EXAGGERATING. I'D NEVER ACTUALLY...
NEIL, I KNOW YOU'RE BEING... HUMOROUS, BUT I STILL SENSE A LOT OF OUTWARD HOSTILITY.
I'D LIKE YOU TO FOCUS MORE ON THE NECESSARY STEPS TOWARDS IMPROVING YOUR MOOD. ASK YOURSELF, "WHAT WOULD REALLY MAKE ME FEEL HAPPY AND ALIVE?"
HOT HORNY GIRLS
24 HOUR PRIVATE OUTCALLS
MISTY (CAUCASIAN)
BRANDY (LATINA)
MIKO (ASIAN)
DESTINY (BLACK)
TCH...
CLICK CLICK
schedule. Release your last name, and home or work number only when you feel comfortable.
WOMEN SEEKING MEN
Gorgeous Looks SWF, 5'6", good figure, auburn/brown, enjoys dancing, dining out, movies, travel, music, theatre, outdoors, seeking SWM, handsome, high morals, good career. ROM # 4802 7/19
Asian Fever Beautiful, blonde SWF, young 30, seeks handsome, charismatic SA mate for exploring exotic dining, Asian
YEAH, HI... MY NAME'S NEIL. I'M 34, UH, 5'10", NORMAL WEIGHT. I'M INTERESTED IN, YOU KNOW... MOVIES, MUSIC, OUTDOORS... WHATEVER.

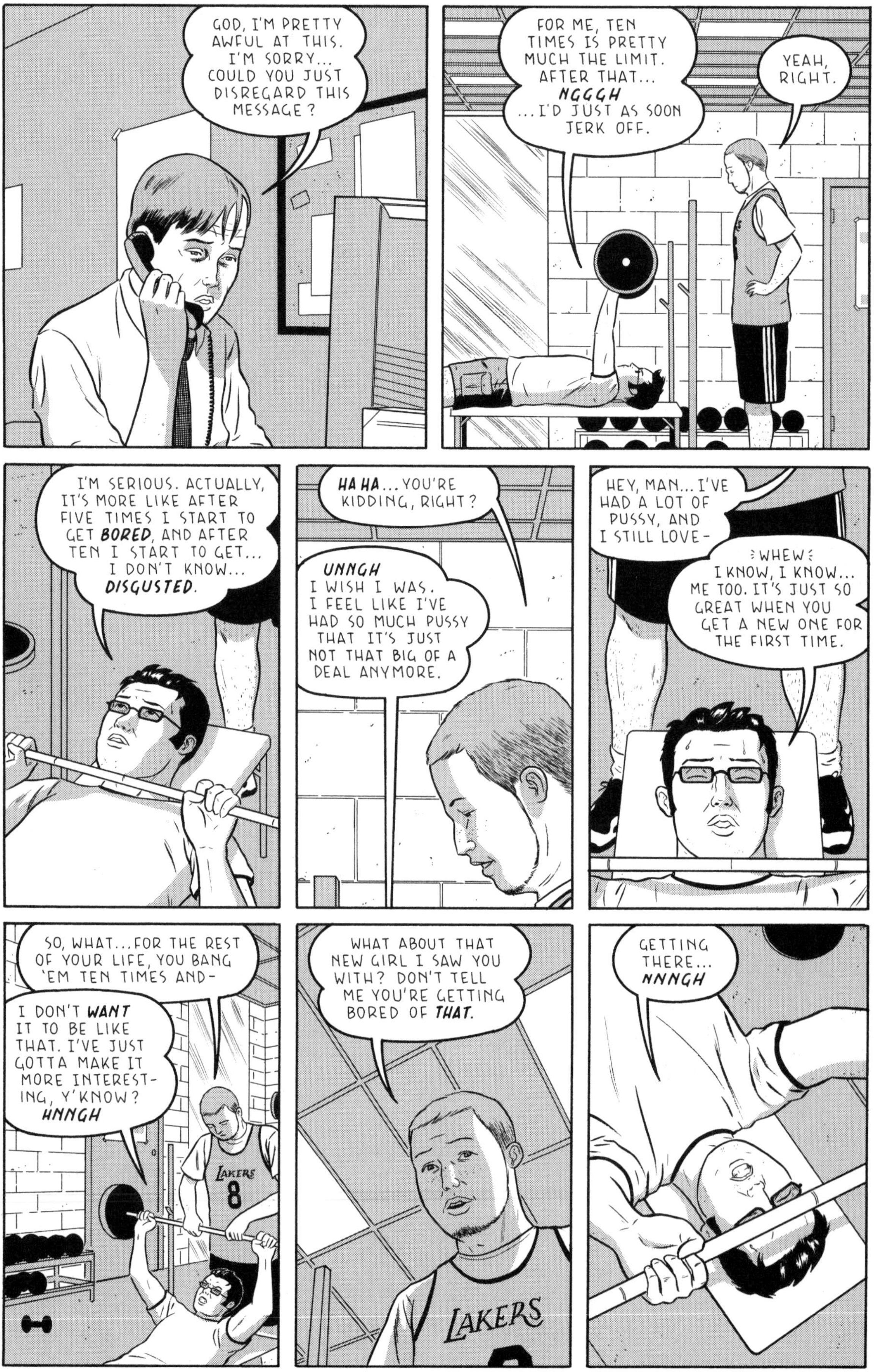
GOD, I'M PRETTY AWFUL AT THIS. I'M SORRY... COULD YOU JUST DISREGARD THIS MESSAGE?
FOR ME, TEN TIMES IS PRETTY MUCH THE LIMIT. AFTER THAT... NGGGH ...I'D JUST AS SOON JERK OFF.
YEAH, RIGHT.
I'M SERIOUS. ACTUALLY, IT'S MORE LIKE AFTER FIVE TIMES I START TO GET BORED, AND AFTER TEN I START TO GET... I DON'T KNOW... DISGUSTED.
HA HA... YOU'RE KIDDING, RIGHT?
UNNGH I WISH I WAS. I FEEL LIKE I'VE HAD SO MUCH PUSSY THAT IT'S JUST NOT THAT BIG OF A DEAL ANYMORE.
HEY, MAN... I'VE HAD A LOT OF PUSSY, AND I STILL LOVE-
WHEW I KNOW, I KNOW... ME TOO. IT'S JUST SO GREAT WHEN YOU GET A NEW ONE FOR THE FIRST TIME.
SO, WHAT... FOR THE REST OF YOUR LIFE, YOU BANG 'EM TEN TIMES AND-
I DON'T WANT IT TO BE LIKE THAT. I'VE JUST GOTTA MAKE IT MORE INTERESTING, Y'KNOW? HNNGH
LAKERS 8
WHAT ABOUT THAT NEW GIRL I SAW YOU WITH? DON'T TELL ME YOU'RE GETTING BORED OF THAT.
LAKERS
GETTING THERE... NNNGH

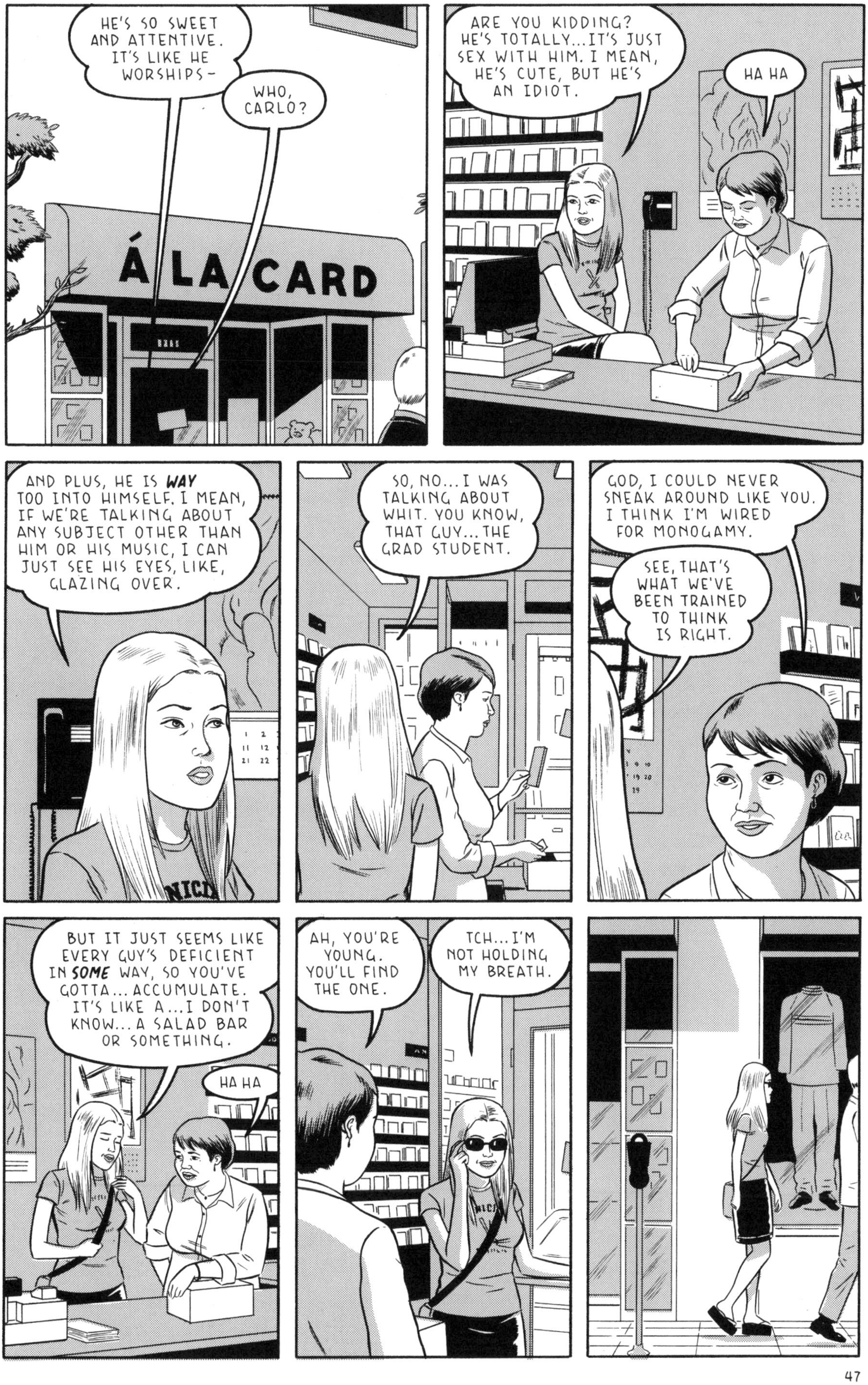
HE'S SO SWEET AND ATTENTIVE. IT'S LIKE HE WORSHIPS–
WHO, CARLO?
Á LA CARD
ARE YOU KIDDING? HE'S TOTALLY... IT'S JUST SEX WITH HIM. I MEAN, HE'S CUTE, BUT HE'S AN IDIOT.
HA HA
AND PLUS, HE IS **WAY** TOO INTO HIMSELF. I MEAN, IF WE'RE TALKING ABOUT ANY SUBJECT OTHER THAN HIM OR HIS MUSIC, I CAN JUST SEE HIS EYES, LIKE, GLAZING OVER.
SO, NO... I WAS TALKING ABOUT WHIT. YOU KNOW, THAT GUY... THE GRAD STUDENT.
GOD, I COULD NEVER SNEAK AROUND LIKE YOU. I THINK I'M WIRED FOR MONOGAMY.
SEE, THAT'S WHAT WE'VE BEEN TRAINED TO THINK IS RIGHT.
BUT IT JUST SEEMS LIKE EVERY GUY'S DEFICIENT IN **SOME** WAY, SO YOU'VE GOTTA... ACCUMULATE. IT'S LIKE A... I DON'T KNOW... A SALAD BAR OR SOMETHING.
HA HA
AH, YOU'RE YOUNG. YOU'LL FIND THE ONE.
TCH... I'M NOT HOLDING MY BREATH.

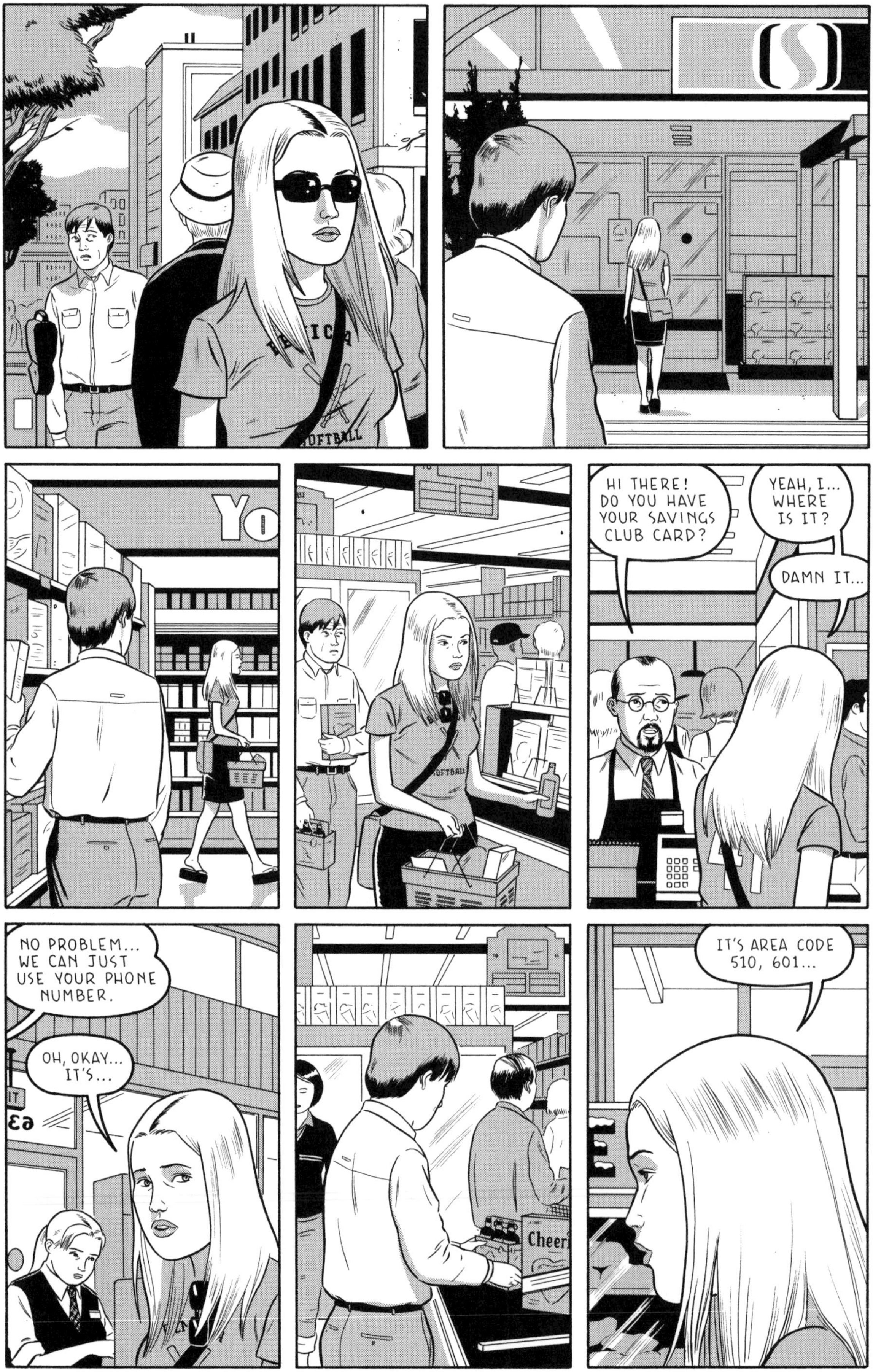
HI THERE! DO YOU HAVE YOUR SAVINGS CLUB CARD?
YEAH, I... WHERE IS IT?
DAMN IT...
NO PROBLEM... WE CAN JUST USE YOUR PHONE NUMBER.
OH, OKAY... IT'S...
IT'S AREA CODE 510, 601...

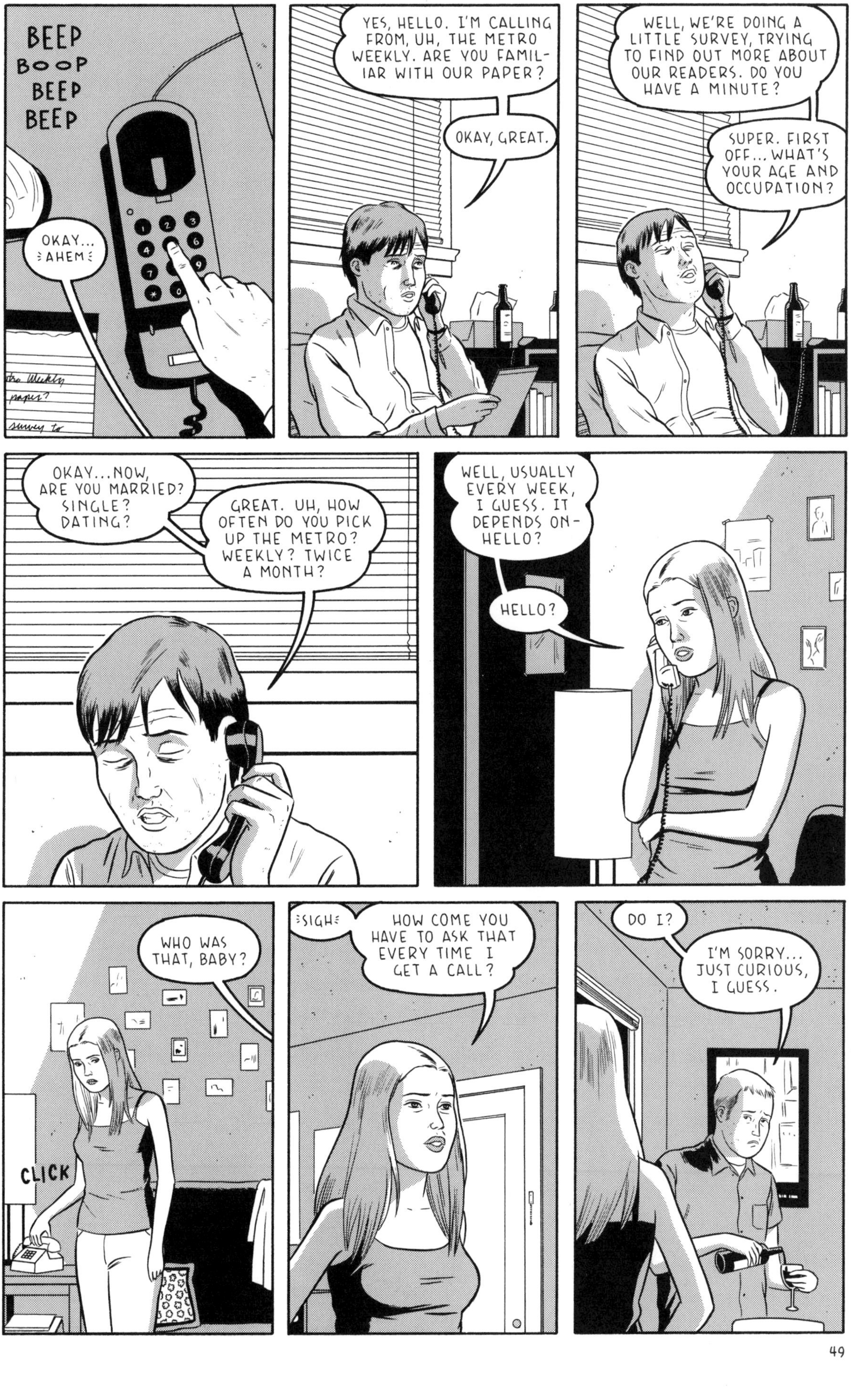
BEEP
BOOP
BEEP
BEEP
OKAY... AHEM
YES, HELLO. I'M CALLING FROM, UH, THE METRO WEEKLY. ARE YOU FAMIL-IAR WITH OUR PAPER?
OKAY, GREAT.
WELL, WE'RE DOING A LITTLE SURVEY, TRYING TO FIND OUT MORE ABOUT OUR READERS. DO YOU HAVE A MINUTE?
SUPER. FIRST OFF... WHAT'S YOUR AGE AND OCCUPATION?
OKAY...NOW, ARE YOU MARRIED? SINGLE? DATING?
GREAT. UH, HOW OFTEN DO YOU PICK UP THE METRO? WEEKLY? TWICE A MONTH?
WELL, USUALLY EVERY WEEK, I GUESS. IT DEPENDS ON—HELLO?
HELLO?
WHO WAS THAT, BABY?
CLICK
SIGH
HOW COME YOU HAVE TO ASK THAT EVERY TIME I GET A CALL?
DO I?
I'M SORRY... JUST CURIOUS, I GUESS.

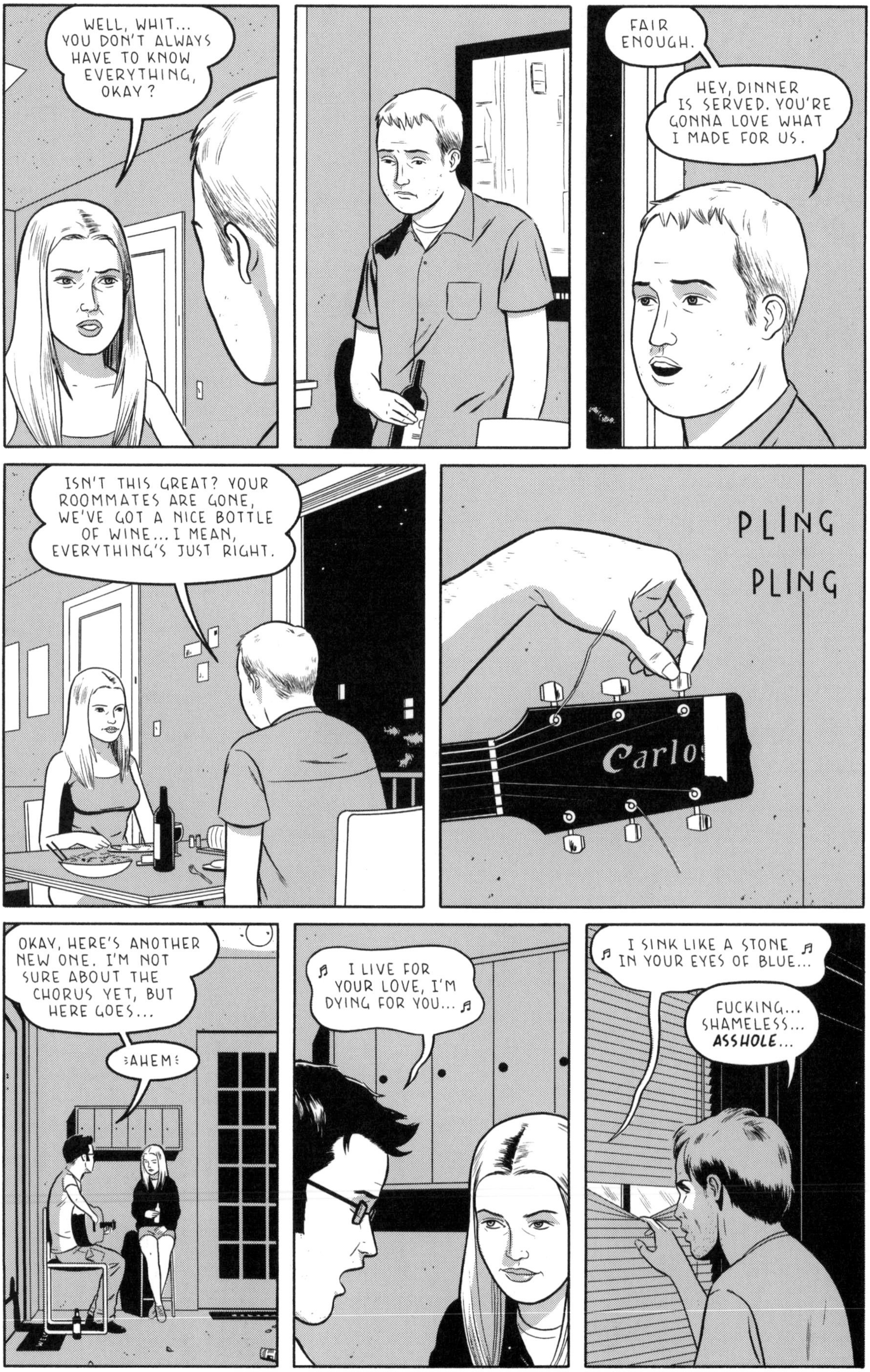
WELL, WHIT... YOU DON'T ALWAYS HAVE TO KNOW EVERYTHING, OKAY?
FAIR ENOUGH.
HEY, DINNER IS SERVED. YOU'RE GONNA LOVE WHAT I MADE FOR US.
ISN'T THIS GREAT? YOUR ROOMMATES ARE GONE, WE'VE GOT A NICE BOTTLE OF WINE... I MEAN, EVERYTHING'S JUST RIGHT.
PLING
PLING
Carlos
OKAY, HERE'S ANOTHER NEW ONE. I'M NOT SURE ABOUT THE CHORUS YET, BUT HERE GOES...
AHEM
♫ I LIVE FOR YOUR LOVE, I'M DYING FOR YOU... ♫
♫ I SINK LIKE A STONE IN YOUR EYES OF BLUE... ♫
FUCKING... SHAMELESS... **ASSHOLE**...

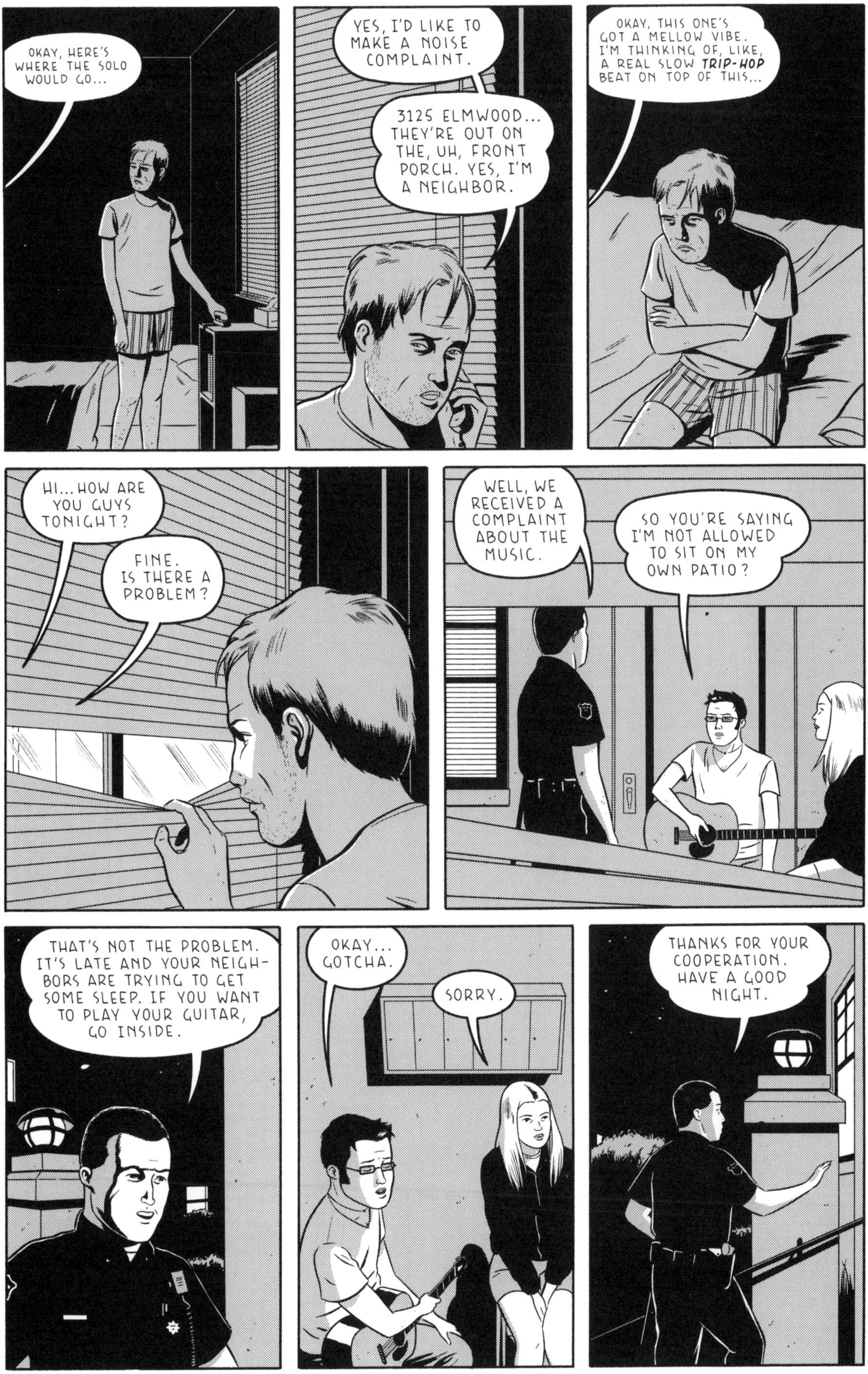
OKAY, HERE'S WHERE THE SOLO WOULD GO...
YES, I'D LIKE TO MAKE A NOISE COMPLAINT.
3125 ELMWOOD... THEY'RE OUT ON THE, UH, FRONT PORCH. YES, I'M A NEIGHBOR.
OKAY, THIS ONE'S GOT A MELLOW VIBE. I'M THINKING OF, LIKE, A REAL SLOW **TRIP-HOP** BEAT ON TOP OF THIS...
HI... HOW ARE YOU GUYS TONIGHT?
FINE. IS THERE A PROBLEM?
WELL, WE RECEIVED A COMPLAINT ABOUT THE MUSIC.
SO YOU'RE SAYING I'M NOT ALLOWED TO SIT ON MY OWN PATIO?
THAT'S NOT THE PROBLEM. IT'S LATE AND YOUR NEIGHBORS ARE TRYING TO GET SOME SLEEP. IF YOU WANT TO PLAY YOUR GUITAR, GO INSIDE.
OKAY... GOTCHA.
SORRY.
THANKS FOR YOUR COOPERATION. HAVE A GOOD NIGHT.

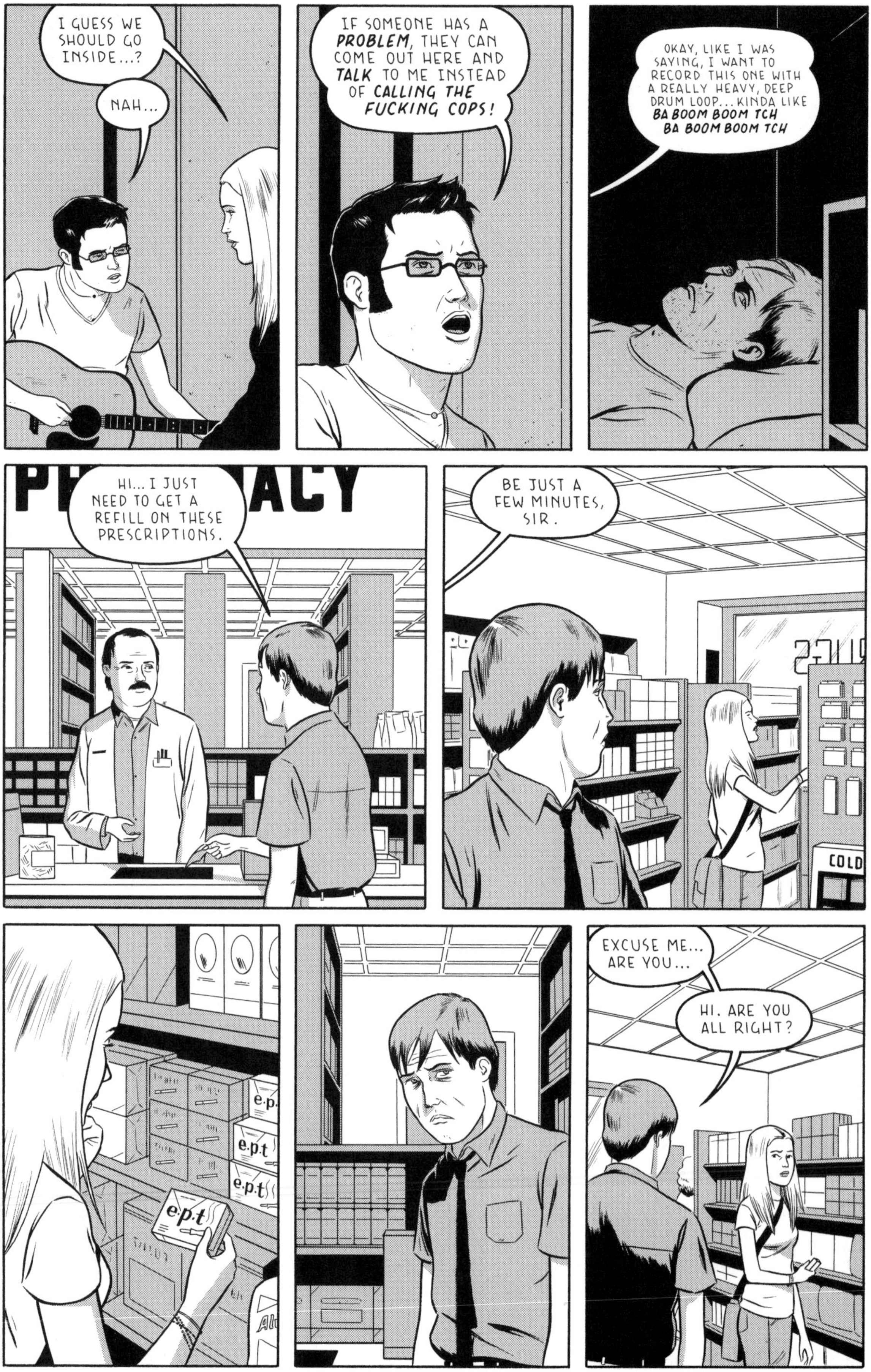
I GUESS WE SHOULD GO INSIDE...?
NAH...
IF SOMEONE HAS A **PROBLEM**, THEY CAN COME OUT HERE AND **TALK** TO ME INSTEAD OF **CALLING THE FUCKING COPS!**
OKAY, LIKE I WAS SAYING, I WANT TO RECORD THIS ONE WITH A REALLY HEAVY, DEEP DRUM LOOP... KINDA LIKE **BA BOOM BOOM TCH BA BOOM BOOM TCH**
ACY
HI... I JUST NEED TO GET A REFILL ON THESE PRESCRIPTIONS.
BE JUST A FEW MINUTES, SIR.
COLD
e.p.t
EXCUSE ME... ARE YOU...
HI. ARE YOU ALL RIGHT?

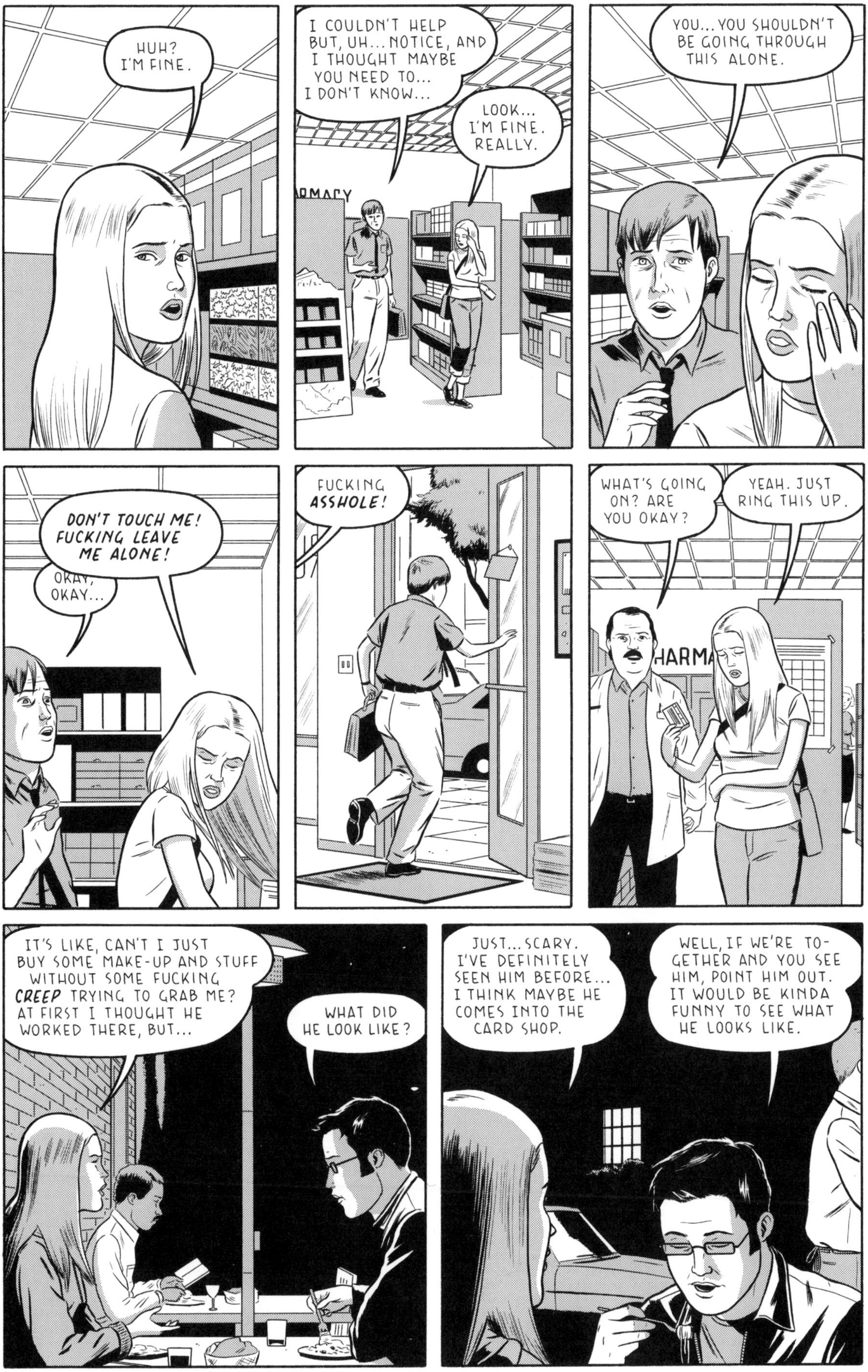
HUH? I'M FINE.
I COULDN'T HELP BUT, UH... NOTICE, AND I THOUGHT MAYBE YOU NEED TO... I DON'T KNOW...
LOOK... I'M FINE. REALLY.
YOU... YOU SHOULDN'T BE GOING THROUGH THIS ALONE.
DON'T TOUCH ME! FUCKING LEAVE ME ALONE!
OKAY, OKAY...
FUCKING ASSHOLE!
WHAT'S GOING ON? ARE YOU OKAY?
YEAH. JUST RING THIS UP.
IT'S LIKE, CAN'T I JUST BUY SOME MAKE-UP AND STUFF WITHOUT SOME FUCKING CREEP TRYING TO GRAB ME? AT FIRST I THOUGHT HE WORKED THERE, BUT...
WHAT DID HE LOOK LIKE?
JUST... SCARY. I'VE DEFINITELY SEEN HIM BEFORE... I THINK MAYBE HE COMES INTO THE CARD SHOP.
WELL, IF WE'RE TOGETHER AND YOU SEE HIM, POINT HIM OUT. IT WOULD BE KINDA FUNNY TO SEE WHAT HE LOOKS LIKE.

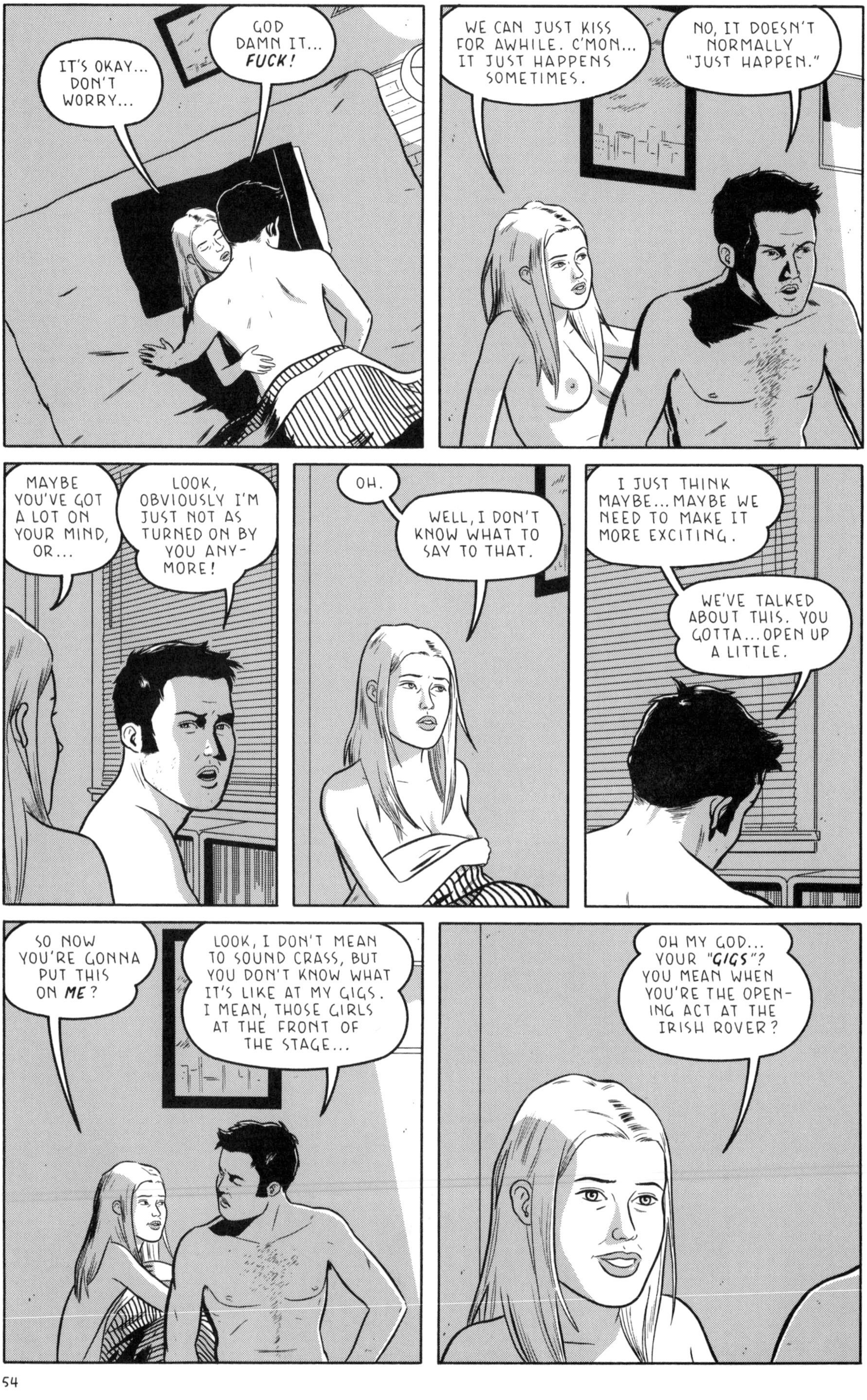
IT'S OKAY... DON'T WORRY...
GOD DAMN IT... FUCK!
WE CAN JUST KISS FOR AWHILE. C'MON... IT JUST HAPPENS SOMETIMES.
NO, IT DOESN'T NORMALLY "JUST HAPPEN."
MAYBE YOU'VE GOT A LOT ON YOUR MIND, OR...
LOOK, OBVIOUSLY I'M JUST NOT AS TURNED ON BY YOU ANYMORE!
OH.
WELL, I DON'T KNOW WHAT TO SAY TO THAT.
I JUST THINK MAYBE... MAYBE WE NEED TO MAKE IT MORE EXCITING.
WE'VE TALKED ABOUT THIS. YOU GOTTA... OPEN UP A LITTLE.
SO NOW YOU'RE GONNA PUT THIS ON ME?
LOOK, I DON'T MEAN TO SOUND CRASS, BUT YOU DON'T KNOW WHAT IT'S LIKE AT MY GIGS. I MEAN, THOSE GIRLS AT THE FRONT OF THE STAGE...
OH MY GOD... YOUR "GIGS"? YOU MEAN WHEN YOU'RE THE OPENING ACT AT THE IRISH ROVER?

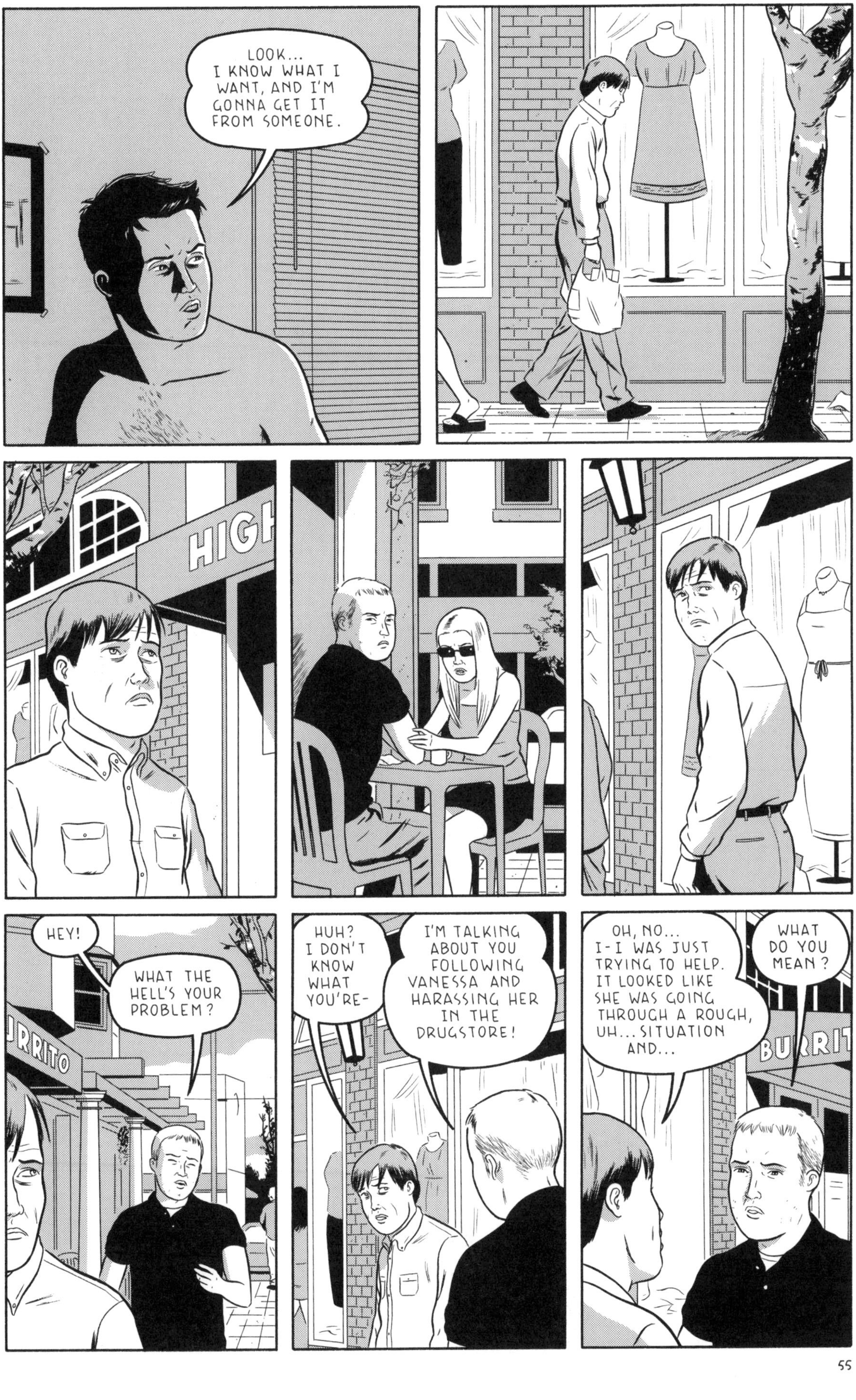
LOOK... I KNOW WHAT I WANT, AND I'M GONNA GET IT FROM SOMEONE.
HIGH
HEY!
WHAT THE HELL'S YOUR PROBLEM?
BURRITO
HUH? I DON'T KNOW WHAT YOU'RE-
I'M TALKING ABOUT YOU FOLLOWING VANESSA AND HARASSING HER IN THE DRUGSTORE!
OH, NO... I-I WAS JUST TRYING TO HELP. IT LOOKED LIKE SHE WAS GOING THROUGH A ROUGH, UH... SITUATION AND...
WHAT DO YOU MEAN?
BURRIT

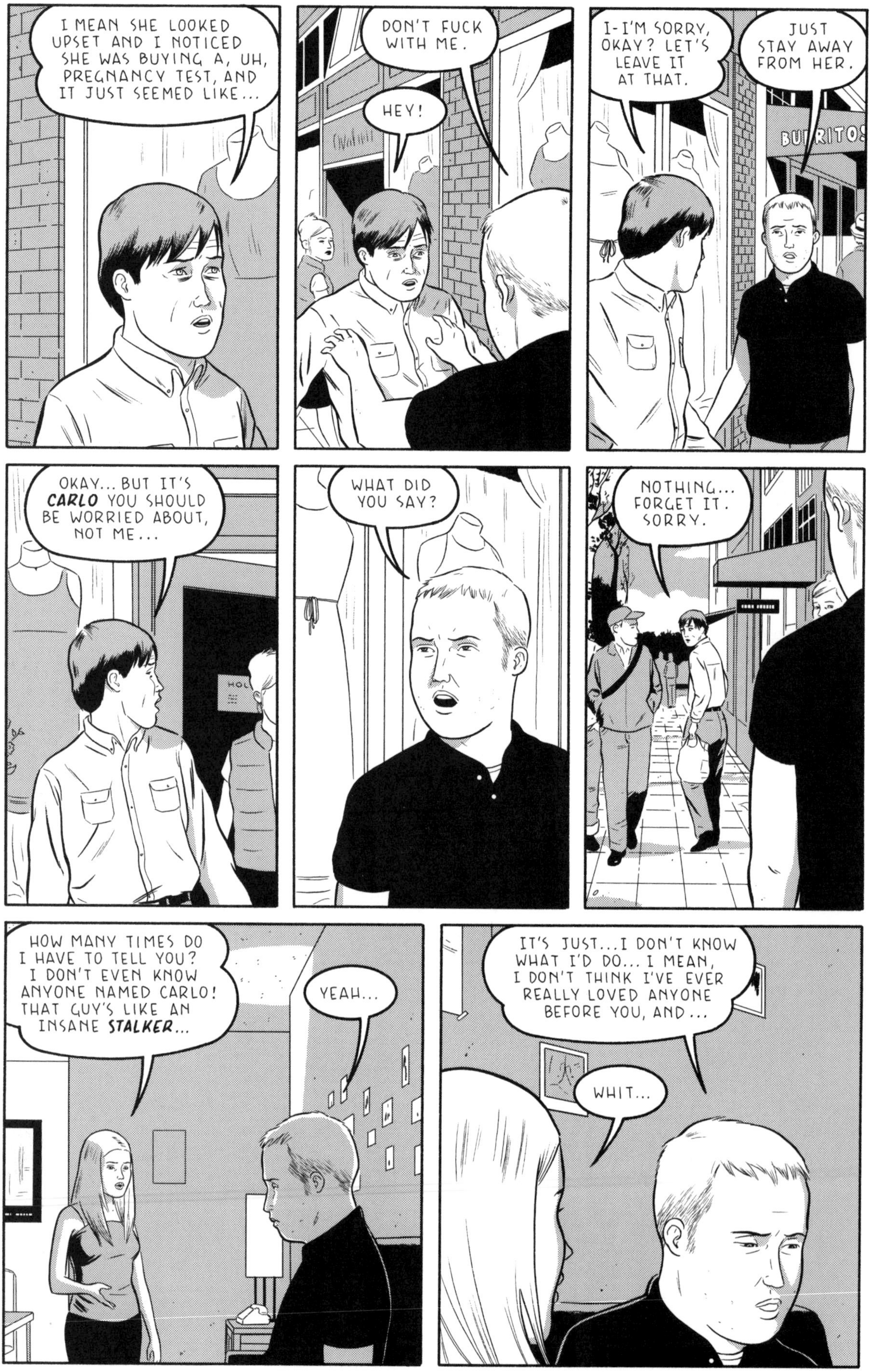
I MEAN SHE LOOKED UPSET AND I NOTICED SHE WAS BUYING A, UH, PREGNANCY TEST, AND IT JUST SEEMED LIKE...
DON'T FUCK WITH ME.
HEY!
I-I'M SORRY, OKAY? LET'S LEAVE IT AT THAT.
JUST STAY AWAY FROM HER.
BURRITOS
OKAY... BUT IT'S **CARLO** YOU SHOULD BE WORRIED ABOUT, NOT ME...
WHAT DID YOU SAY?
NOTHING... FORGET IT. SORRY.
HOW MANY TIMES DO I HAVE TO TELL YOU? I DON'T EVEN KNOW ANYONE NAMED CARLO! THAT GUY'S LIKE AN INSANE **STALKER**...
YEAH...
IT'S JUST... I DON'T KNOW WHAT I'D DO... I MEAN, I DON'T THINK I'VE EVER REALLY LOVED ANYONE BEFORE YOU, AND...
WHIT...

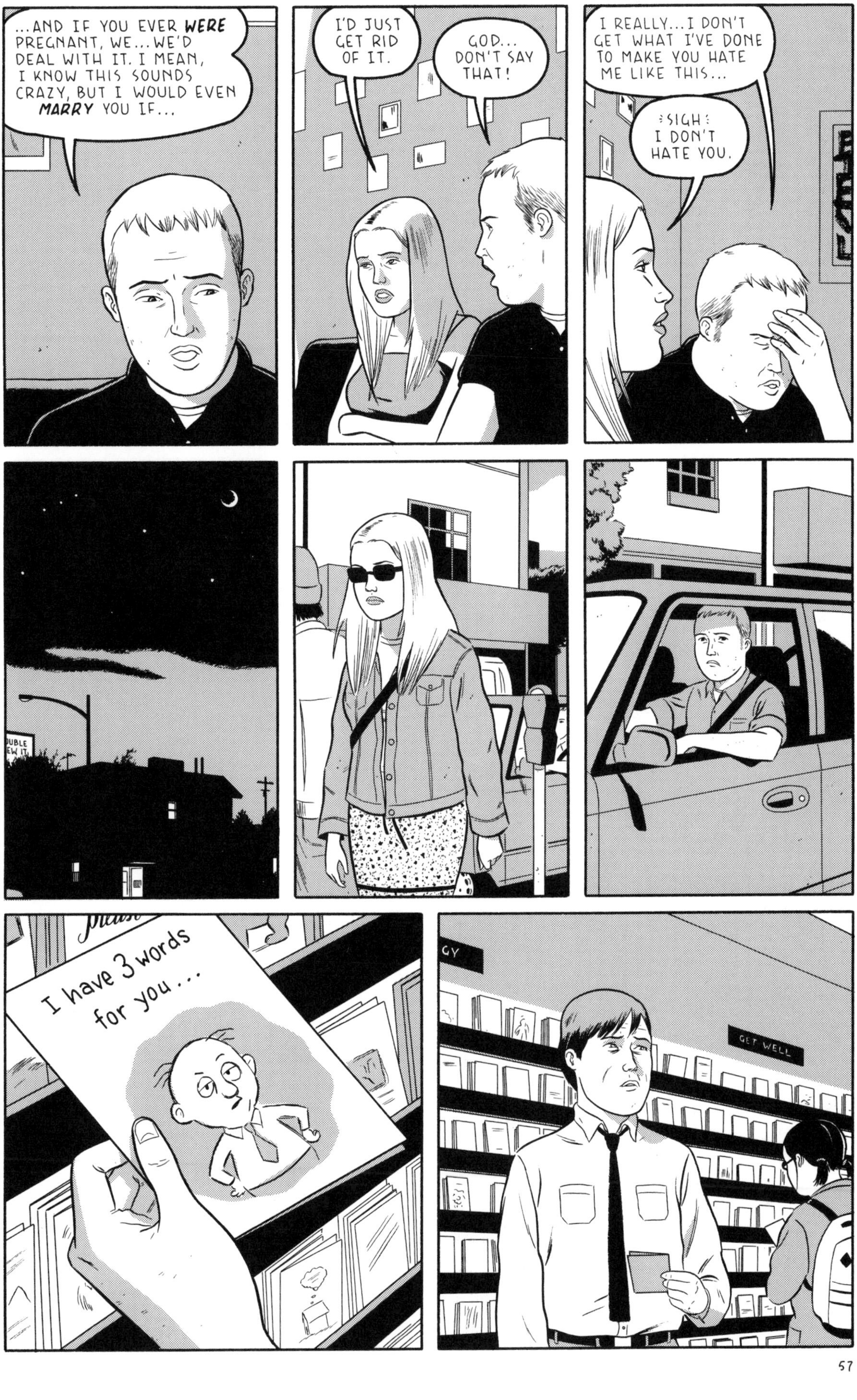
...AND IF YOU EVER WERE PREGNANT, WE... WE'D DEAL WITH IT. I MEAN, I KNOW THIS SOUNDS CRAZY, BUT I WOULD EVEN MARRY YOU IF...
I'D JUST GET RID OF IT.
GOD... DON'T SAY THAT!
I REALLY... I DON'T GET WHAT I'VE DONE TO MAKE YOU HATE ME LIKE THIS...
SIGH I DON'T HATE YOU.
I have 3 words for you...
GET WELL

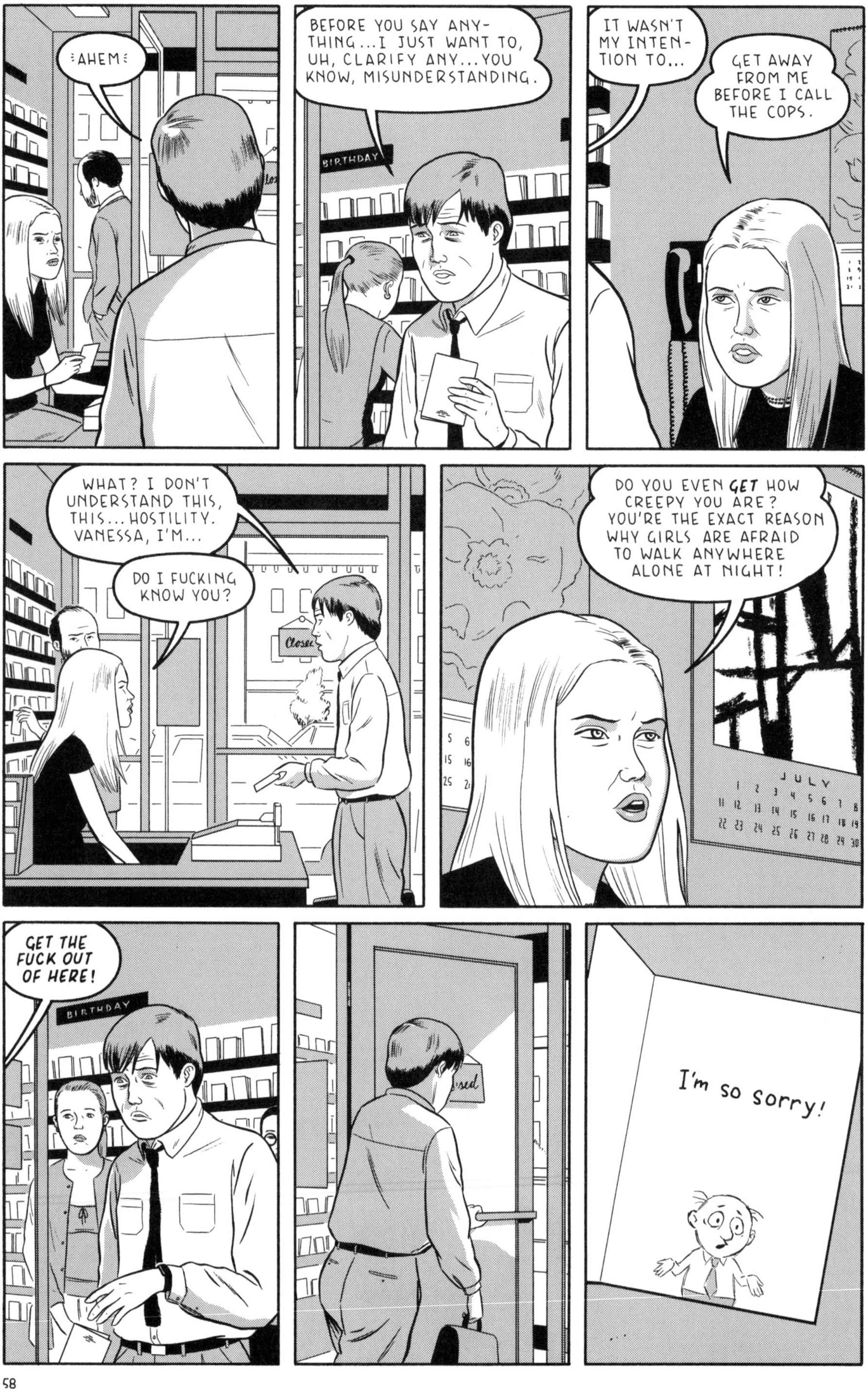
AHEM
BEFORE YOU SAY ANYTHING... I JUST WANT TO, UH, CLARIFY ANY... YOU KNOW, MISUNDERSTANDING.
BIRTHDAY
IT WASN'T MY INTENTION TO...
GET AWAY FROM ME BEFORE I CALL THE COPS.
WHAT? I DON'T UNDERSTAND THIS, THIS... HOSTILITY. VANESSA, I'M...
DO I FUCKING KNOW YOU?
DO YOU EVEN **GET** HOW CREEPY YOU ARE? YOU'RE THE EXACT REASON WHY GIRLS ARE AFRAID TO WALK ANYWHERE ALONE AT NIGHT!
JULY
GET THE FUCK OUT OF HERE!
BIRTHDAY
I'm so sorry!

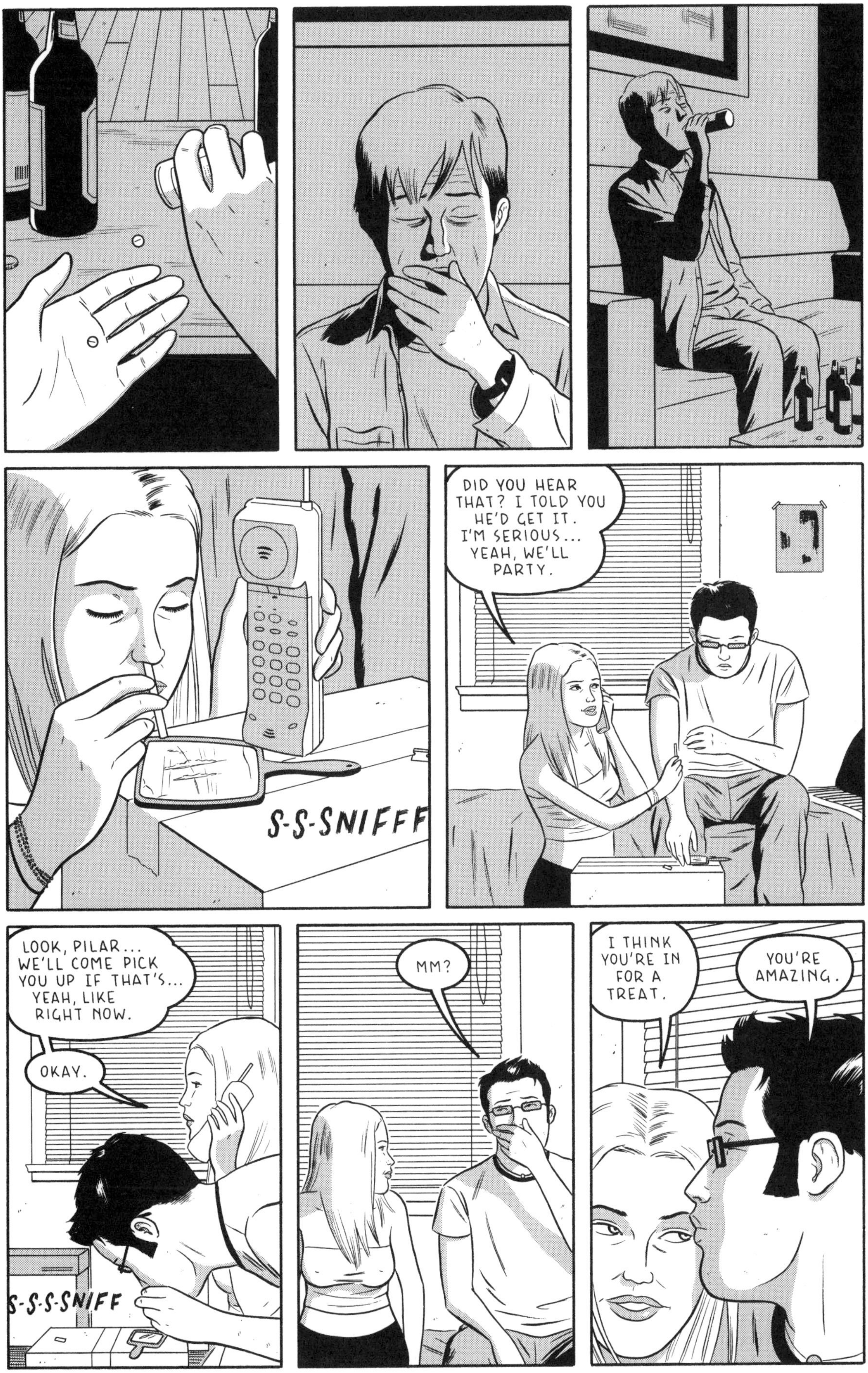
DID YOU HEAR THAT? I TOLD YOU HE'D GET IT. I'M SERIOUS... YEAH, WE'LL PARTY.
S-S-SNIFFF
LOOK, PILAR... WE'LL COME PICK YOU UP IF THAT'S... YEAH, LIKE RIGHT NOW.
OKAY.
S-S-S-SNIFF
MM?
I THINK YOU'RE IN FOR A TREAT.
YOU'RE AMAZING.

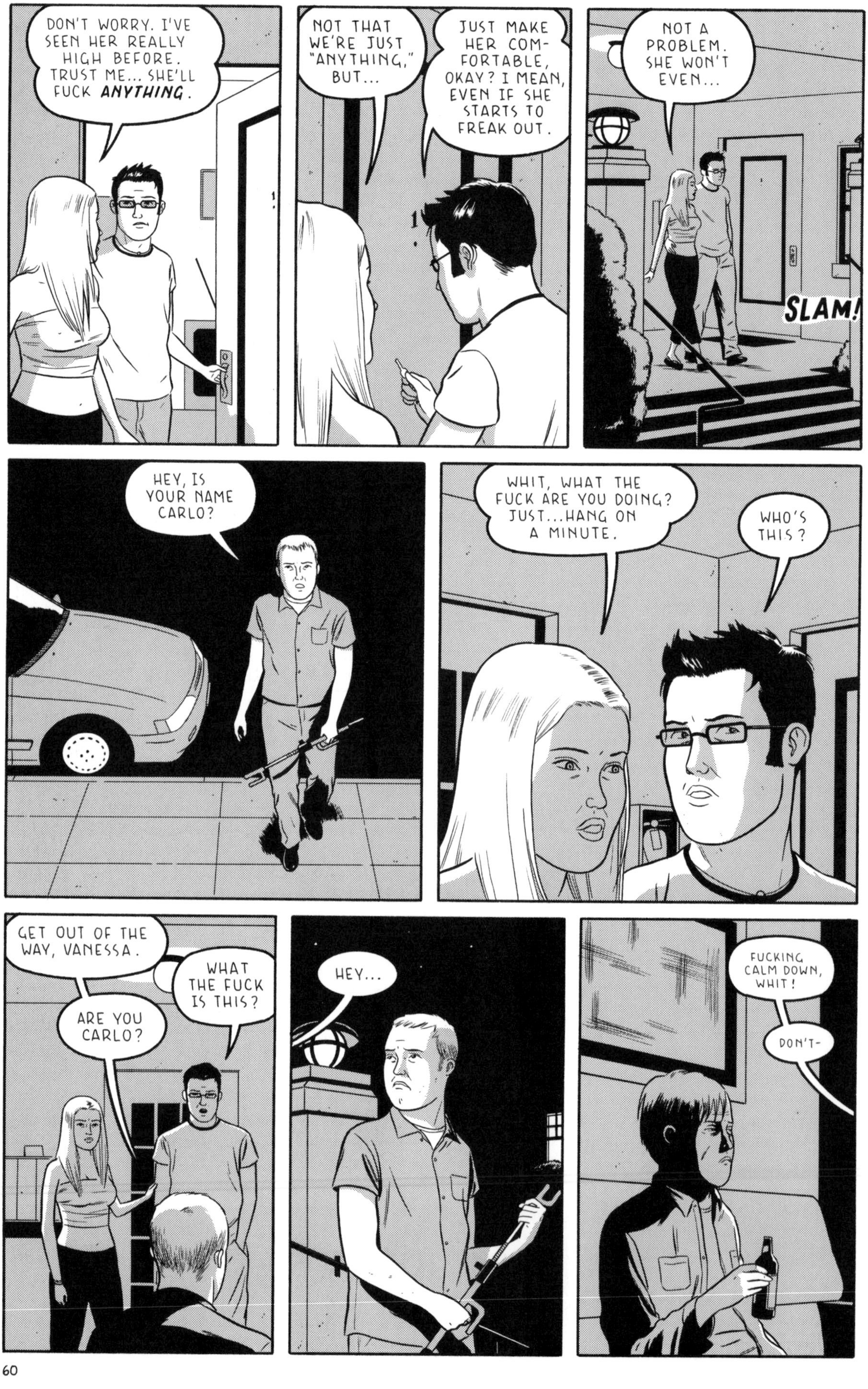
DON'T WORRY. I'VE SEEN HER REALLY HIGH BEFORE. TRUST ME... SHE'LL FUCK **ANYTHING**.
NOT THAT WE'RE JUST "ANYTHING," BUT...
JUST MAKE HER COMFORTABLE, OKAY? I MEAN, EVEN IF SHE STARTS TO FREAK OUT.
NOT A PROBLEM. SHE WON'T EVEN...
SLAM!
HEY, IS YOUR NAME CARLO?
WHIT, WHAT THE FUCK ARE YOU DOING? JUST...HANG ON A MINUTE.
WHO'S THIS?
GET OUT OF THE WAY, VANESSA.
ARE YOU CARLO?
WHAT THE FUCK IS THIS?
HEY...
FUCKING CALM DOWN, WHIT!
DON'T-

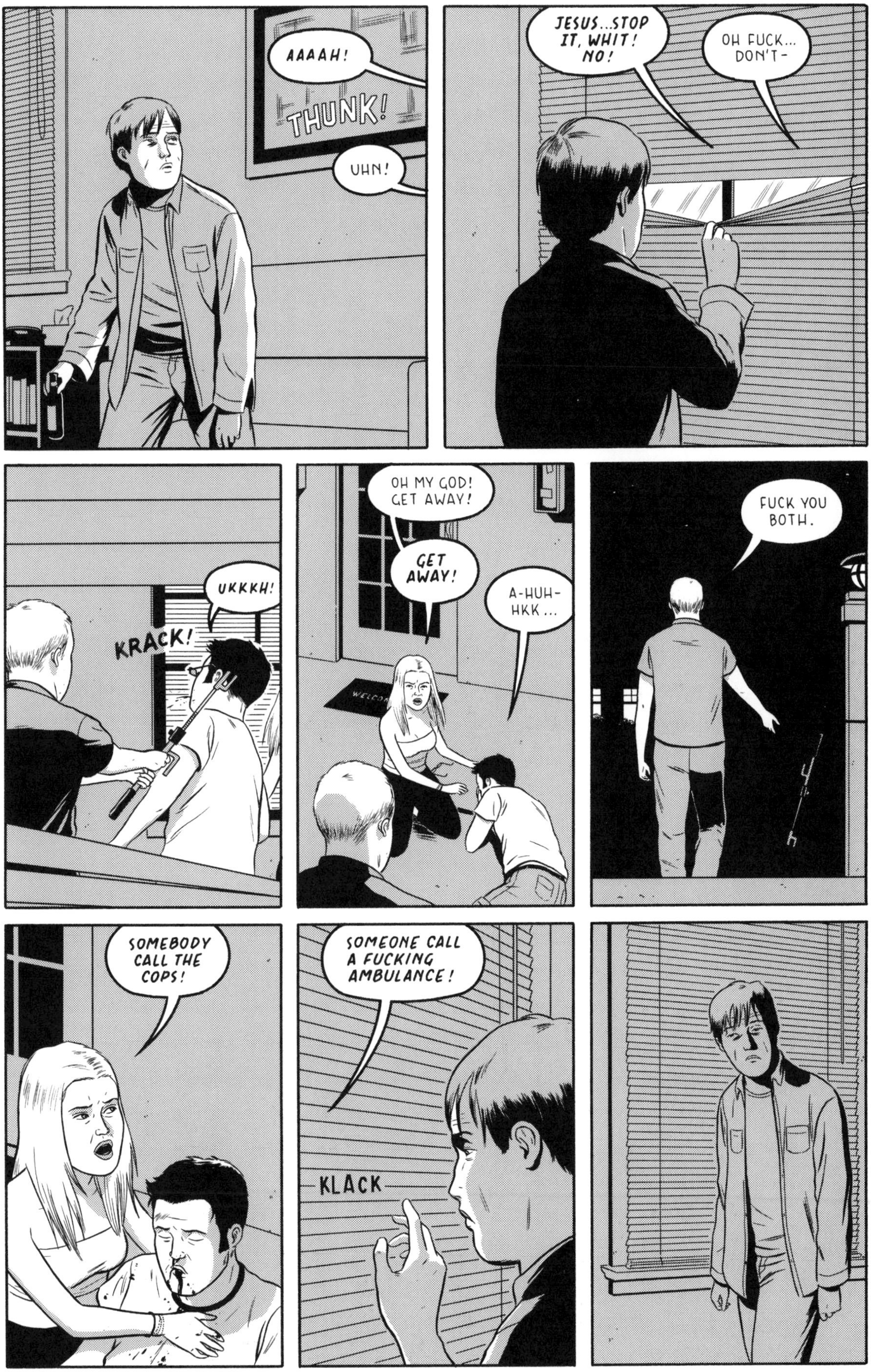
AAAAH!
THUNK!
UHN!
JESUS...STOP IT, WHIT! NO!
OH FUCK... DON'T-
UKKKH!
KRACK!
OH MY GOD! GET AWAY!
GET AWAY!
A-HUH-HKK...
FUCK YOU BOTH.
SOMEBODY CALL THE COPS!
SOMEONE CALL A FUCKING AMBULANCE!
KLACK

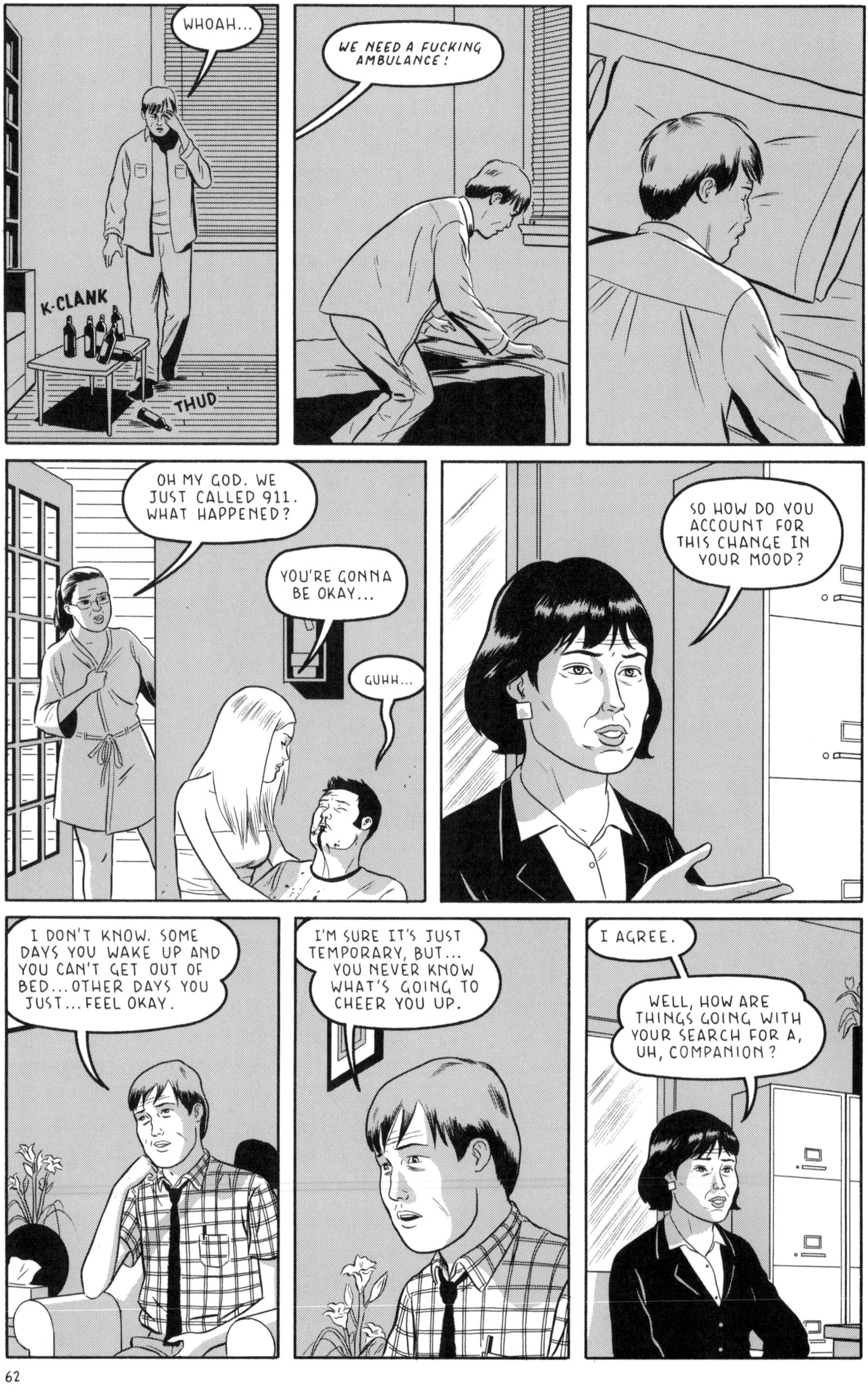
WHOAH...
K-CLANK
THUD
WE NEED A FUCKING AMBULANCE!
OH MY GOD. WE JUST CALLED 911. WHAT HAPPENED?
YOU'RE GONNA BE OKAY...
GUHH...
SO HOW DO YOU ACCOUNT FOR THIS CHANGE IN YOUR MOOD?
I DON'T KNOW. SOME DAYS YOU WAKE UP AND YOU CAN'T GET OUT OF BED... OTHER DAYS YOU JUST... FEEL OKAY.
I'M SURE IT'S JUST TEMPORARY, BUT... YOU NEVER KNOW WHAT'S GOING TO CHEER YOU UP.
I AGREE.
WELL, HOW ARE THINGS GOING WITH YOUR SEARCH FOR A, UH, COMPANION?

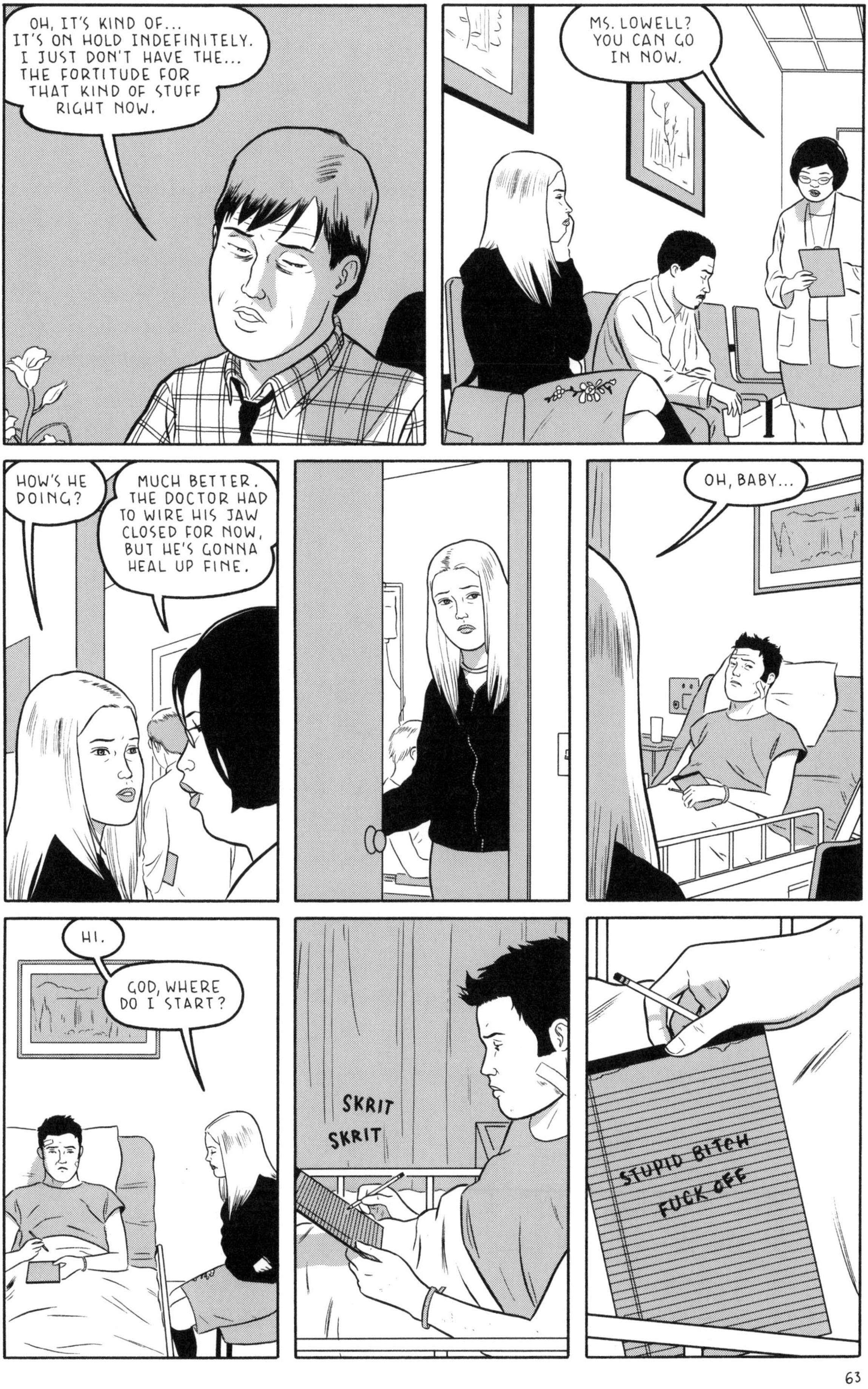
OH, IT'S KIND OF... IT'S ON HOLD INDEFINITELY. I JUST DON'T HAVE THE... THE FORTITUDE FOR THAT KIND OF STUFF RIGHT NOW.
MS. LOWELL? YOU CAN GO IN NOW.
HOW'S HE DOING?
MUCH BETTER. THE DOCTOR HAD TO WIRE HIS JAW CLOSED FOR NOW, BUT HE'S GONNA HEAL UP FINE.
OH, BABY...
HI.
GOD, WHERE DO I START?
SKRIT
SKRIT
STUPID BITCH
FUCK OFF

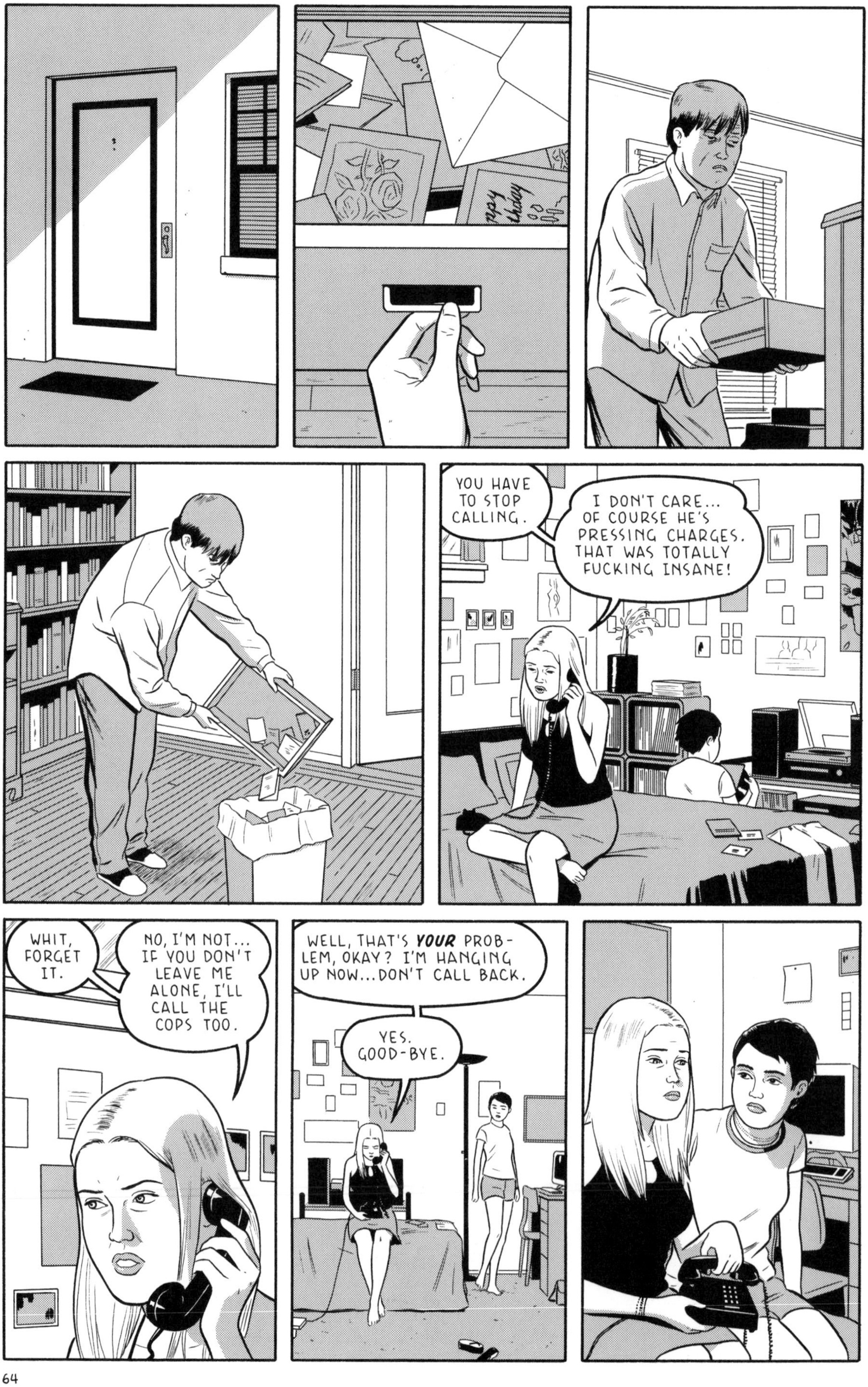
YOU HAVE TO STOP CALLING.
I DON'T CARE... OF COURSE HE'S PRESSING CHARGES. THAT WAS TOTALLY FUCKING INSANE!
WHIT, FORGET IT.
NO, I'M NOT... IF YOU DON'T LEAVE ME ALONE, I'LL CALL THE COPS TOO.
WELL, THAT'S *YOUR* PROBLEM, OKAY? I'M HANGING UP NOW... DON'T CALL BACK.
YES. GOOD-BYE.

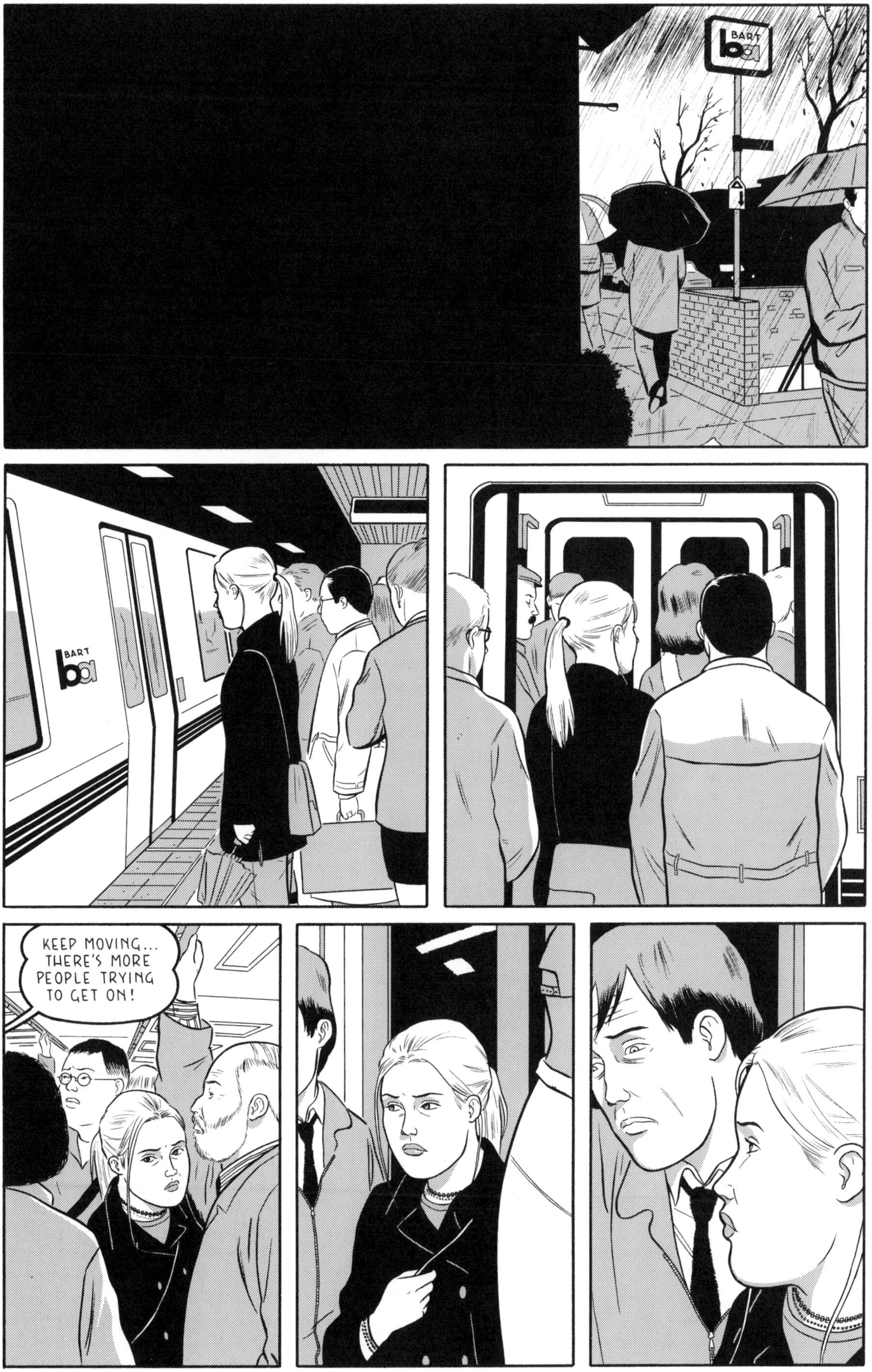
BART
BART
KEEP MOVING... THERE'S MORE PEOPLE TRYING TO GET ON!

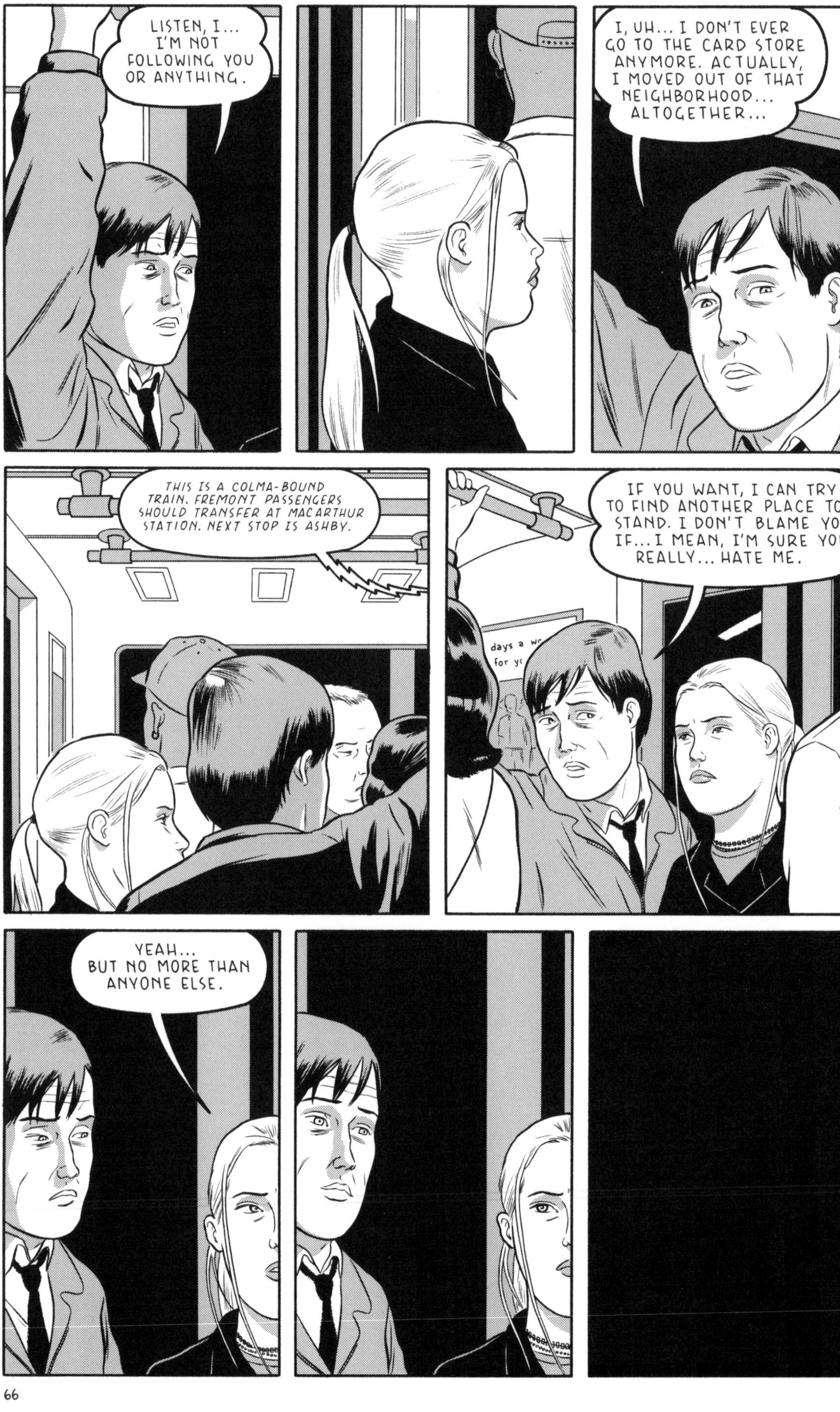
LISTEN, I... I'M NOT FOLLOWING YOU OR ANYTHING.
I, UH... I DON'T EVER GO TO THE CARD STORE ANYMORE. ACTUALLY, I MOVED OUT OF THAT NEIGHBORHOOD... ALTOGETHER...
THIS IS A COLMA-BOUND TRAIN. FREMONT PASSENGERS SHOULD TRANSFER AT MACARTHUR STATION. NEXT STOP IS ASHBY.
IF YOU WANT, I CAN TRY TO FIND ANOTHER PLACE TO STAND. I DON'T BLAME YOU IF... I MEAN, I'M SURE YOU REALLY... HATE ME.
YEAH... BUT NO MORE THAN ANYONE ELSE.

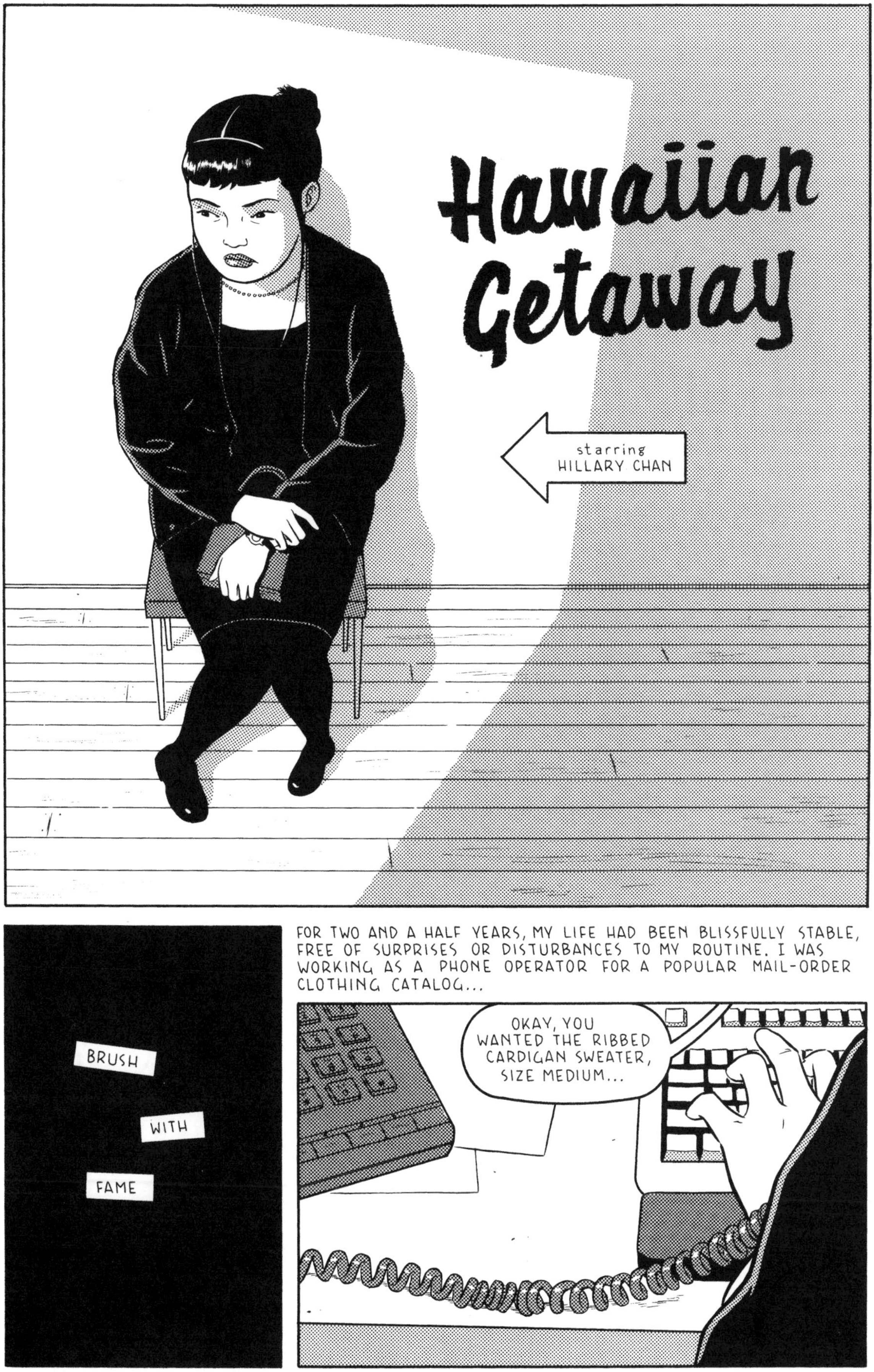
Hawaiian Getaway
starring HILLARY CHAN
BRUSH
WITH
FAME
FOR TWO AND A HALF YEARS, MY LIFE HAD BEEN BLISSFULLY STABLE, FREE OF SURPRISES OR DISTURBANCES TO MY ROUTINE. I WAS WORKING AS A PHONE OPERATOR FOR A POPULAR MAIL-ORDER CLOTHING CATALOG...
OKAY, YOU WANTED THE RIBBED CARDIGAN SWEATER, SIZE MEDIUM...

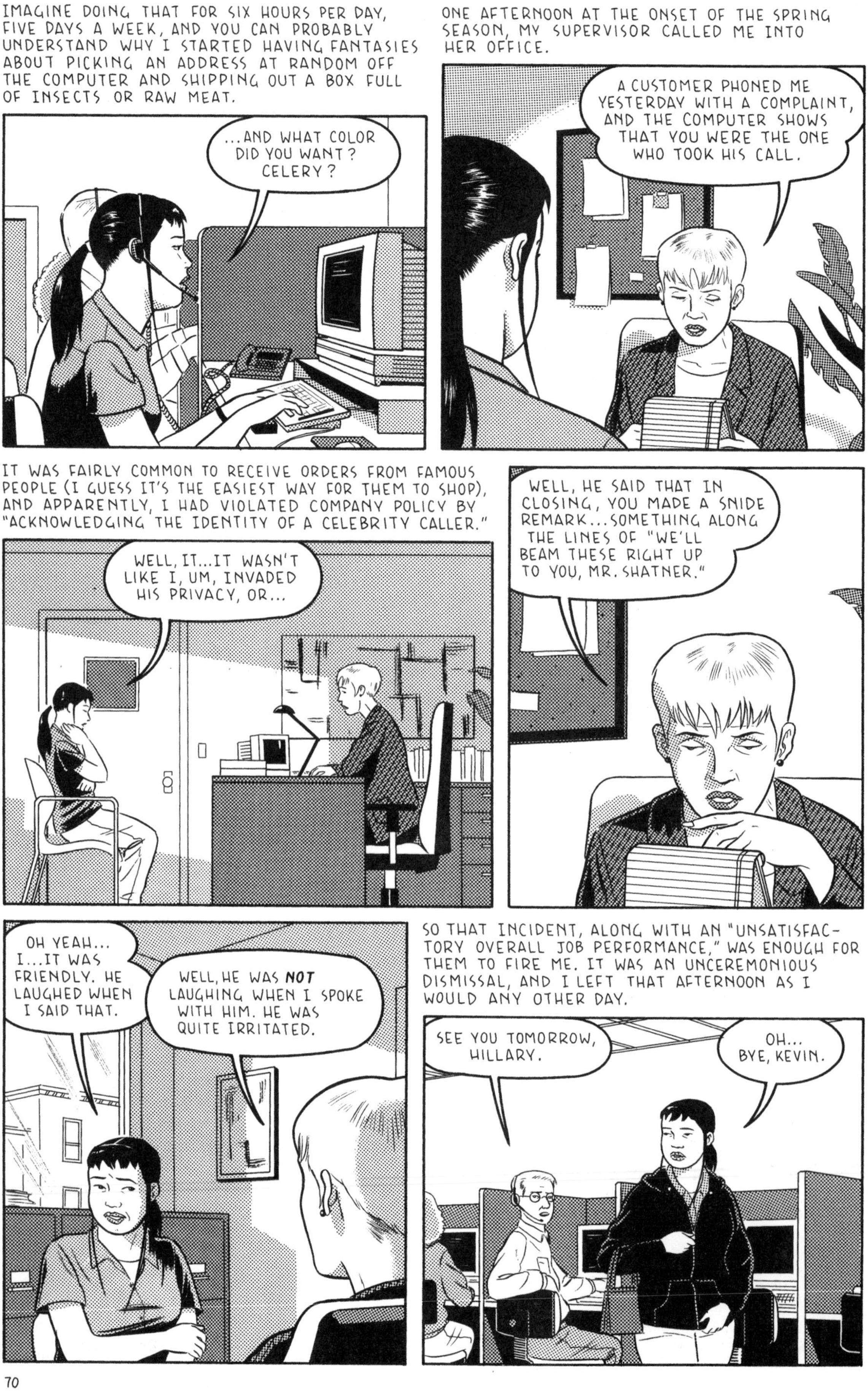
IMAGINE DOING THAT FOR SIX HOURS PER DAY, FIVE DAYS A WEEK, AND YOU CAN PROBABLY UNDERSTAND WHY I STARTED HAVING FANTASIES ABOUT PICKING AN ADDRESS AT RANDOM OFF THE COMPUTER AND SHIPPING OUT A BOX FULL OF INSECTS OR RAW MEAT.
...AND WHAT COLOR DID YOU WANT? CELERY?
ONE AFTERNOON AT THE ONSET OF THE SPRING SEASON, MY SUPERVISOR CALLED ME INTO HER OFFICE.
A CUSTOMER PHONED ME YESTERDAY WITH A COMPLAINT, AND THE COMPUTER SHOWS THAT YOU WERE THE ONE WHO TOOK HIS CALL.
IT WAS FAIRLY COMMON TO RECEIVE ORDERS FROM FAMOUS PEOPLE (I GUESS IT'S THE EASIEST WAY FOR THEM TO SHOP), AND APPARENTLY, I HAD VIOLATED COMPANY POLICY BY "ACKNOWLEDGING THE IDENTITY OF A CELEBRITY CALLER."
WELL, IT...IT WASN'T LIKE I, UM, INVADED HIS PRIVACY, OR...
WELL, HE SAID THAT IN CLOSING, YOU MADE A SNIDE REMARK...SOMETHING ALONG THE LINES OF "WE'LL BEAM THESE RIGHT UP TO YOU, MR. SHATNER."
OH YEAH... I...IT WAS FRIENDLY. HE LAUGHED WHEN I SAID THAT.
WELL, HE WAS **NOT** LAUGHING WHEN I SPOKE WITH HIM. HE WAS QUITE IRRITATED.
SO THAT INCIDENT, ALONG WITH AN "UNSATISFACTORY OVERALL JOB PERFORMANCE," WAS ENOUGH FOR THEM TO FIRE ME. IT WAS AN UNCEREMONIOUS DISMISSAL, AND I LEFT THAT AFTERNOON AS I WOULD ANY OTHER DAY.
SEE YOU TOMORROW, HILLARY.
OH... BYE, KEVIN.

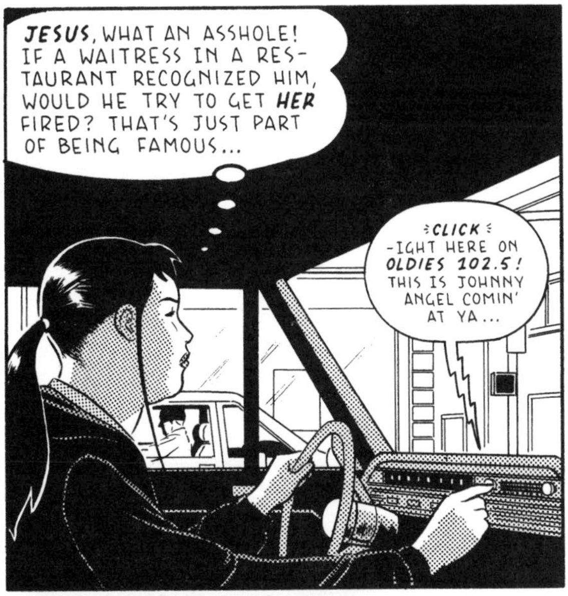
JESUS, WHAT AN ASSHOLE! IF A WAITRESS IN A RESTAURANT RECOGNIZED HIM, WOULD HE TRY TO GET HER FIRED? THAT'S JUST PART OF BEING FAMOUS...
CLICK -IGHT HERE ON OLDIES 102.5! THIS IS JOHNNY ANGEL COMIN' AT YA...

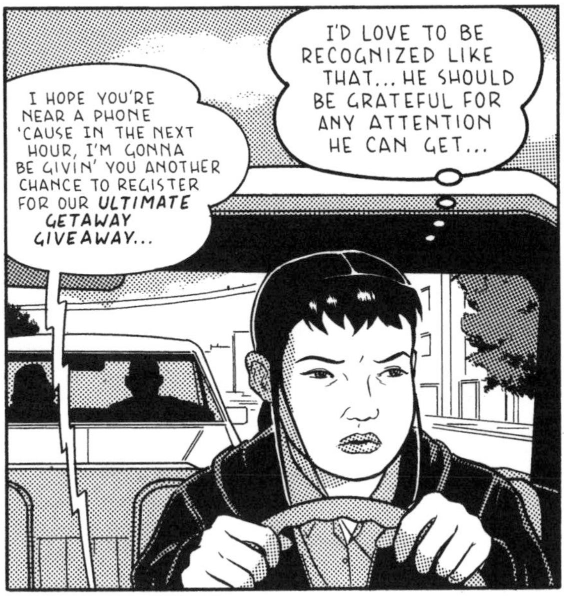
I HOPE YOU'RE NEAR A PHONE 'CAUSE IN THE NEXT HOUR, I'M GONNA BE GIVIN' YOU ANOTHER CHANCE TO REGISTER FOR OUR ULTIMATE GETAWAY GIVEAWAY...
I'D LOVE TO BE RECOGNIZED LIKE THAT... HE SHOULD BE GRATEFUL FOR ANY ATTENTION HE CAN GET...

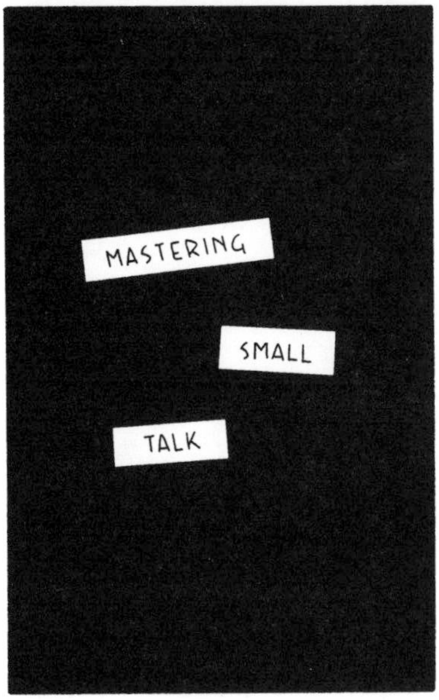
MASTERING
SMALL
TALK

I KNOW, ANSWERING PHONES SEEMS LIKE A DREARY JOB FOR SOMEONE OF MY INTELLECT AND EDUCATION, BUT IT WAS, IN A WAY, PERFECTLY SUITED TO MY DISPOSITION. THE RIGHT WORDS ARE ALWAYS IN MY HEAD; IT'S JUST A MATTER OF SPITTING THEM OUT. THAT'S MY MAIN PROBLEM.

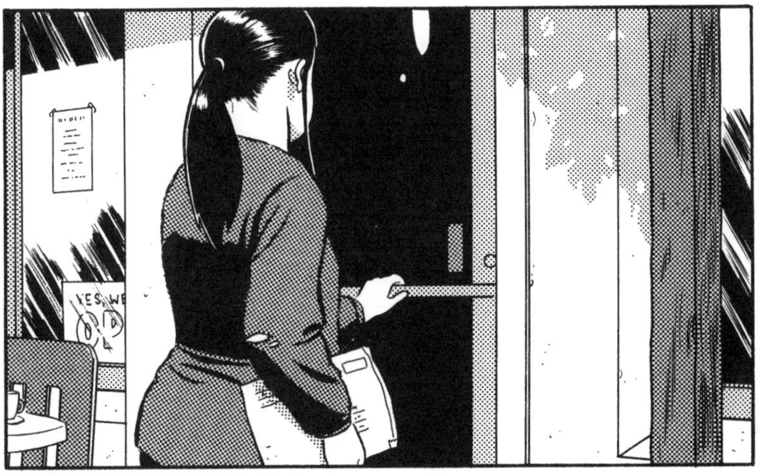

WHEN I'M TALKING ON THE PHONE, I'M USUALLY MORE RELAXED AND, THUS, MORE ARTICULATE. BUT WHEN I'M FACE-TO-FACE WITH SOMEONE (ESPECIALLY A STRANGER), I END UP SOUNDING LIKE SOME MUMBLING, GLAZED-OVER PANHANDLER.

SOMETIMES I FEEL LIKE THERE'S A SIGN FLOATING ABOVE MY HEAD THAT SAYS SOMETHING LIKE "WARNING: AVOID CONTACT WITH THIS PERSON." I WAS TOLD ONCE THAT I LOOK "NATURALLY STANDOFFISH," WHICH I COULD NOT UNDERSTAND.

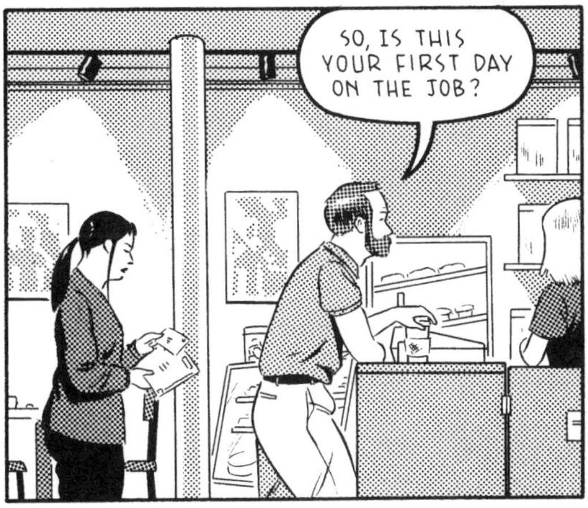
SO, IS THIS YOUR FIRST DAY ON THE JOB?

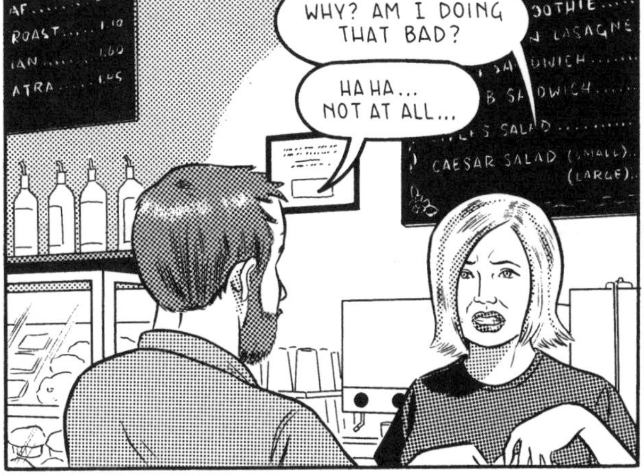
WHY? AM I DOING THAT BAD?
HA HA... NOT AT ALL...
CAESAR SALAD

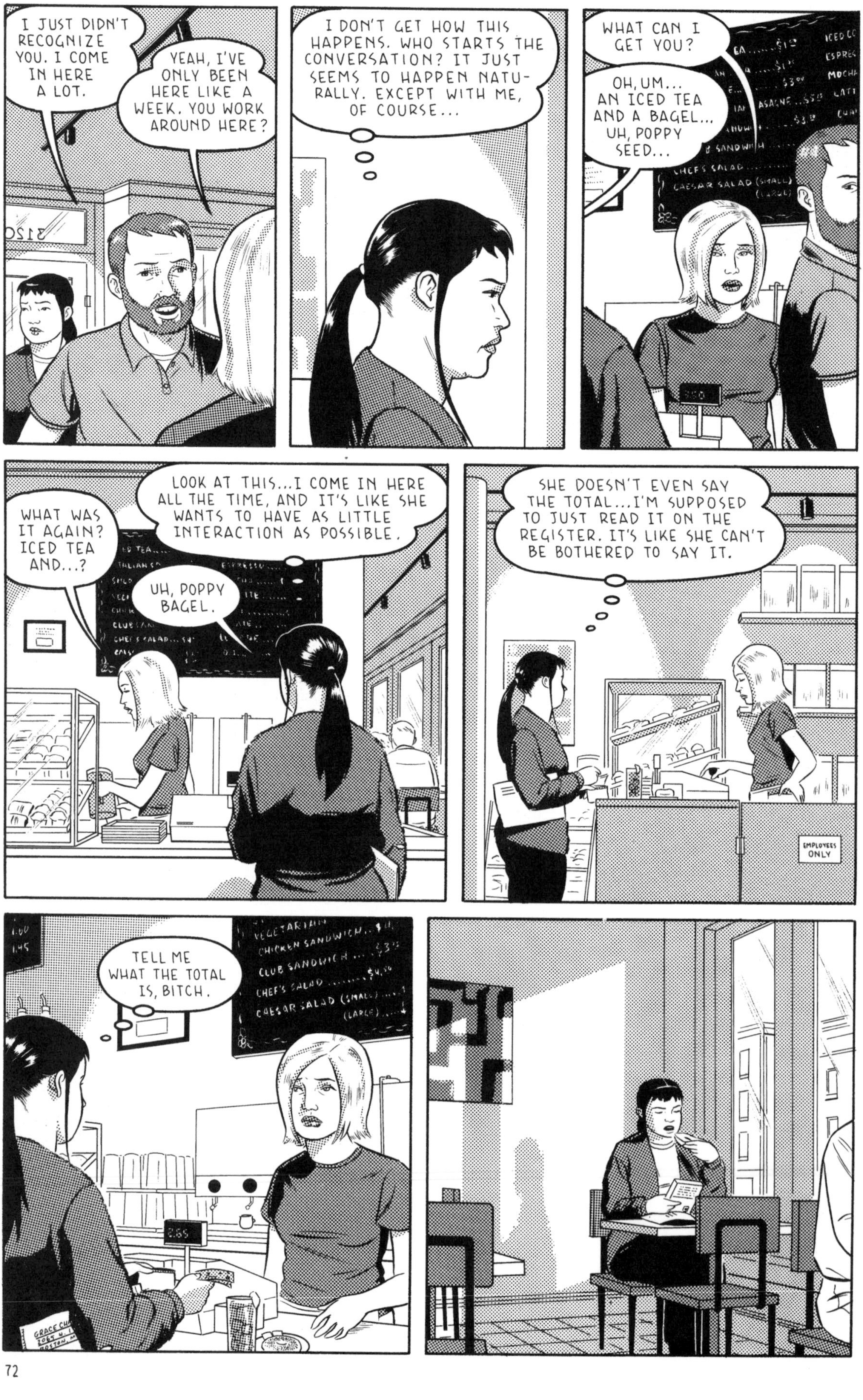
I JUST DIDN'T RECOGNIZE YOU. I COME IN HERE A LOT.
YEAH, I'VE ONLY BEEN HERE LIKE A WEEK. YOU WORK AROUND HERE?
I DON'T GET HOW THIS HAPPENS. WHO STARTS THE CONVERSATION? IT JUST SEEMS TO HAPPEN NATURALLY. EXCEPT WITH ME, OF COURSE...
WHAT CAN I GET YOU?
OH, UM... AN ICED TEA AND A BAGEL... UH, POPPY SEED...
WHAT WAS IT AGAIN? ICED TEA AND...?
LOOK AT THIS...I COME IN HERE ALL THE TIME, AND IT'S LIKE SHE WANTS TO HAVE AS LITTLE INTERACTION AS POSSIBLE.
UH, POPPY BAGEL.
SHE DOESN'T EVEN SAY THE TOTAL...I'M SUPPOSED TO JUST READ IT ON THE REGISTER. IT'S LIKE SHE CAN'T BE BOTHERED TO SAY IT.
EMPLOYEES ONLY
TELL ME WHAT THE TOTAL IS, BITCH.
VEGETARIAN
CHICKEN SANDWICH
CLUB SANDWICH
CHEF'S SALAD
CAESAR SALAD (SMALL)
(LARGE)
2.65

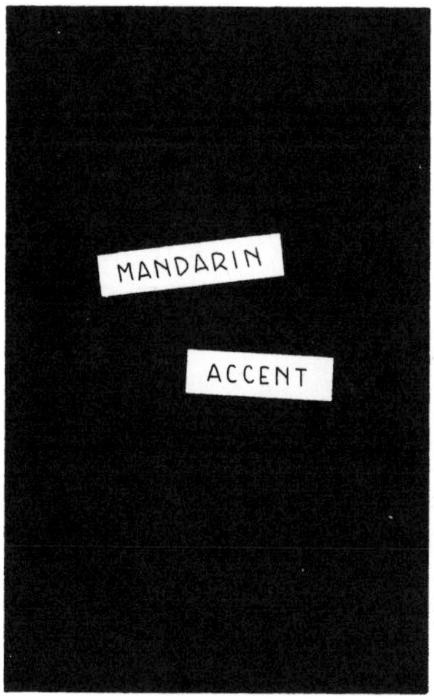
MANDARIN
ACCENT

EVEN THOUGH MY PARENTS LIVE IN NEW JERSEY (TO SAY NOTHING OF THE FACT THAT I MOVED AWAY FROM HOME ALMOST TEN YEARS AGO), MY MOM STILL CALLS ON A REGULAR BASIS TO NAG, BELITTLE, AND CRITICIZE ME. I KNOW THAT'S NOT HER INTENT, BUT I CAN'T HELP FEELING LIKE I'M ALWAYS ON THE DEFENSIVE.

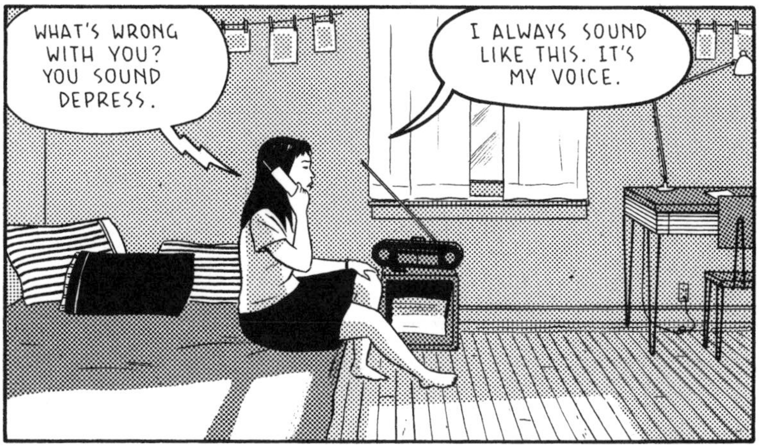
WHAT'S WRONG WITH YOU? YOU SOUND DEPRESS.
I ALWAYS SOUND LIKE THIS. IT'S MY VOICE.

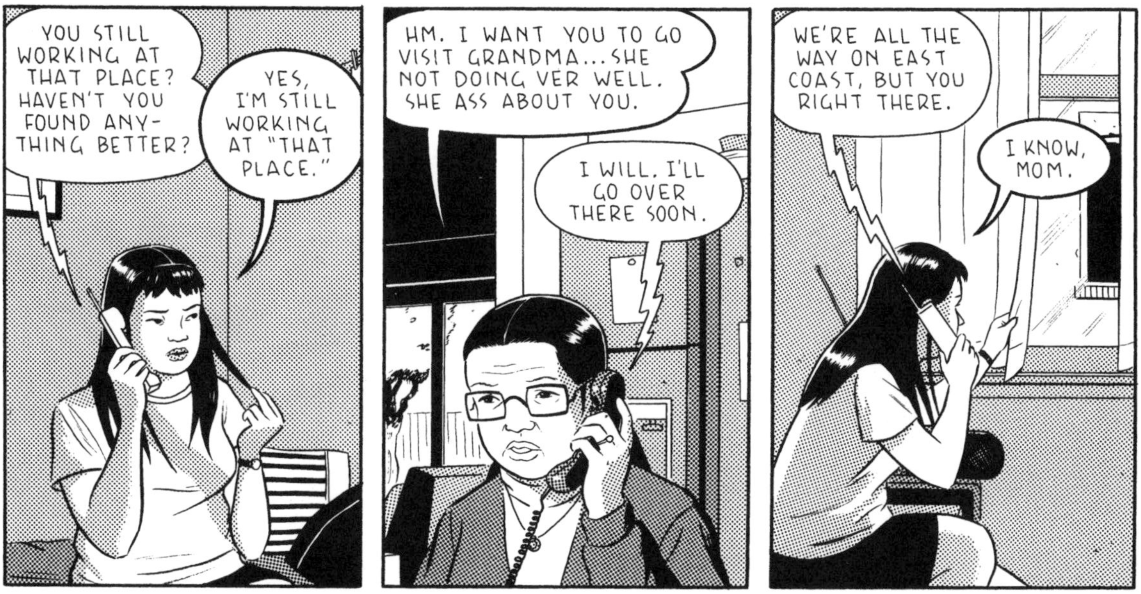
YOU STILL WORKING AT THAT PLACE? HAVEN'T YOU FOUND ANYTHING BETTER?
YES, I'M STILL WORKING AT "THAT PLACE."
HM. I WANT YOU TO GO VISIT GRANDMA... SHE NOT DOING VER WELL. SHE ASS ABOUT YOU.
I WILL. I'LL GO OVER THERE SOON.
WE'RE ALL THE WAY ON EAST COAST, BUT YOU RIGHT THERE.
I KNOW, MOM.

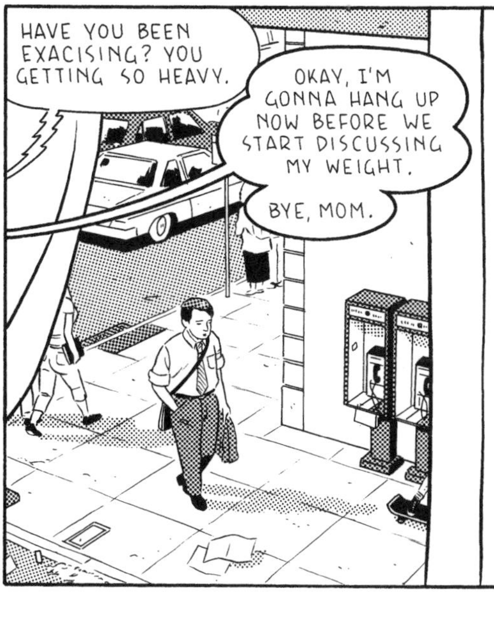
HAVE YOU BEEN EXACISING? YOU GETTING SO HEAVY.
OKAY, I'M GONNA HANG UP NOW BEFORE WE START DISCUSSING MY WEIGHT.
BYE, MOM.

WHEN I'M NOT POLITELY DEFLECTING HER INSULTS, I'M TRYING MY BEST TO IGNORE HER MASTERFUL GUILT-INSTILLING TECHNIQUES.

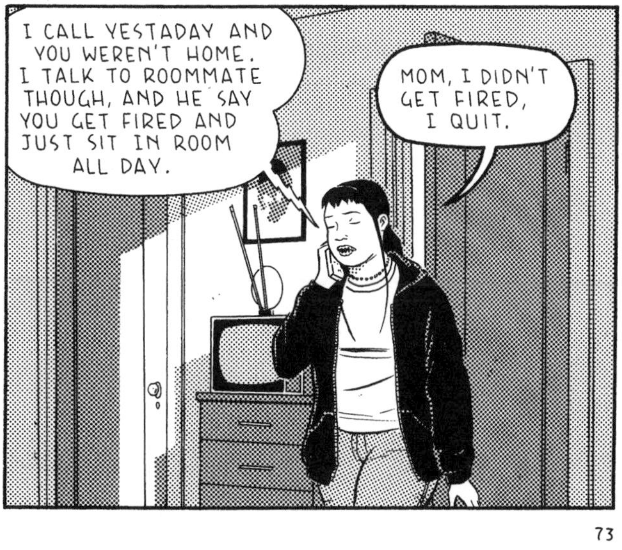
I CALL YESTADAY AND YOU WEREN'T HOME. I TALK TO ROOMMATE THOUGH, AND HE SAY YOU GET FIRED AND JUST SIT IN ROOM ALL DAY.
MOM, I DIDN'T GET FIRED, I QUIT.

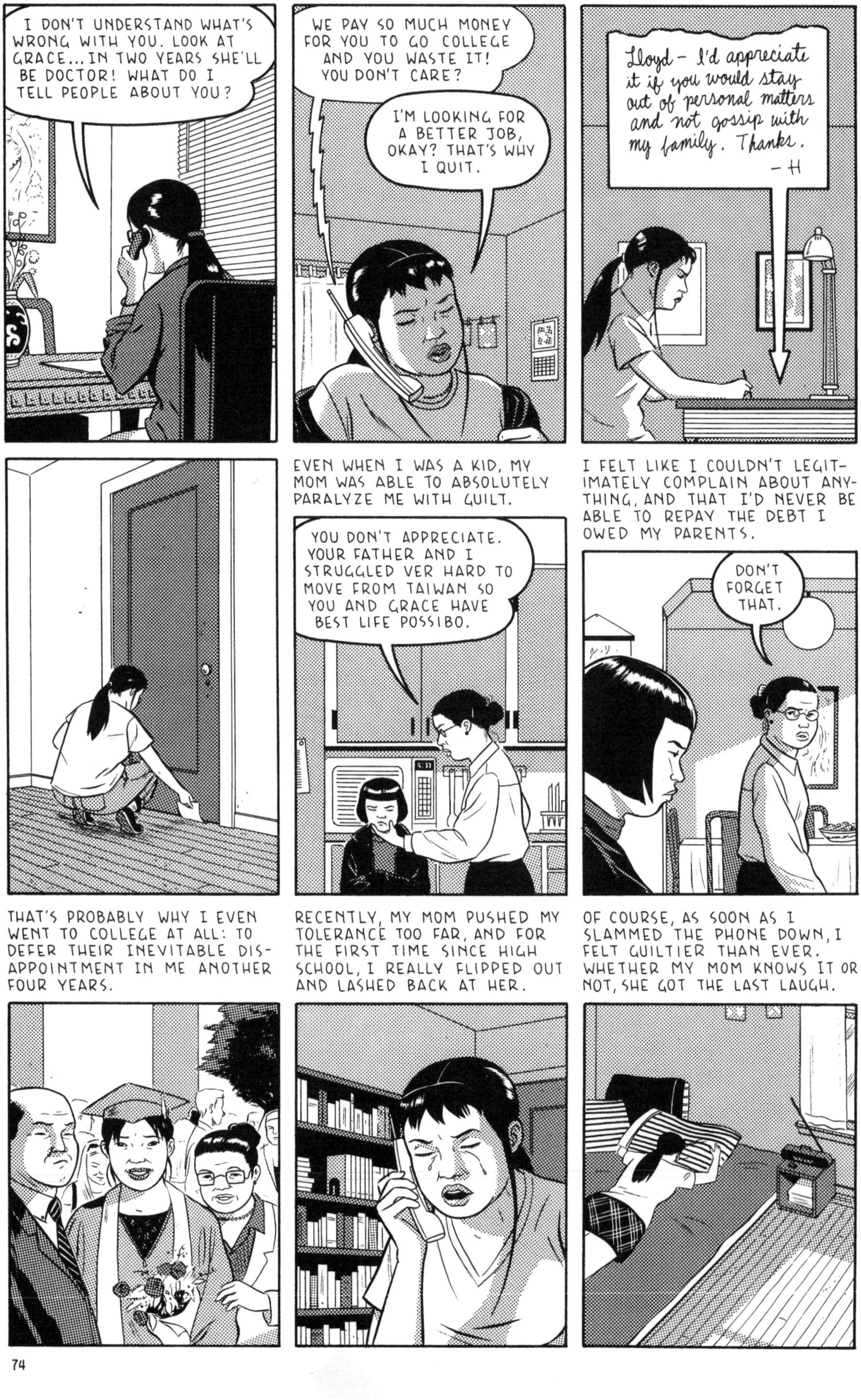
I DON'T UNDERSTAND WHAT'S WRONG WITH YOU. LOOK AT GRACE... IN TWO YEARS SHE'LL BE DOCTOR! WHAT DO I TELL PEOPLE ABOUT YOU?
WE PAY SO MUCH MONEY FOR YOU TO GO COLLEGE AND YOU WASTE IT! YOU DON'T CARE?
I'M LOOKING FOR A BETTER JOB, OKAY? THAT'S WHY I QUIT.
Lloyd - I'd appreciate it if you would stay out of personal matters and not gossip with my family. Thanks. -H
EVEN WHEN I WAS A KID, MY MOM WAS ABLE TO ABSOLUTELY PARALYZE ME WITH GUILT.
YOU DON'T APPRECIATE. YOUR FATHER AND I STRUGGLED VER HARD TO MOVE FROM TAIWAN SO YOU AND GRACE HAVE BEST LIFE POSSIBO.
I FELT LIKE I COULDN'T LEGITIMATELY COMPLAIN ABOUT ANYTHING, AND THAT I'D NEVER BE ABLE TO REPAY THE DEBT I OWED MY PARENTS.
DON'T FORGET THAT.
THAT'S PROBABLY WHY I EVEN WENT TO COLLEGE AT ALL: TO DEFER THEIR INEVITABLE DISAPPOINTMENT IN ME ANOTHER FOUR YEARS.
RECENTLY, MY MOM PUSHED MY TOLERANCE TOO FAR, AND FOR THE FIRST TIME SINCE HIGH SCHOOL, I REALLY FLIPPED OUT AND LASHED BACK AT HER.
OF COURSE, AS SOON AS I SLAMMED THE PHONE DOWN, I FELT GUILTIER THAN EVER. WHETHER MY MOM KNOWS IT OR NOT, SHE GOT THE LAST LAUGH.

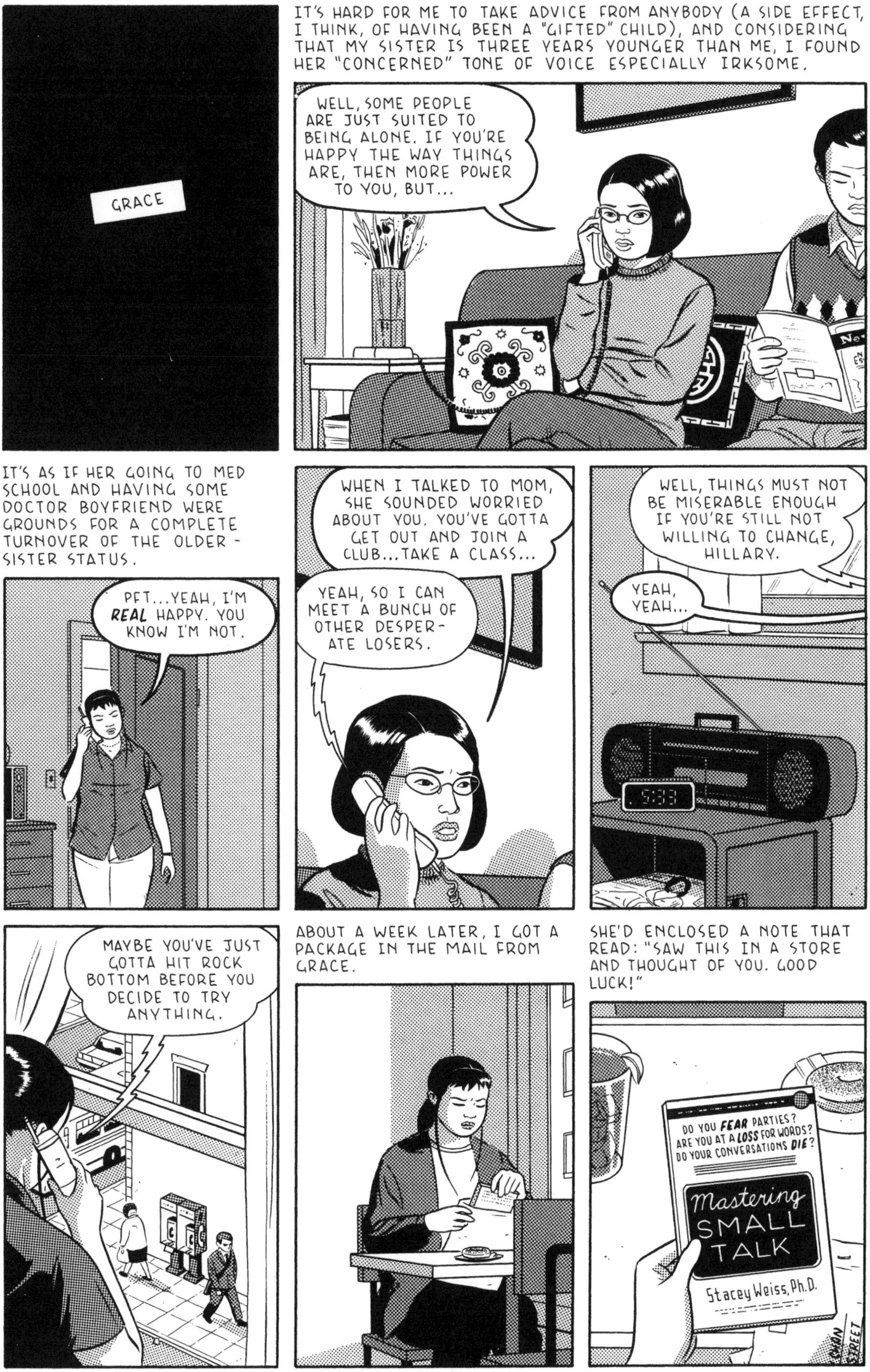
GRACE
IT'S HARD FOR ME TO TAKE ADVICE FROM ANYBODY (A SIDE EFFECT, I THINK, OF HAVING BEEN A "GIFTED" CHILD), AND CONSIDERING THAT MY SISTER IS THREE YEARS YOUNGER THAN ME, I FOUND HER "CONCERNED" TONE OF VOICE ESPECIALLY IRKSOME.
WELL, SOME PEOPLE ARE JUST SUITED TO BEING ALONE. IF YOU'RE HAPPY THE WAY THINGS ARE, THEN MORE POWER TO YOU, BUT...
IT'S AS IF HER GOING TO MED SCHOOL AND HAVING SOME DOCTOR BOYFRIEND WERE GROUNDS FOR A COMPLETE TURNOVER OF THE OLDER-SISTER STATUS.
PFT...YEAH, I'M **REAL** HAPPY. YOU KNOW I'M NOT.
WHEN I TALKED TO MOM, SHE SOUNDED WORRIED ABOUT YOU. YOU'VE GOTTA GET OUT AND JOIN A CLUB...TAKE A CLASS...
YEAH, SO I CAN MEET A BUNCH OF OTHER DESPERATE LOSERS.
WELL, THINGS MUST NOT BE MISERABLE ENOUGH IF YOU'RE STILL NOT WILLING TO CHANGE, HILLARY.
YEAH, YEAH...
MAYBE YOU'VE JUST GOTTA HIT ROCK BOTTOM BEFORE YOU DECIDE TO TRY ANYTHING.
ABOUT A WEEK LATER, I GOT A PACKAGE IN THE MAIL FROM GRACE.
SHE'D ENCLOSED A NOTE THAT READ: "SAW THIS IN A STORE AND THOUGHT OF YOU. GOOD LUCK!"
DO YOU **FEAR** PARTIES? ARE YOU AT A **LOSS** FOR WORDS? DO YOUR CONVERSATIONS **DIE**?
Mastering SMALL TALK
Stacey Weiss, Ph.D.

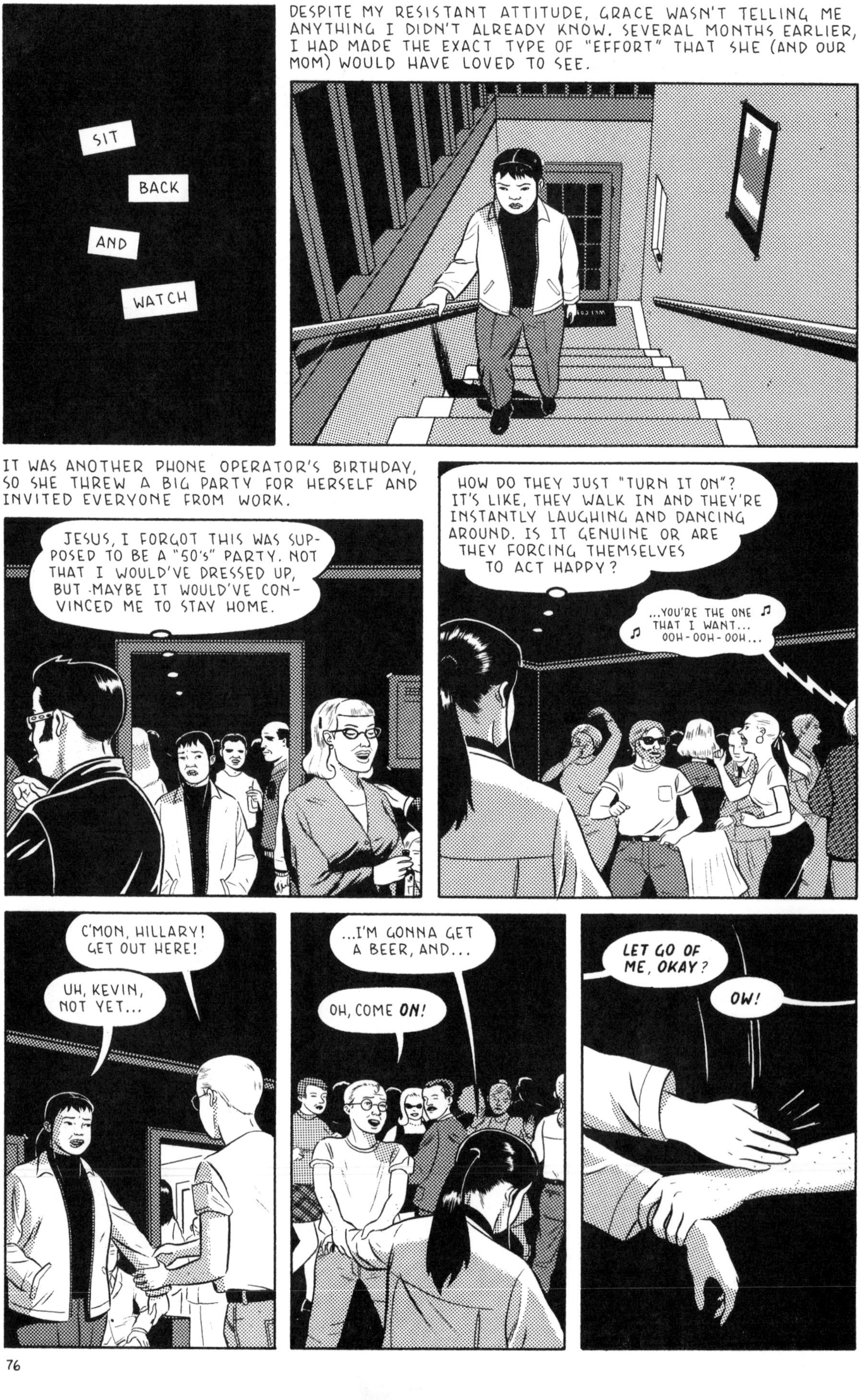
DESPITE MY RESISTANT ATTITUDE, GRACE WASN'T TELLING ME ANYTHING I DIDN'T ALREADY KNOW. SEVERAL MONTHS EARLIER, I HAD MADE THE EXACT TYPE OF "EFFORT" THAT SHE (AND OUR MOM) WOULD HAVE LOVED TO SEE.
SIT
BACK
AND
WATCH
IT WAS ANOTHER PHONE OPERATOR'S BIRTHDAY, SO SHE THREW A BIG PARTY FOR HERSELF AND INVITED EVERYONE FROM WORK.
JESUS, I FORGOT THIS WAS SUPPOSED TO BE A "50's" PARTY. NOT THAT I WOULD'VE DRESSED UP, BUT MAYBE IT WOULD'VE CONVINCED ME TO STAY HOME.
HOW DO THEY JUST "TURN IT ON"? IT'S LIKE, THEY WALK IN AND THEY'RE INSTANTLY LAUGHING AND DANCING AROUND. IS IT GENUINE OR ARE THEY FORCING THEMSELVES TO ACT HAPPY?
♫ ...YOU'RE THE ONE THAT I WANT... OOH-OOH-OOH... ♫
C'MON, HILLARY! GET OUT HERE!
UH, KEVIN, NOT YET...
...I'M GONNA GET A BEER, AND...
OH, COME ON!
LET GO OF ME, OKAY?
OW!

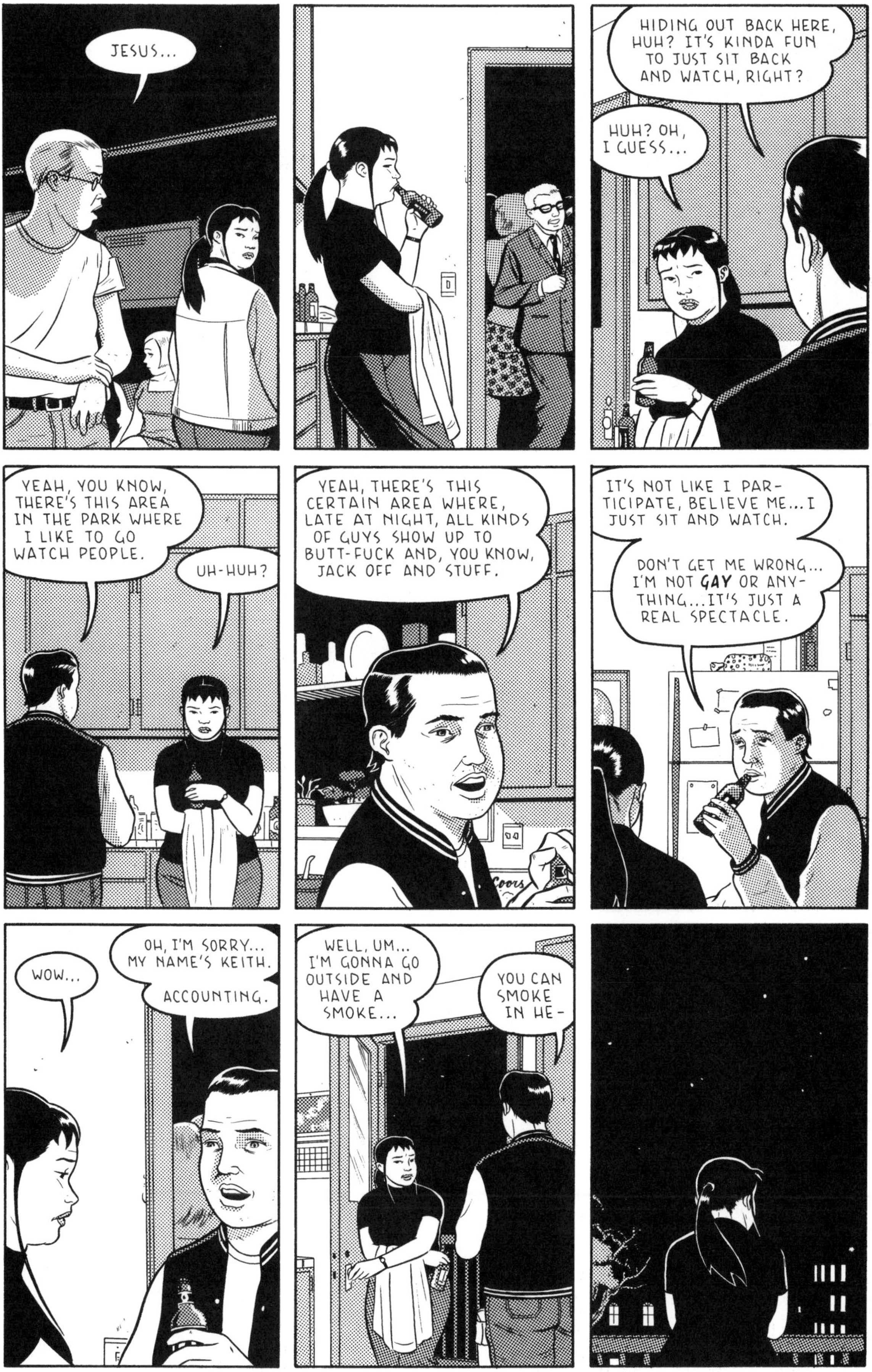
JESUS...
HIDING OUT BACK HERE, HUH? IT'S KINDA FUN TO JUST SIT BACK AND WATCH, RIGHT?
HUH? OH, I GUESS...
YEAH, YOU KNOW, THERE'S THIS AREA IN THE PARK WHERE I LIKE TO GO WATCH PEOPLE.
UH-HUH?
YEAH, THERE'S THIS CERTAIN AREA WHERE, LATE AT NIGHT, ALL KINDS OF GUYS SHOW UP TO BUTT-FUCK AND, YOU KNOW, JACK OFF AND STUFF.
Coors
IT'S NOT LIKE I PARTICIPATE, BELIEVE ME... I JUST SIT AND WATCH.
DON'T GET ME WRONG... I'M NOT GAY OR ANYTHING... IT'S JUST A REAL SPECTACLE.
WOW...
OH, I'M SORRY... MY NAME'S KEITH.
ACCOUNTING.
WELL, UM... I'M GONNA GO OUTSIDE AND HAVE A SMOKE...
YOU CAN SMOKE IN HE-

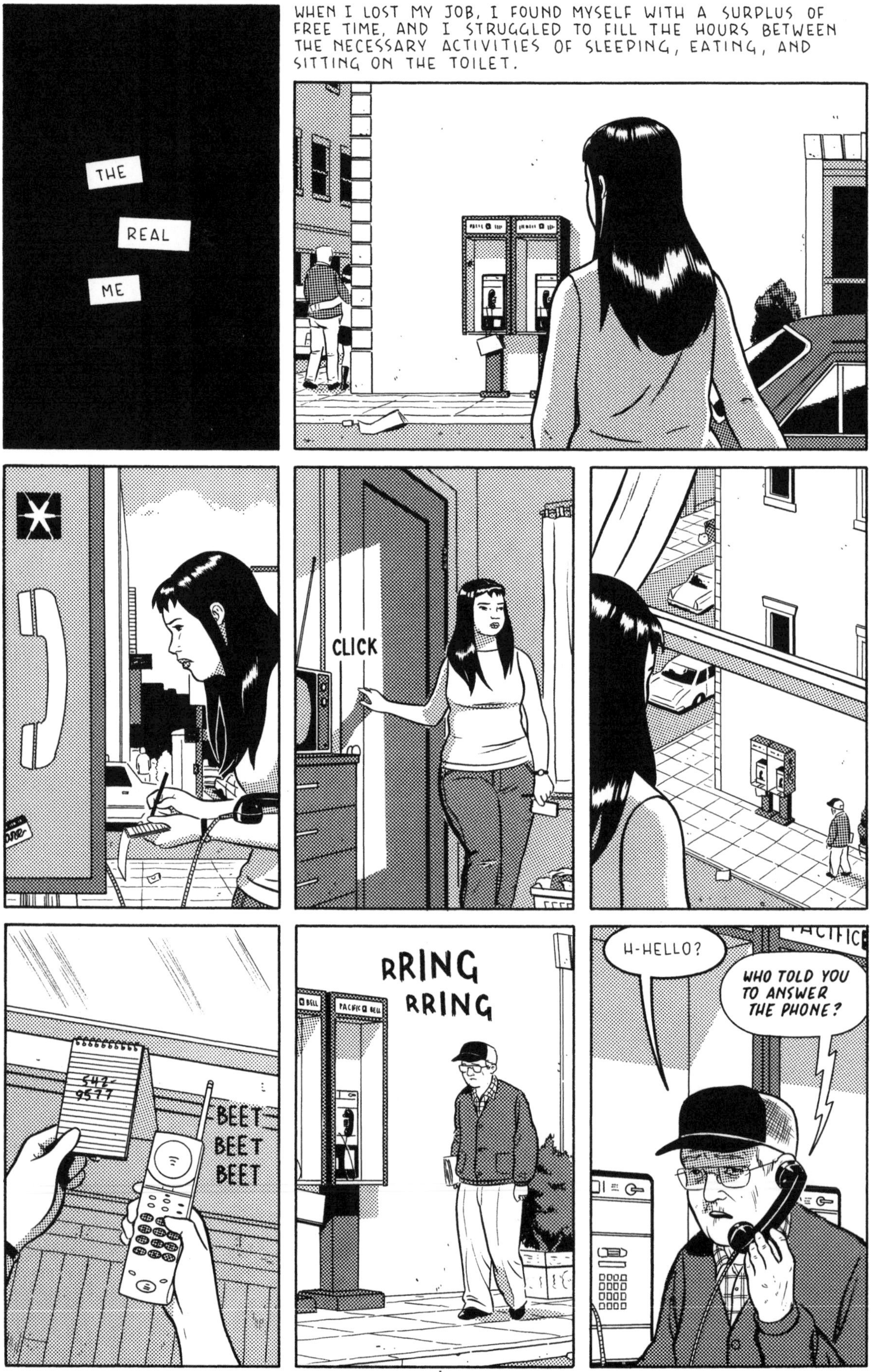
THE
REAL
ME
WHEN I LOST MY JOB, I FOUND MYSELF WITH A SURPLUS OF FREE TIME, AND I STRUGGLED TO FILL THE HOURS BETWEEN THE NECESSARY ACTIVITIES OF SLEEPING, EATING, AND SITTING ON THE TOILET.
CLICK
542-9577
BEET
BEET
BEET
RRING
RRING
H-HELLO?
WHO TOLD YOU TO ANSWER THE PHONE?

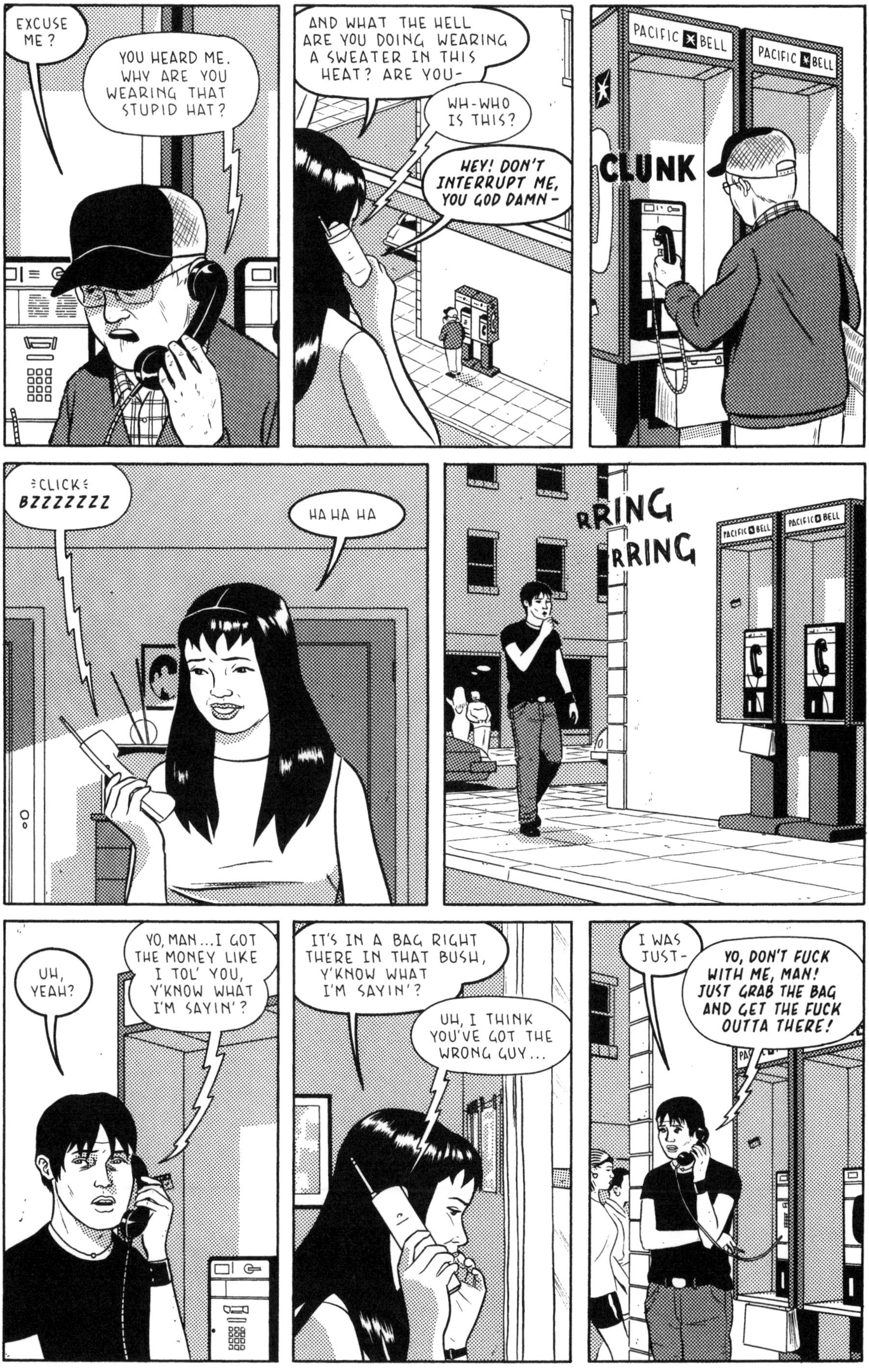
EXCUSE ME?
YOU HEARD ME. WHY ARE YOU WEARING THAT STUPID HAT?
AND WHAT THE HELL ARE YOU DOING WEARING A SWEATER IN THIS HEAT? ARE YOU-
WH-WHO IS THIS?
HEY! DON'T INTERRUPT ME, YOU GOD DAMN-
PACIFIC BELL
PACIFIC BELL
CLUNK
CLICK
BZZZZZZZ
HA HA HA
RRING
RRING
PACIFIC BELL
PACIFIC BELL
UH, YEAH?
YO, MAN...I GOT THE MONEY LIKE I TOL' YOU, Y'KNOW WHAT I'M SAYIN'?
IT'S IN A BAG RIGHT THERE IN THAT BUSH, Y'KNOW WHAT I'M SAYIN'?
UH, I THINK YOU'VE GOT THE WRONG GUY...
I WAS JUST-
YO, DON'T FUCK WITH ME, MAN! JUST GRAB THE BAG AND GET THE FUCK OUTTA THERE!

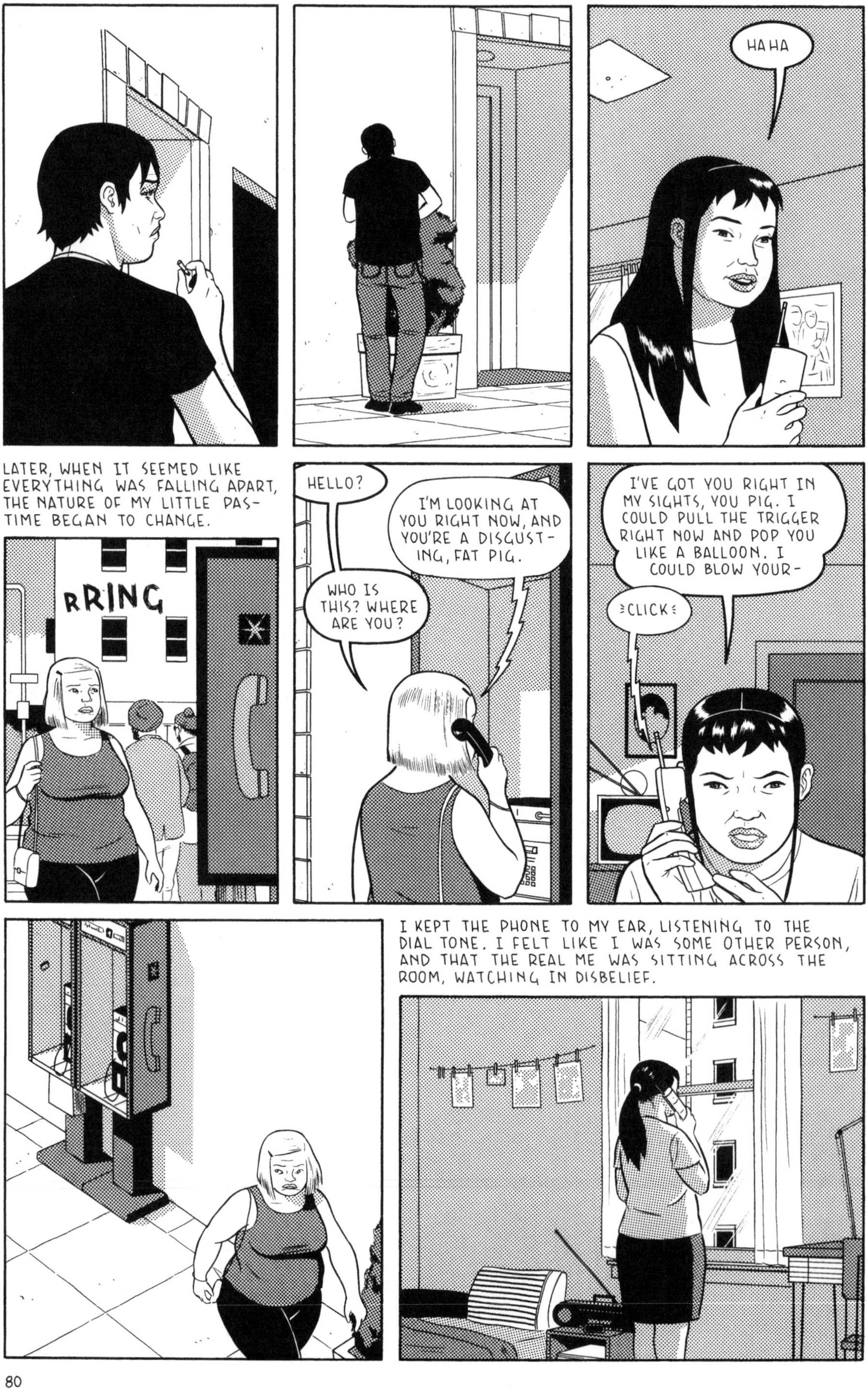
HA HA
LATER, WHEN IT SEEMED LIKE EVERYTHING WAS FALLING APART, THE NATURE OF MY LITTLE PAS-TIME BEGAN TO CHANGE.
RRING
HELLO?
I'M LOOKING AT YOU RIGHT NOW, AND YOU'RE A DISGUST-ING, FAT PIG.
WHO IS THIS? WHERE ARE YOU?
I'VE GOT YOU RIGHT IN MY SIGHTS, YOU PIG. I COULD PULL THE TRIGGER RIGHT NOW AND POP YOU LIKE A BALLOON. I COULD BLOW YOUR-
CLICK
I KEPT THE PHONE TO MY EAR, LISTENING TO THE DIAL TONE. I FELT LIKE I WAS SOME OTHER PERSON, AND THAT THE REAL ME WAS SITTING ACROSS THE ROOM, WATCHING IN DISBELIEF.

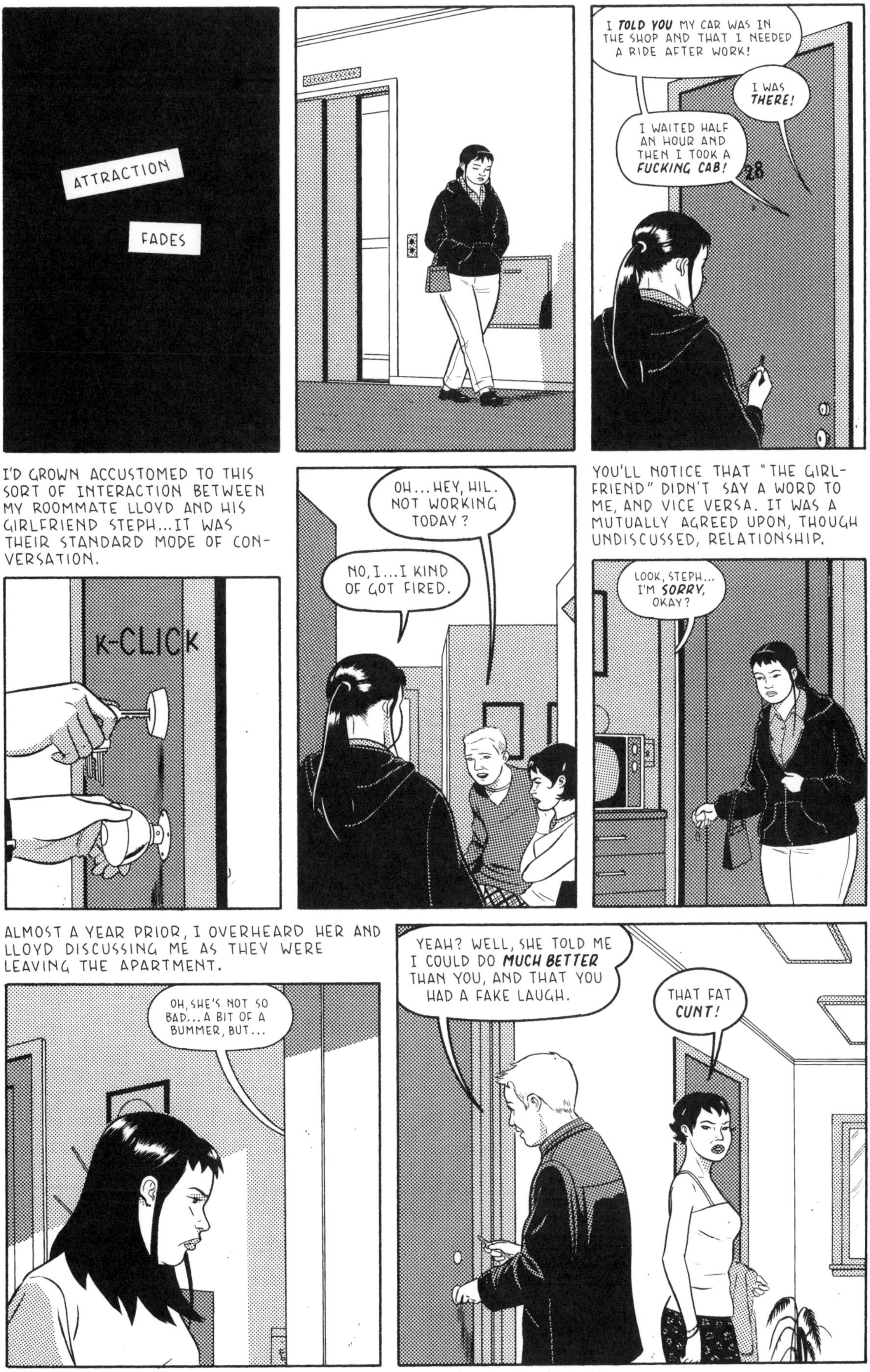
ATTRACTION
FADES
I TOLD YOU MY CAR WAS IN THE SHOP AND THAT I NEEDED A RIDE AFTER WORK!
I WAS THERE!
I WAITED HALF AN HOUR AND THEN I TOOK A FUCKING CAB!
28
I'D GROWN ACCUSTOMED TO THIS SORT OF INTERACTION BETWEEN MY ROOMMATE LLOYD AND HIS GIRLFRIEND STEPH...IT WAS THEIR STANDARD MODE OF CONVERSATION.
K-CLICK
OH... HEY, HIL. NOT WORKING TODAY?
NO, I...I KIND OF GOT FIRED.
YOU'LL NOTICE THAT "THE GIRLFRIEND" DIDN'T SAY A WORD TO ME, AND VICE VERSA. IT WAS A MUTUALLY AGREED UPON, THOUGH UNDISCUSSED, RELATIONSHIP.
LOOK, STEPH... I'M SORRY, OKAY?
ALMOST A YEAR PRIOR, I OVERHEARD HER AND LLOYD DISCUSSING ME AS THEY WERE LEAVING THE APARTMENT.
OH, SHE'S NOT SO BAD... A BIT OF A BUMMER, BUT...
YEAH? WELL, SHE TOLD ME I COULD DO MUCH BETTER THAN YOU, AND THAT YOU HAD A FAKE LAUGH.
THAT FAT CUNT!

AFTER SEVERAL WEEKS OF KEEPING MY MOUTH SHUT, I FELT COMPELLED TO OFFER MY UNSOLICITED OPINION ON STEPH TO LLOYD.

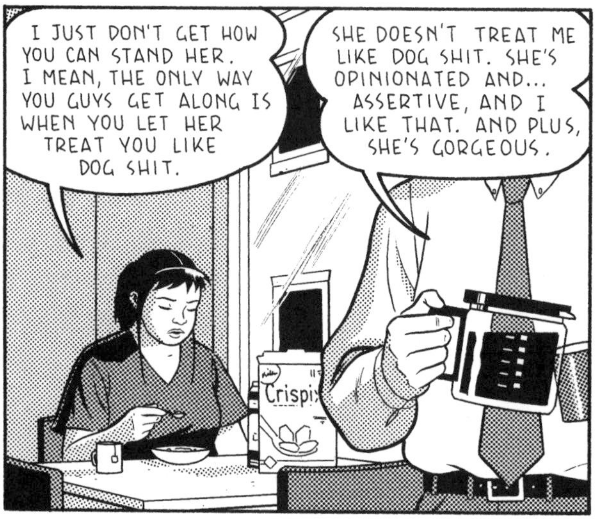
I JUST DON'T GET HOW YOU CAN STAND HER. I MEAN, THE ONLY WAY YOU GUYS GET ALONG IS WHEN YOU LET HER TREAT YOU LIKE DOG SHIT.
SHE DOESN'T TREAT ME LIKE DOG SHIT. SHE'S OPINIONATED AND... ASSERTIVE, AND I LIKE THAT. AND PLUS, SHE'S GORGEOUS.
Crispix

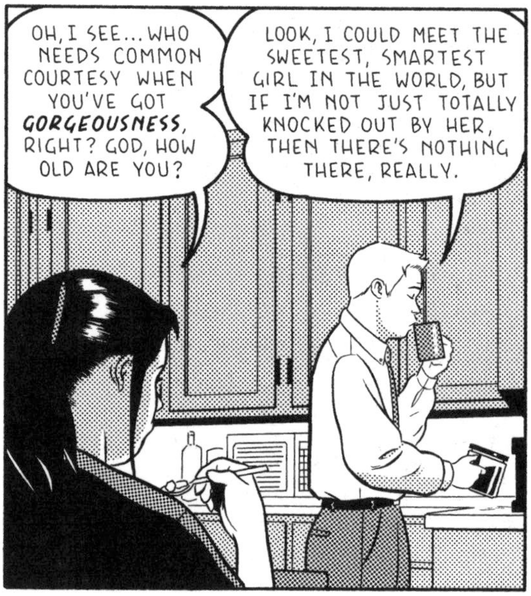
OH, I SEE... WHO NEEDS COMMON COURTESY WHEN YOU'VE GOT **GORGEOUSNESS**, RIGHT? GOD, HOW OLD ARE YOU?
LOOK, I COULD MEET THE SWEETEST, SMARTEST GIRL IN THE WORLD, BUT IF I'M NOT JUST TOTALLY KNOCKED OUT BY HER, THEN THERE'S NOTHING THERE, REALLY.

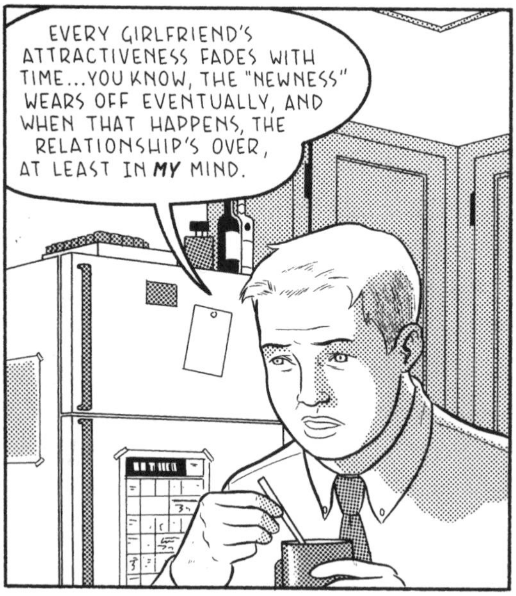
EVERY GIRLFRIEND'S ATTRACTIVENESS FADES WITH TIME... YOU KNOW, THE "NEWNESS" WEARS OFF EVENTUALLY, AND WHEN THAT HAPPENS, THE RELATIONSHIP'S OVER, AT LEAST IN **MY** MIND.

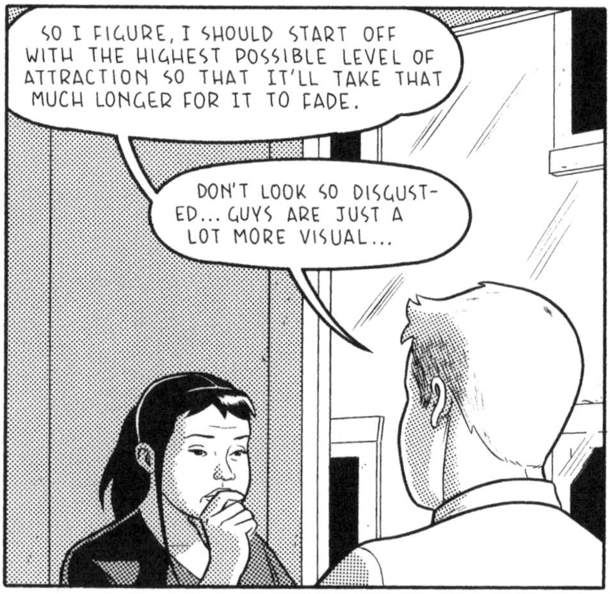
SO I FIGURE, I SHOULD START OFF WITH THE HIGHEST POSSIBLE LEVEL OF ATTRACTION SO THAT IT'LL TAKE THAT MUCH LONGER FOR IT TO FADE.
DON'T LOOK SO DISGUSTED... GUYS ARE JUST A LOT MORE VISUAL...

I COULDN'T HELP BUT THINK THAT HIS "ATTRACTION FADES" SPIEL WAS A SUBTLE JAB IN MY DIRECTION, LIKE A RETALIATION FOR CRITICIZING STEPH. A YEAR AND A HALF EARLIER, RIGHT WHEN I MOVED IN, LLOYD AND I STAYED UP ALL NIGHT, HUMPING EACH OTHER TO EXHAUSTION.

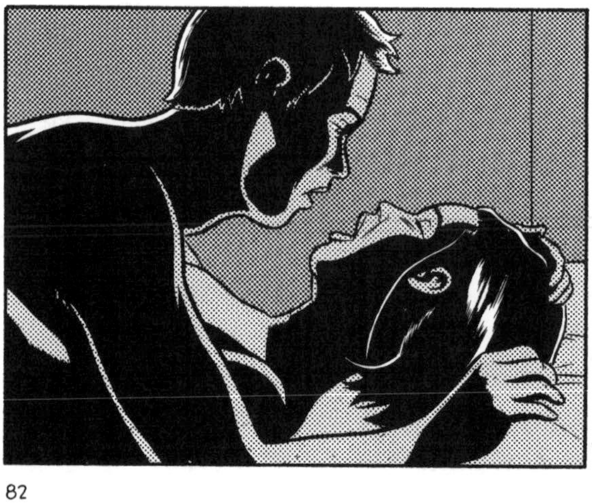

AFTER THREE NIGHTS OF THAT, HE MADE IT CLEAR THAT WE WERE STRICTLY ROOMMATES, AND HE NEVER AGAIN EXPRESSED EVEN THE SLIGHTEST BIT OF INTEREST IN ME.

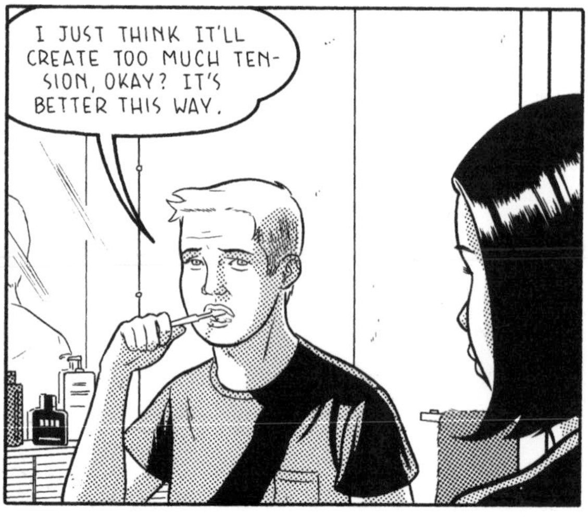
I JUST THINK IT'LL CREATE TOO MUCH TENSION, OKAY? IT'S BETTER THIS WAY.

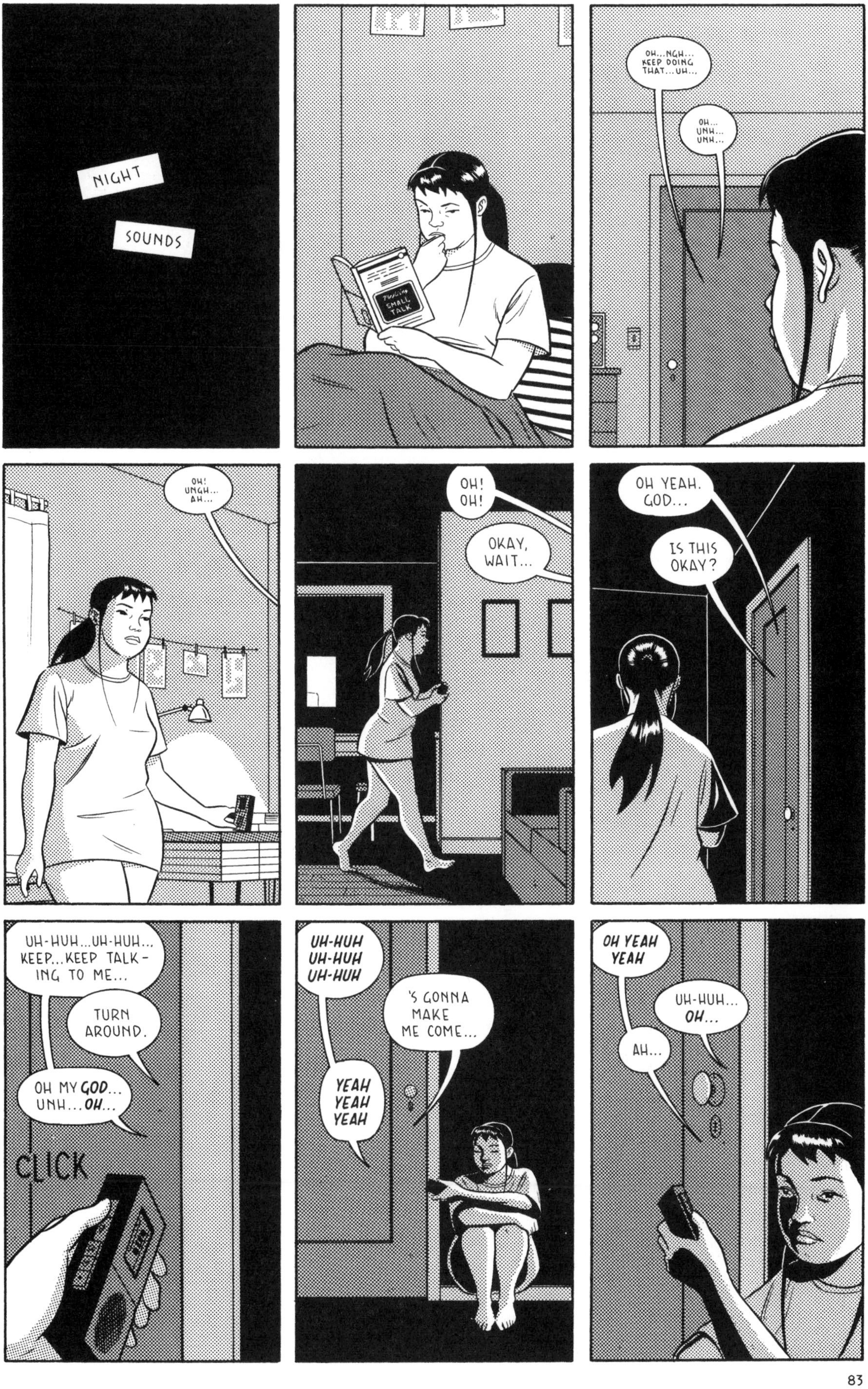
NIGHT
SOUNDS
SMALL TALK
OH...NGH... KEEP DOING THAT...UH...
OH... UNH... UNH...
OH! UNGH... AH...
OH! OH!
OKAY, WAIT...
OH YEAH. GOD...
IS THIS OKAY?
UH-HUH...UH-HUH... KEEP...KEEP TALK-ING TO ME...
TURN AROUND.
OH MY **GOD**... UNH...**OH**...
CLICK
UH-HUH UH-HUH UH-HUH
'S GONNA MAKE ME COME...
YEAH YEAH YEAH
OH YEAH YEAH
UH-HUH... **OH**...
AH...

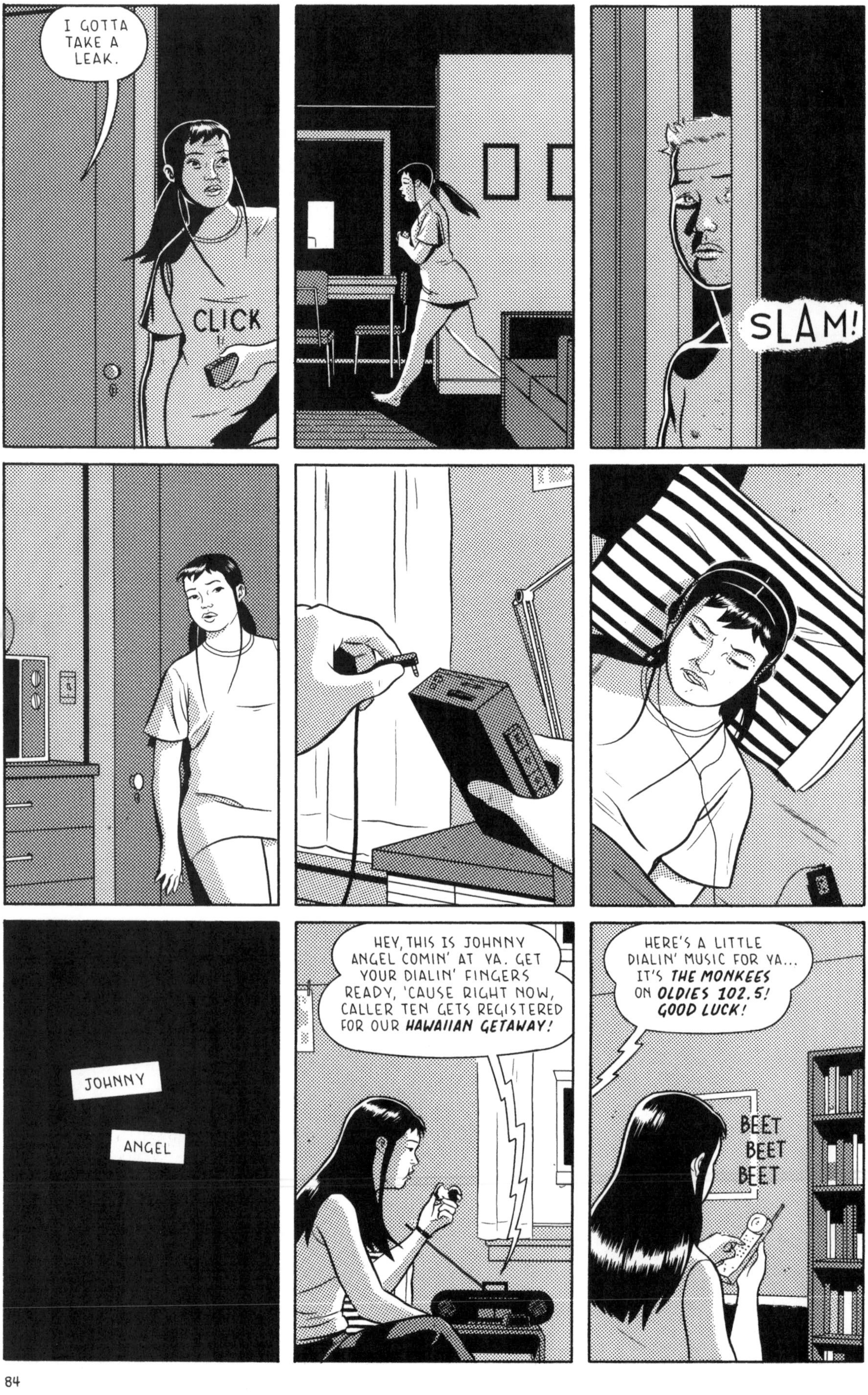
I GOTTA TAKE A LEAK.
CLICK
SLAM!
JOHNNY
ANGEL
HEY, THIS IS JOHNNY ANGEL COMIN' AT YA. GET YOUR DIALIN' FINGERS READY, 'CAUSE RIGHT NOW, CALLER TEN GETS REGISTERED FOR OUR HAWAIIAN GETAWAY!
HERE'S A LITTLE DIALIN' MUSIC FOR YA... IT'S THE MONKEES ON OLDIES 102.5! GOOD LUCK!
BEET BEET BEET

OF COURSE THE LINE WAS BUSY, SO I BEGAN A FRENETIC TWO-HANDED SYSTEM OF HANGING UP AND HITTING REDIAL AS FAST AS POSSIBLE. I COULDN'T STOP... IT WAS THAT SLOT-MACHINE KIND OF FEELING. I MUST'VE TRIED THIRTY, FORTY TIMES UNTIL...

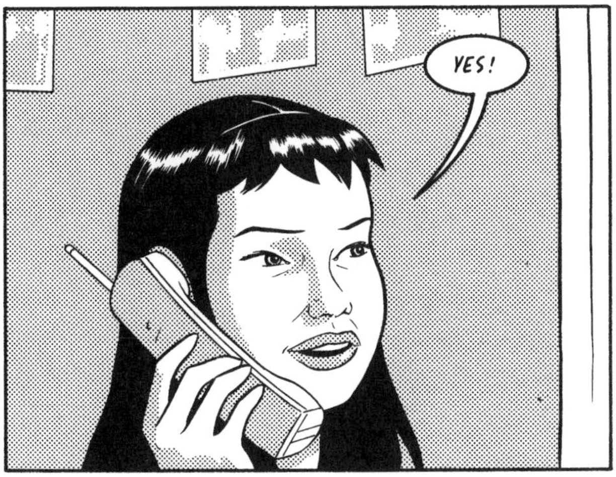
YES!

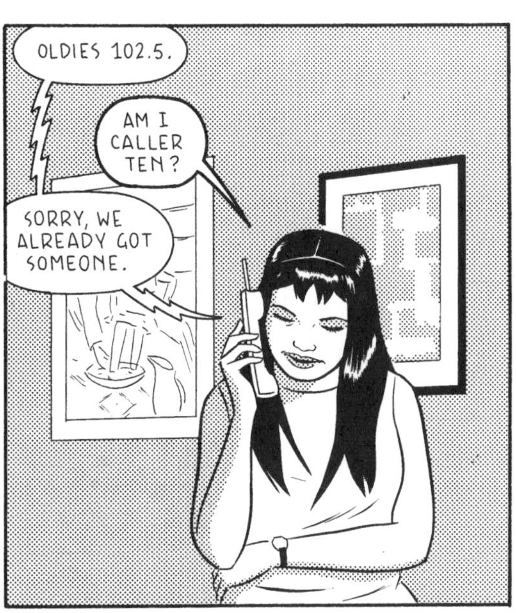
OLDIES 102.5.
AM I CALLER TEN?
SORRY, WE ALREADY GOT SOMEONE.

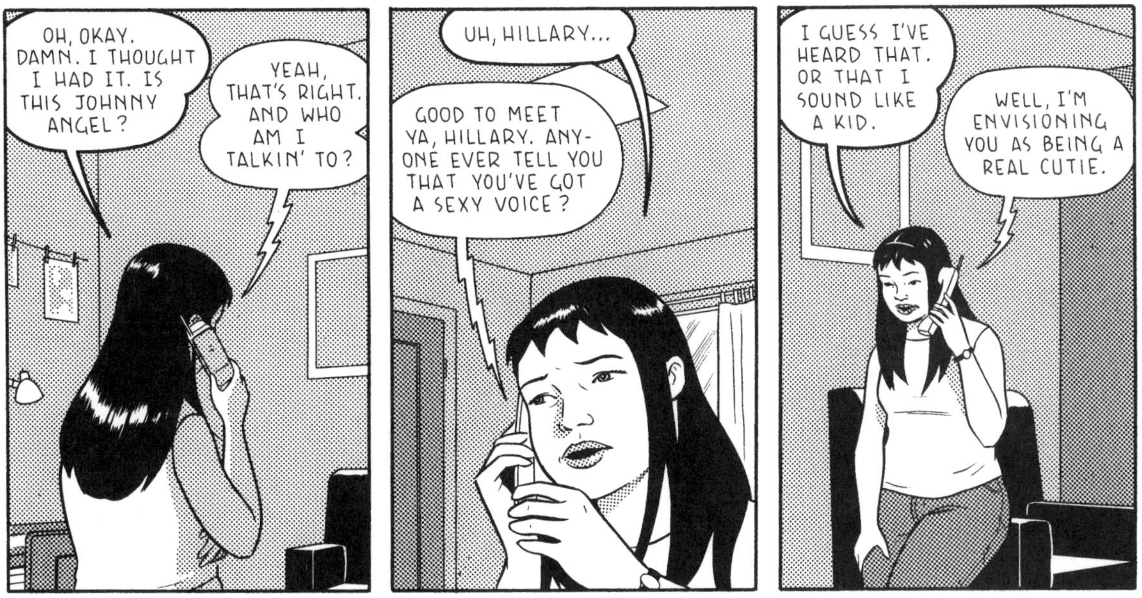
OH, OKAY. DAMN. I THOUGHT I HAD IT. IS THIS JOHNNY ANGEL?
YEAH, THAT'S RIGHT. AND WHO AM I TALKIN' TO?
UH, HILLARY...
GOOD TO MEET YA, HILLARY. ANYONE EVER TELL YOU THAT YOU'VE GOT A SEXY VOICE?
I GUESS I'VE HEARD THAT. OR THAT I SOUND LIKE A KID.
WELL, I'M ENVISIONING YOU AS BEING A REAL CUTIE.

SO I AGREED TO MEET HIM THAT WEEKEND AT THE BAR IN A RESTAURANT CALLED THE NIGHT DEPOSIT (HIS CHOICE, BELIEVE ME). HE SAID I'D RECOGNIZE HIM BY HIS "GROOVY" OLDIES 102.5 JACKET, AND I LAUGHED, HOPING HE'D MEANT IT AS A JOKE.

SATURDAY ARRIVED EVENTUALLY, AND AS I PREPARED FOR MY "DATE," I DEVELOPED A SENSATION OF BOTH ANXIETY AND EXCITEMENT. I HAD A MILD CASE OF NAUSEA, AND I KEPT GETTING WHAT FELT LIKE HOT FLASHES.

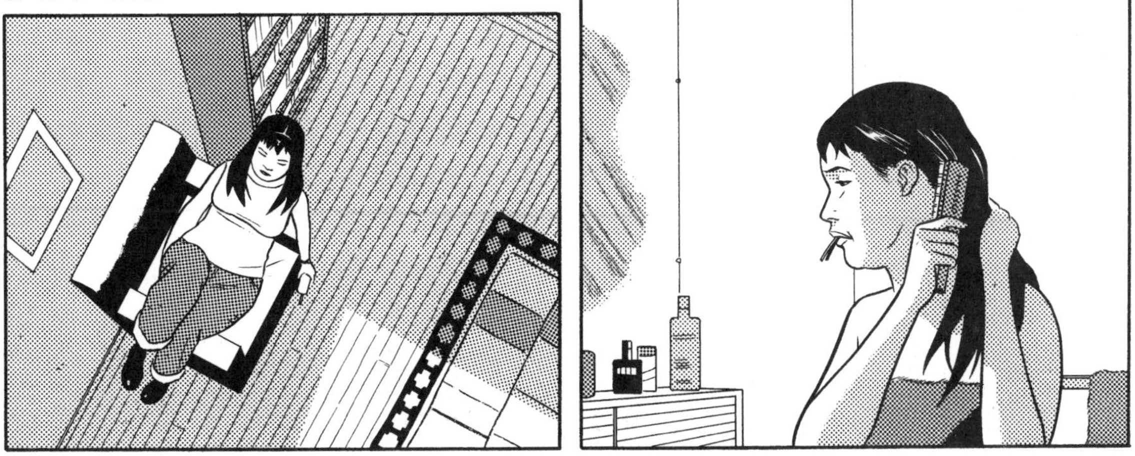

I DROVE PAST THE NIGHT DEPOSIT FOUR TIMES BEFORE PARKING AND GOING INSIDE.

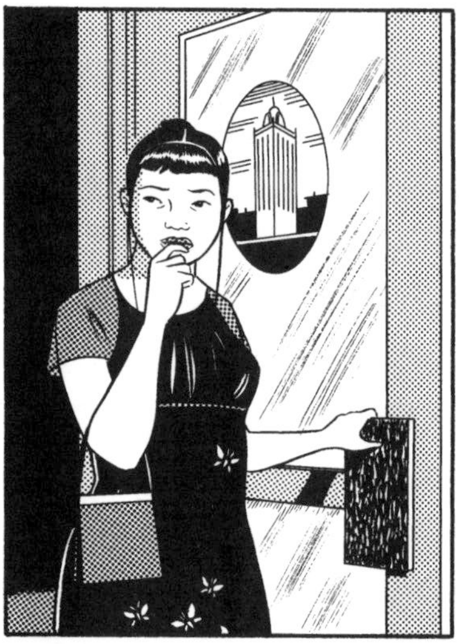

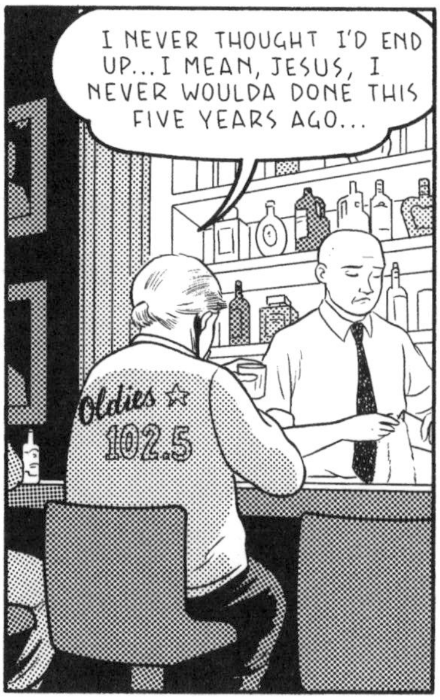
I NEVER THOUGHT I'D END UP...I MEAN, JESUS, I NEVER WOULDA DONE THIS FIVE YEARS AGO...
Oldies ☆ 102.5

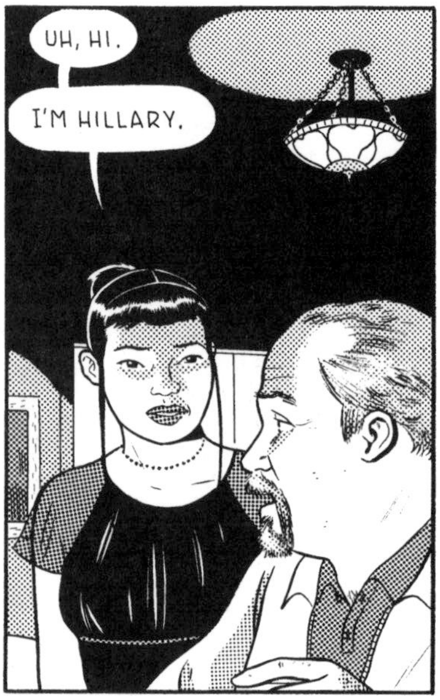
UH, HI.
I'M HILLARY.

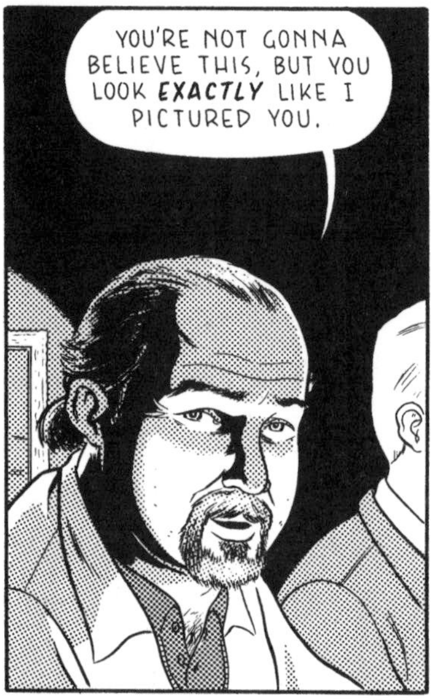
YOU'RE NOT GONNA BELIEVE THIS, BUT YOU LOOK **EXACTLY** LIKE I PICTURED YOU.

OF COURSE HE WAS RIGHT -I DIDN'T BELIEVE HIM- BUT I WAS NEVERTHELESS FLATTERED, OR AT LEAST RELIEVED THAT HE DIDN'T RESPOND WITH A LOOK OF DISAPPOINTMENT WHEN I INTRODUCED MYSELF.

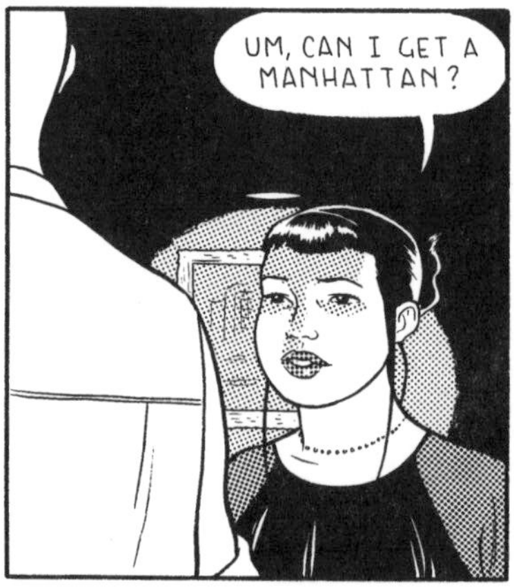
UM, CAN I GET A MANHATTAN?

I COULD TELL THAT HE'D ALREADY BEEN DRINKING FOR AWHILE, AND AFTER TWO COCKTAILS, I WAS PRETTY FLUSHED MYSELF. (I'M A TYPICAL LOW-TOLERANCE ASIAN.)

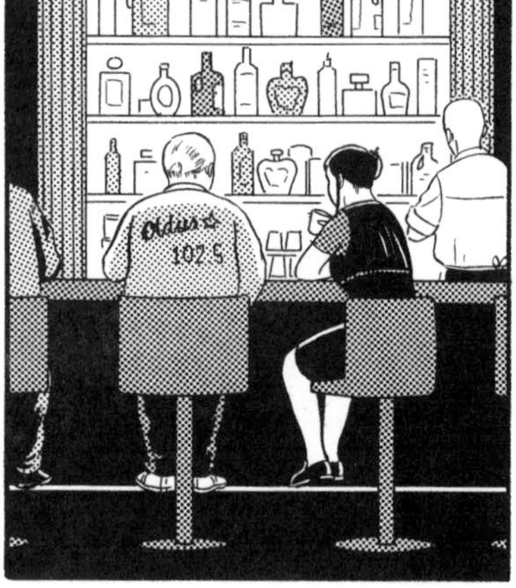

FOR THAT REASON, THE SPECIFICS OF OUR CONVERSATION ESCAPE ME, BUT I RECALL FEELING A TWINGE OF PITY AS HE WHINED ABOUT THE UPS AND DOWNS OF HIS CAREER.

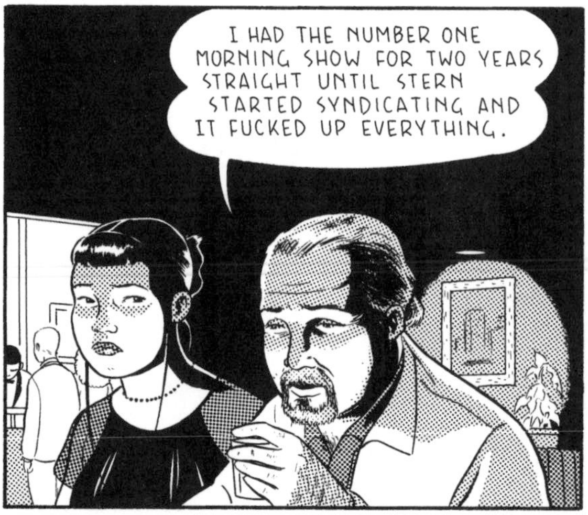
I HAD THE NUMBER ONE MORNING SHOW FOR TWO YEARS STRAIGHT UNTIL STERN STARTED SYNDICATING AND IT FUCKED UP EVERYTHING.

WHEN THE RESTAURANT CLOSED, WE BOTH WOBBLED OUT INTO THE PARKING LOT WHERE HE CONVINCED ME TO SIT IN HIS CAR AND CONTINUE OUR CONVERSATION.

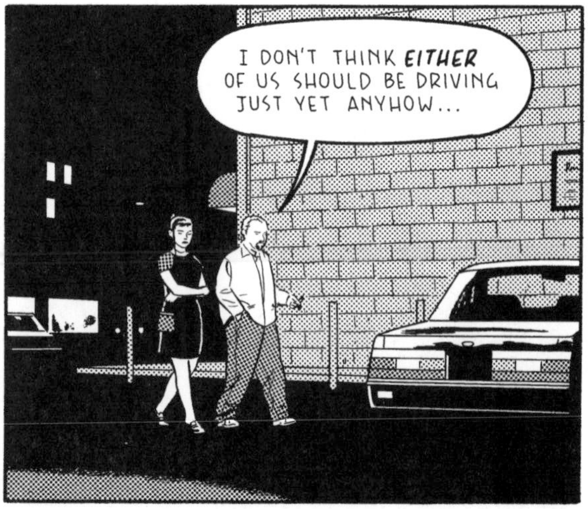
I DON'T THINK **EITHER** OF US SHOULD BE DRIVING JUST YET ANYHOW...

SOMEHOW WE ENDED UP MAKING OUT. I KNOW, THE IDEA OF AN OLD GUY LIKE THAT SEEMS REPELLENT, BUT IT WAS OKAY ONCE WE STARTED GOING. I BET TWO AND A HALF YEARS WITHOUT ANY PHYSICAL CONTACT WOULD ERODE ANYONE'S STANDARDS.

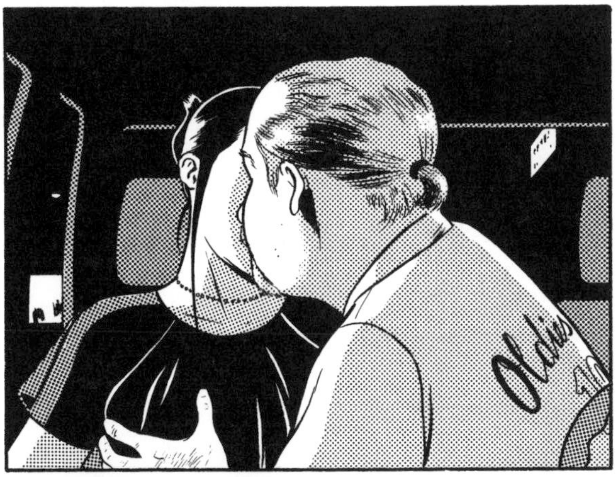

I THINK HE WANTED TO FUCK ME RIGHT THERE IN HIS NISSAN, BUT I ENDED UP JUST J.O.-ING HIM AND GETTING IT OVER WITH.

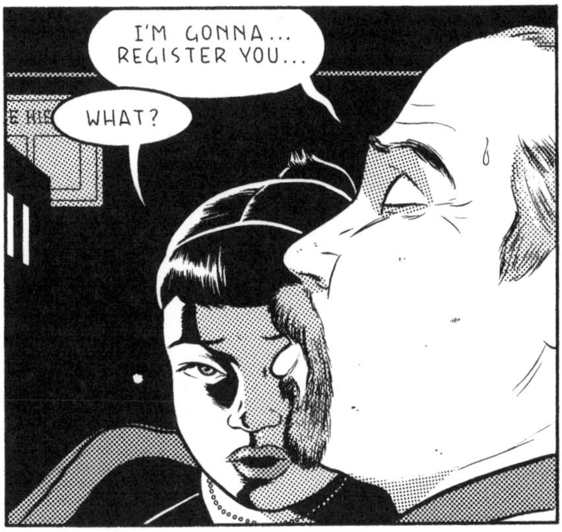
I'M GONNA... REGISTER YOU...
WHAT?

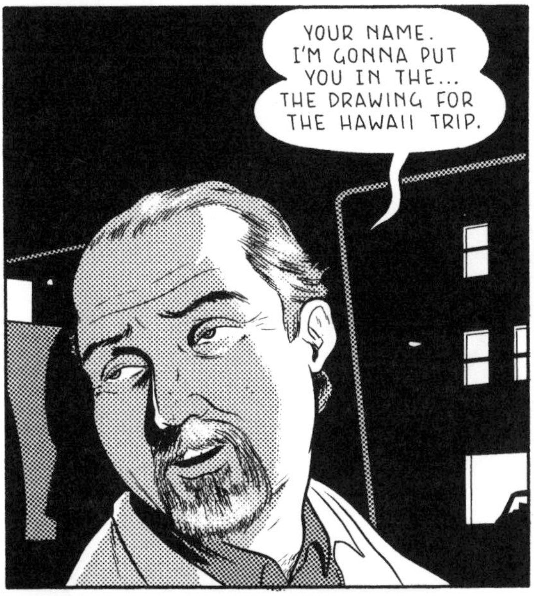
YOUR NAME. I'M GONNA PUT YOU IN THE... THE DRAWING FOR THE HAWAII TRIP.

A FEW MINUTES LATER, I WAS DRIVING HOME. WE DIDN'T EXCHANGE PHONE NUMBERS OR MAKE PLANS TO SEE EACH OTHER AGAIN.

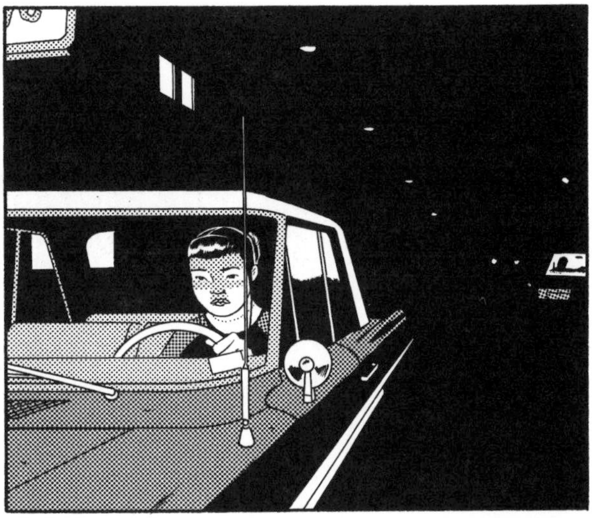

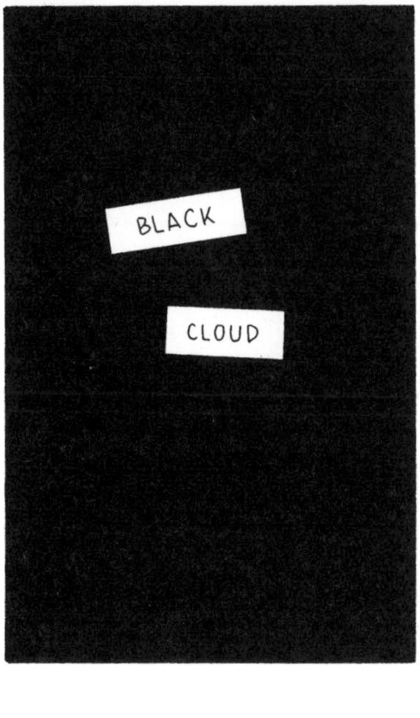
BLACK
CLOUD

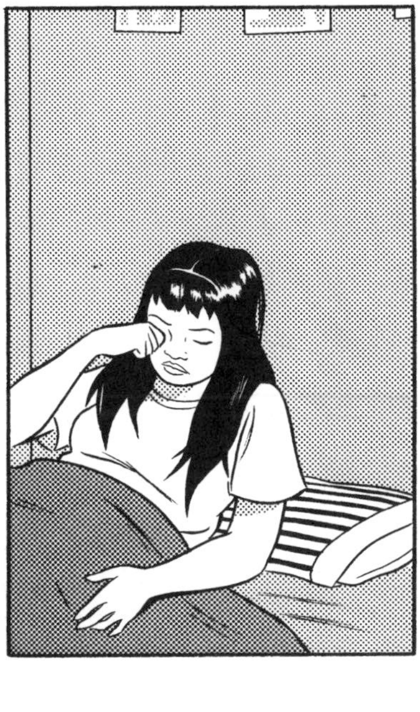

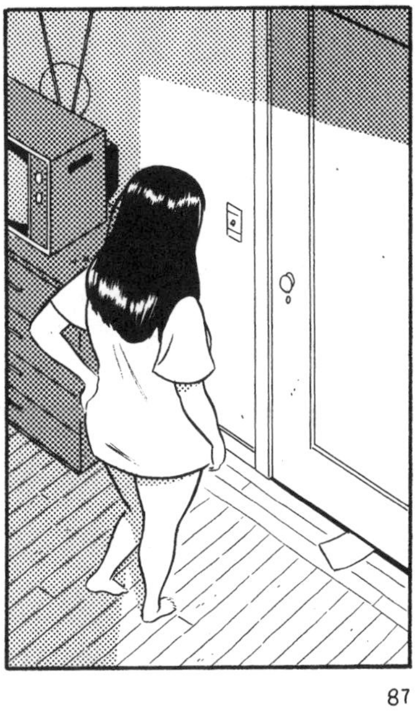

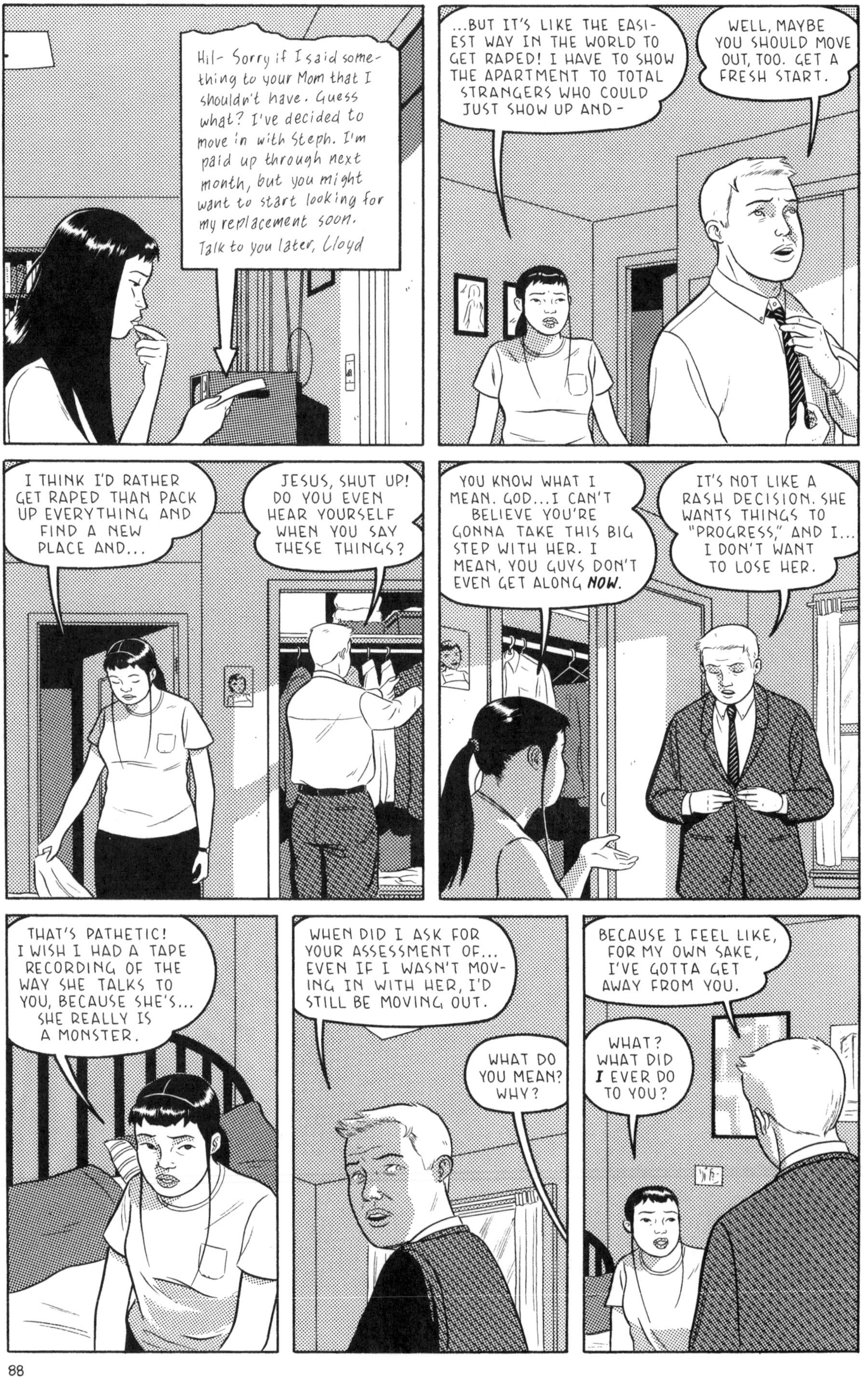
Hi! - Sorry if I said something to your Mom that I shouldn't have. Guess what? I've decided to move in with Steph. I'm paid up through next month, but you might want to start looking for my replacement soon.
Talk to you later, Lloyd
...BUT IT'S LIKE THE EASIEST WAY IN THE WORLD TO GET RAPED! I HAVE TO SHOW THE APARTMENT TO TOTAL STRANGERS WHO COULD JUST SHOW UP AND -
WELL, MAYBE YOU SHOULD MOVE OUT, TOO. GET A FRESH START.
I THINK I'D RATHER GET RAPED THAN PACK UP EVERYTHING AND FIND A NEW PLACE AND...
JESUS, SHUT UP! DO YOU EVEN HEAR YOURSELF WHEN YOU SAY THESE THINGS?
YOU KNOW WHAT I MEAN. GOD...I CAN'T BELIEVE YOU'RE GONNA TAKE THIS BIG STEP WITH HER. I MEAN, YOU GUYS DON'T EVEN GET ALONG NOW.
IT'S NOT LIKE A RASH DECISION. SHE WANTS THINGS TO "PROGRESS," AND I... I DON'T WANT TO LOSE HER.
THAT'S PATHETIC! I WISH I HAD A TAPE RECORDING OF THE WAY SHE TALKS TO YOU, BECAUSE SHE'S... SHE REALLY IS A MONSTER.
WHEN DID I ASK FOR YOUR ASSESSMENT OF... EVEN IF I WASN'T MOVING IN WITH HER, I'D STILL BE MOVING OUT.
WHAT DO YOU MEAN? WHY?
BECAUSE I FEEL LIKE, FOR MY OWN SAKE, I'VE GOTTA GET AWAY FROM YOU.
WHAT? WHAT DID I EVER DO TO YOU?

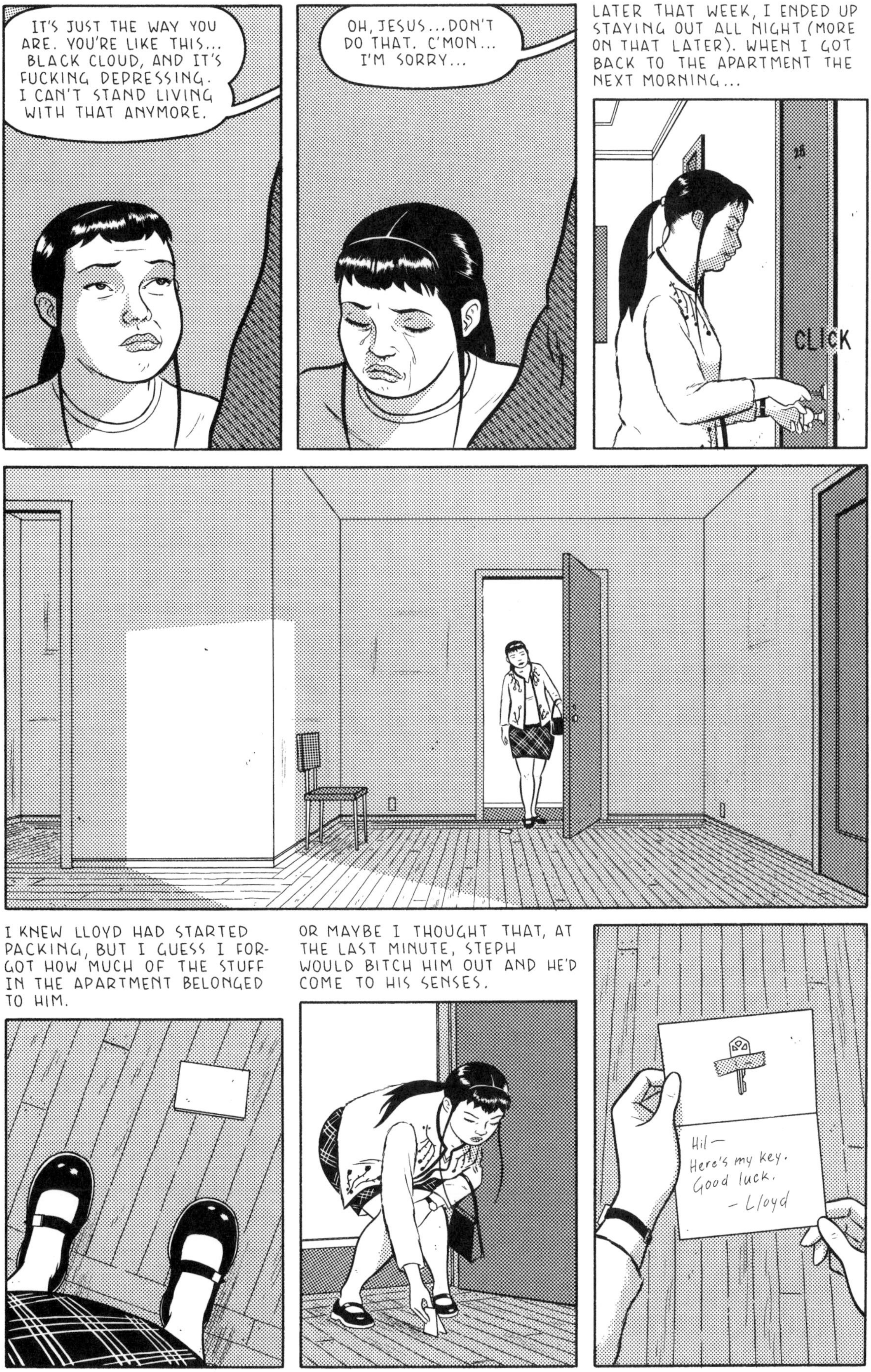
IT'S JUST THE WAY YOU ARE. YOU'RE LIKE THIS... BLACK CLOUD, AND IT'S FUCKING DEPRESSING. I CAN'T STAND LIVING WITH THAT ANYMORE.
OH, JESUS... DON'T DO THAT. C'MON... I'M SORRY...
LATER THAT WEEK, I ENDED UP STAYING OUT ALL NIGHT (MORE ON THAT LATER). WHEN I GOT BACK TO THE APARTMENT THE NEXT MORNING...
CLICK
I KNEW LLOYD HAD STARTED PACKING, BUT I GUESS I FORGOT HOW MUCH OF THE STUFF IN THE APARTMENT BELONGED TO HIM.
OR MAYBE I THOUGHT THAT, AT THE LAST MINUTE, STEPH WOULD BITCH HIM OUT AND HE'D COME TO HIS SENSES.
Hil—
Here's my key.
Good luck.
—Lloyd

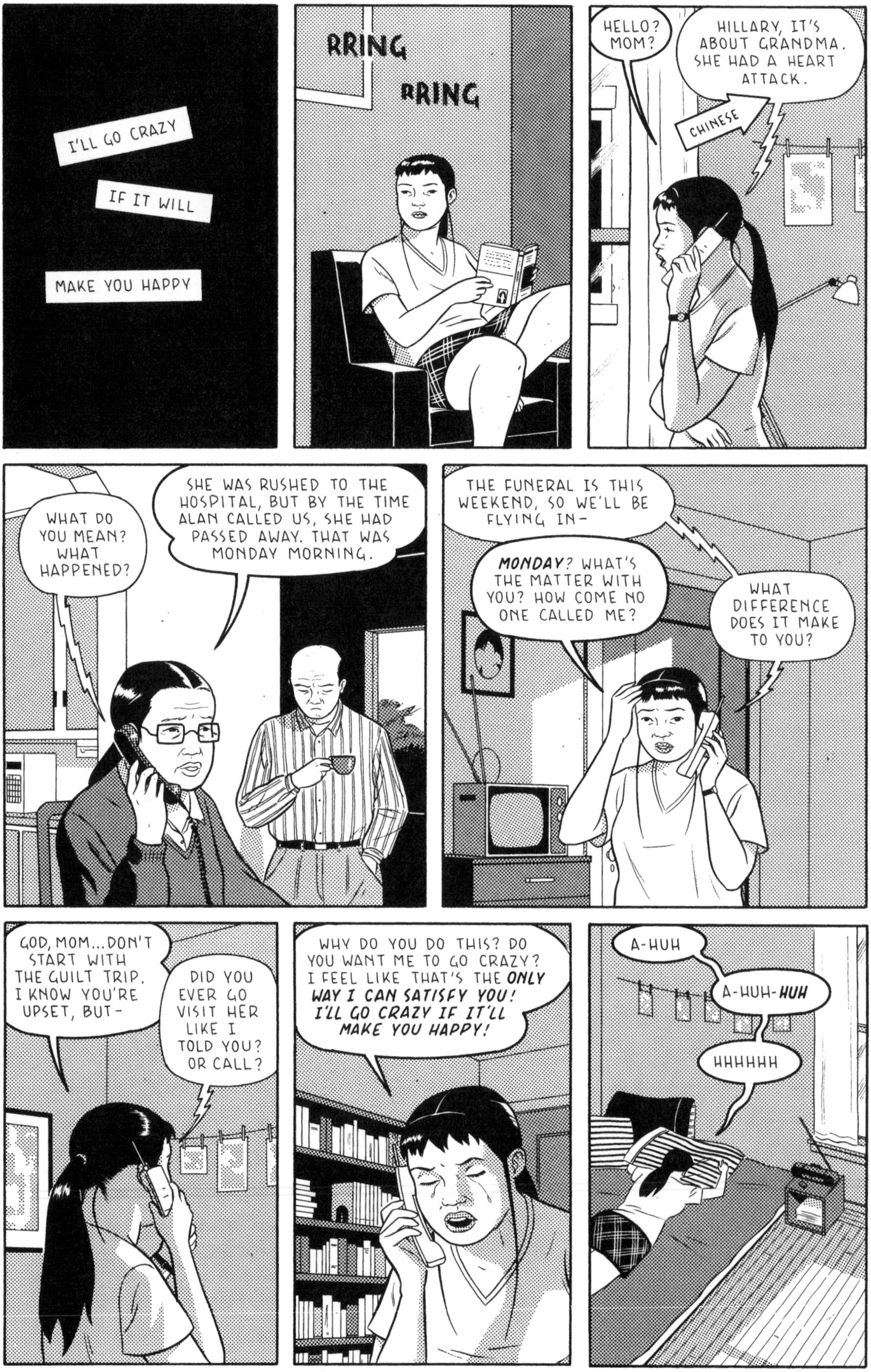

I'LL GO CRAZY
IF IT WILL
MAKE YOU HAPPY
RRING
RRING
HELLO? MOM?
HILLARY, IT'S ABOUT GRANDMA. SHE HAD A HEART ATTACK.
CHINESE
WHAT DO YOU MEAN? WHAT HAPPENED?
SHE WAS RUSHED TO THE HOSPITAL, BUT BY THE TIME ALAN CALLED US, SHE HAD PASSED AWAY. THAT WAS MONDAY MORNING.
THE FUNERAL IS THIS WEEKEND, SO WE'LL BE FLYING IN-
MONDAY? WHAT'S THE MATTER WITH YOU? HOW COME NO ONE CALLED ME?
WHAT DIFFERENCE DOES IT MAKE TO YOU?
GOD, MOM...DON'T START WITH THE GUILT TRIP. I KNOW YOU'RE UPSET, BUT-
DID YOU EVER GO VISIT HER LIKE I TOLD YOU? OR CALL?
WHY DO YOU DO THIS? DO YOU WANT ME TO GO CRAZY? I FEEL LIKE THAT'S THE ONLY WAY I CAN SATISFY YOU! I'LL GO CRAZY IF IT'LL MAKE YOU HAPPY!
A-HUH
A-HUH-HUH
HHHHHH

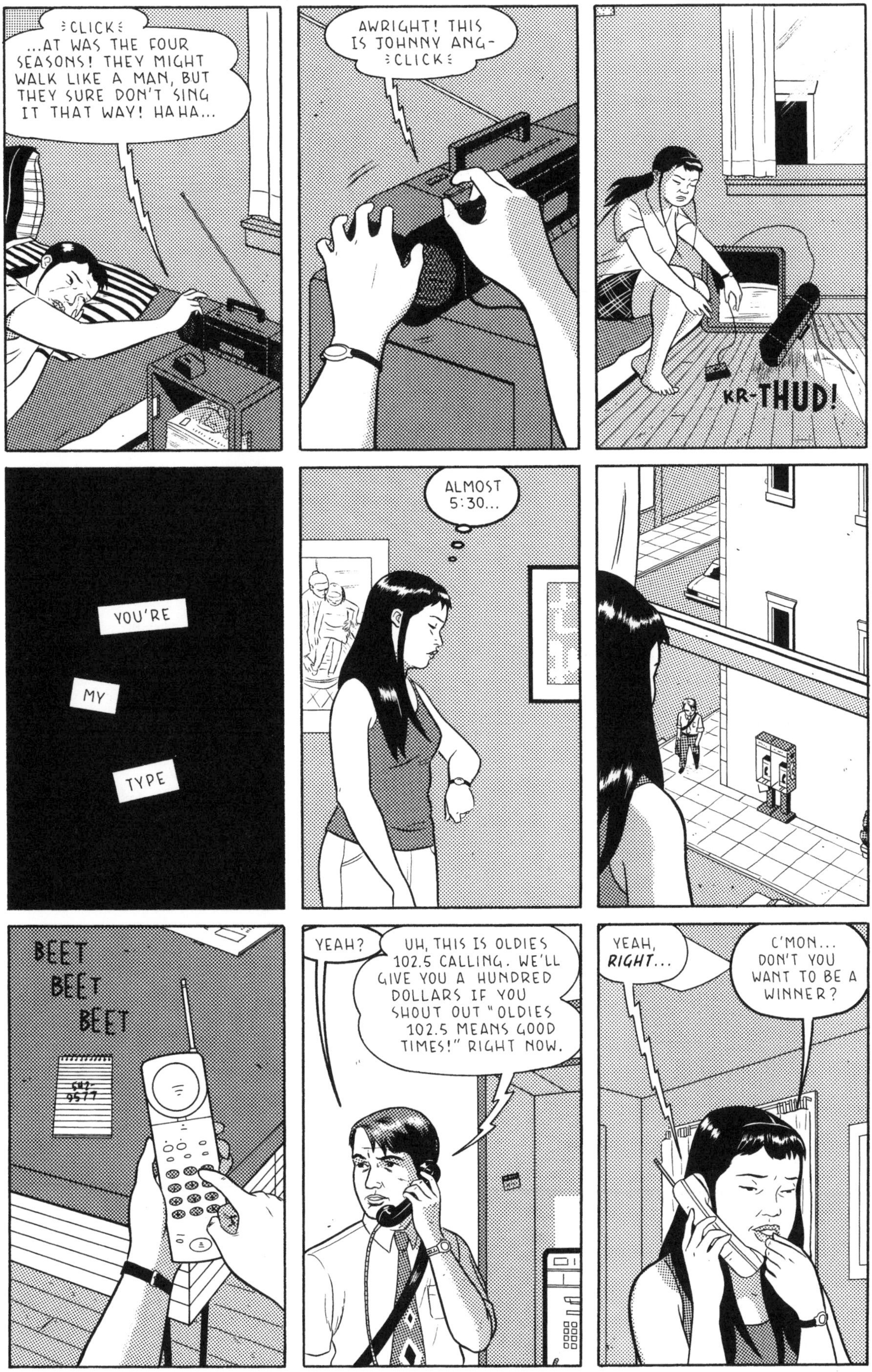
CLICK
...AT WAS THE FOUR SEASONS! THEY MIGHT WALK LIKE A MAN, BUT THEY SURE DON'T SING IT THAT WAY! HAHA...
AWRIGHT! THIS IS JOHNNY ANG- CLICK
KR-THUD!
YOU'RE
MY
TYPE
ALMOST 5:30...
BEET
BEET
BEET
YEAH?
UH, THIS IS OLDIES 102.5 CALLING. WE'LL GIVE YOU A HUNDRED DOLLARS IF YOU SHOUT OUT "OLDIES 102.5 MEANS GOOD TIMES!" RIGHT NOW.
YEAH, RIGHT...
C'MON... DON'T YOU WANT TO BE A WINNER?

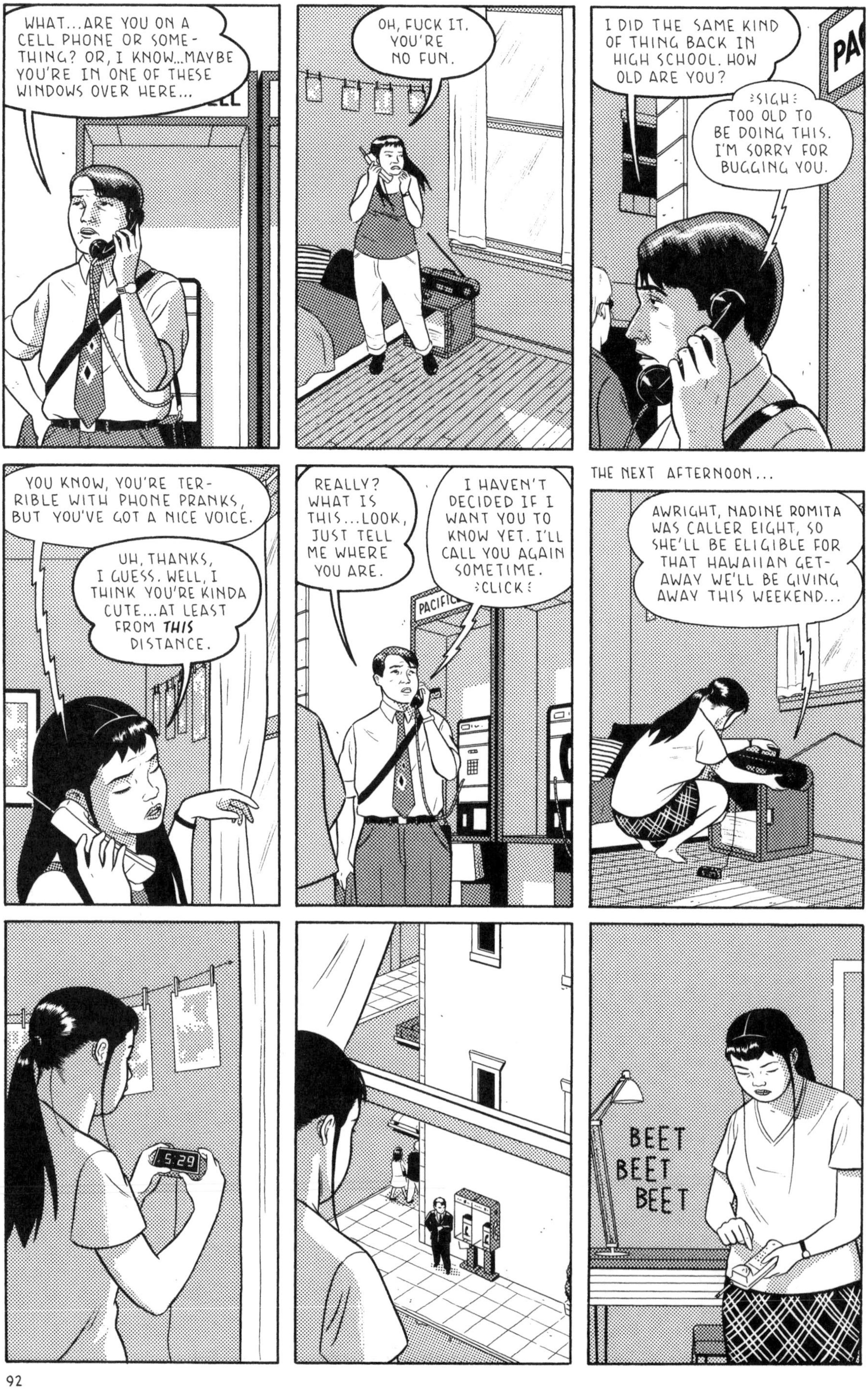
WHAT...ARE YOU ON A CELL PHONE OR SOME-THING? OR, I KNOW...MAYBE YOU'RE IN ONE OF THESE WINDOWS OVER HERE...
OH, FUCK IT. YOU'RE NO FUN.
I DID THE SAME KIND OF THING BACK IN HIGH SCHOOL. HOW OLD ARE YOU?
SIGH TOO OLD TO BE DOING THIS. I'M SORRY FOR BUGGING YOU.
PAC
YOU KNOW, YOU'RE TER-RIBLE WITH PHONE PRANKS, BUT YOU'VE GOT A NICE VOICE.
UH, THANKS, I GUESS. WELL, I THINK YOU'RE KINDA CUTE...AT LEAST FROM **THIS** DISTANCE.
REALLY? WHAT IS THIS...LOOK, JUST TELL ME WHERE YOU ARE.
I HAVEN'T DECIDED IF I WANT YOU TO KNOW YET. I'LL CALL YOU AGAIN SOMETIME. CLICK
PACIFIC
THE NEXT AFTERNOON...
AWRIGHT, NADINE ROMITA WAS CALLER EIGHT, SO SHE'LL BE ELIGIBLE FOR THAT HAWAIIAN GET-AWAY WE'LL BE GIVING AWAY THIS WEEKEND...
5:29
BEET BEET BEET

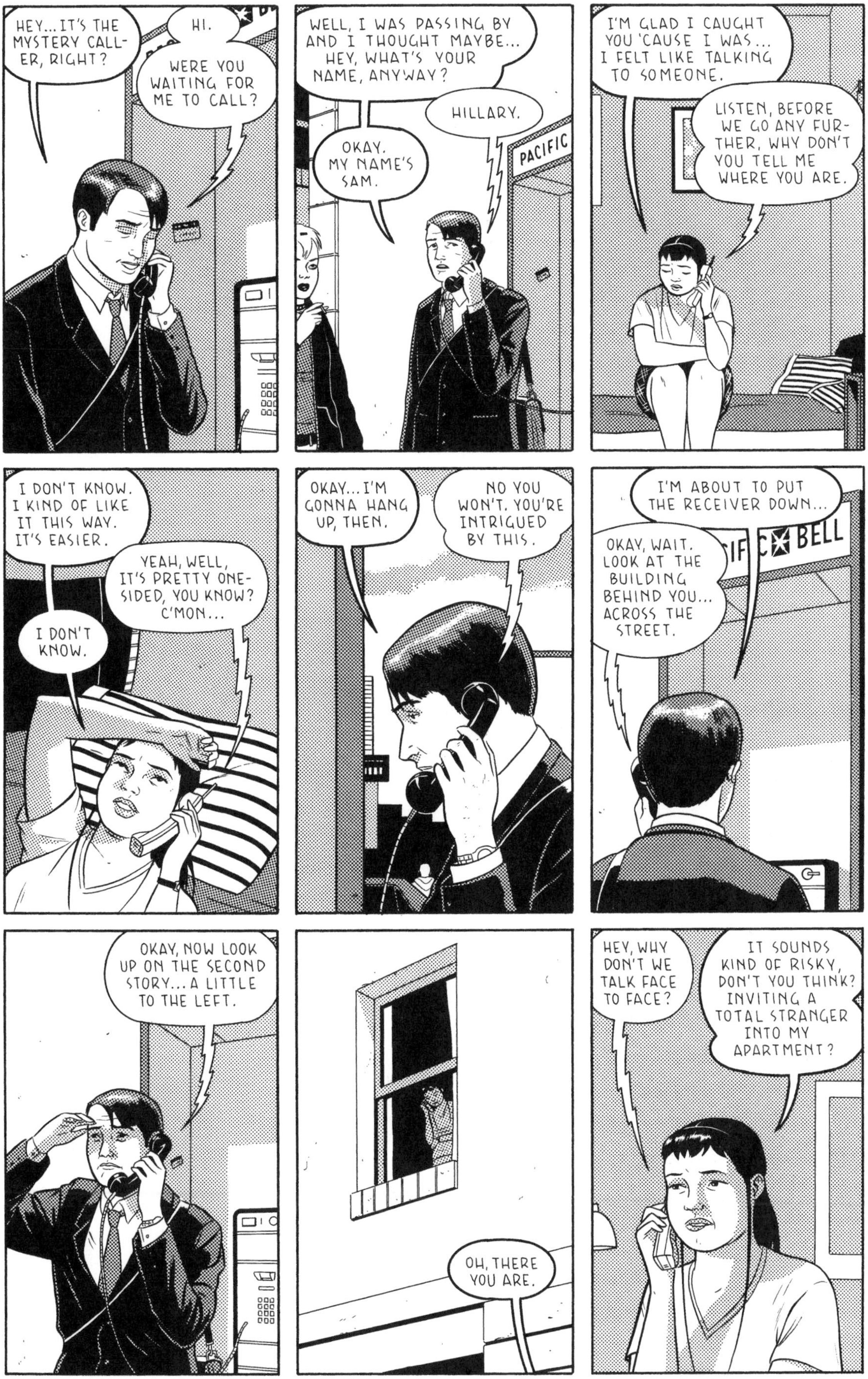
HEY...IT'S THE MYSTERY CALLER, RIGHT?
HI.
WERE YOU WAITING FOR ME TO CALL?
WELL, I WAS PASSING BY AND I THOUGHT MAYBE... HEY, WHAT'S YOUR NAME, ANYWAY?
HILLARY.
OKAY. MY NAME'S SAM.
PACIFIC
I'M GLAD I CAUGHT YOU 'CAUSE I WAS... I FELT LIKE TALKING TO SOMEONE.
LISTEN, BEFORE WE GO ANY FURTHER, WHY DON'T YOU TELL ME WHERE YOU ARE.
I DON'T KNOW. I KIND OF LIKE IT THIS WAY. IT'S EASIER.
YEAH, WELL, IT'S PRETTY ONE-SIDED, YOU KNOW? C'MON...
I DON'T KNOW.
OKAY...I'M GONNA HANG UP, THEN.
NO YOU WON'T. YOU'RE INTRIGUED BY THIS.
I'M ABOUT TO PUT THE RECEIVER DOWN...
OKAY, WAIT. LOOK AT THE BUILDING BEHIND YOU... ACROSS THE STREET.
BELL
OKAY, NOW LOOK UP ON THE SECOND STORY... A LITTLE TO THE LEFT.
OH, THERE YOU ARE.
HEY, WHY DON'T WE TALK FACE TO FACE?
IT SOUNDS KIND OF RISKY, DON'T YOU THINK? INVITING A TOTAL STRANGER INTO MY APARTMENT?

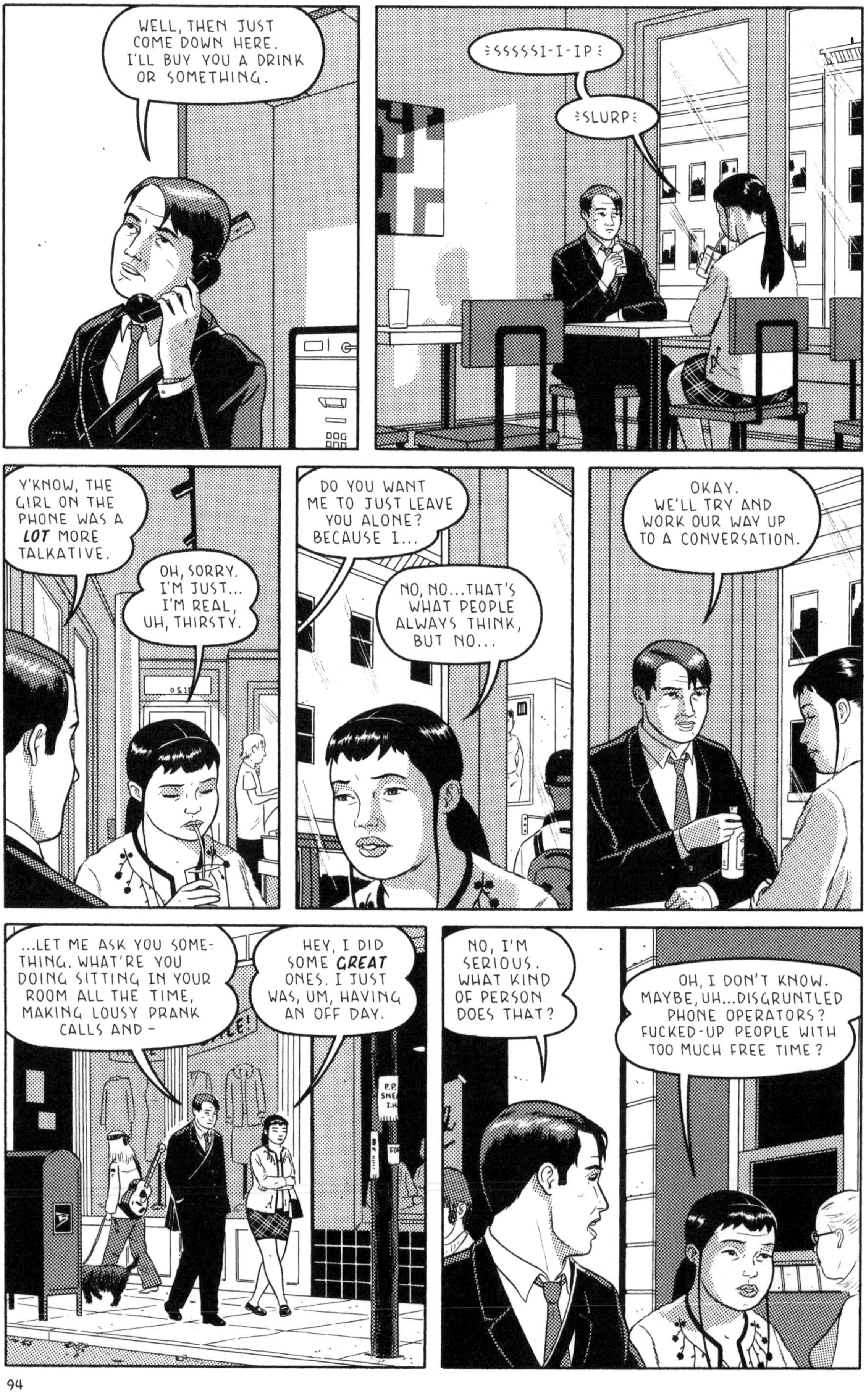
WELL, THEN JUST COME DOWN HERE. I'LL BUY YOU A DRINK OR SOMETHING.
SSSSSI-I-IP
SLURP
Y'KNOW, THE GIRL ON THE PHONE WAS A LOT MORE TALKATIVE.
OH, SORRY. I'M JUST... I'M REAL, UH, THIRSTY.
DO YOU WANT ME TO JUST LEAVE YOU ALONE? BECAUSE I...
NO, NO... THAT'S WHAT PEOPLE ALWAYS THINK, BUT NO...
OKAY. WE'LL TRY AND WORK OUR WAY UP TO A CONVERSATION.
...LET ME ASK YOU SOMETHING. WHAT'RE YOU DOING SITTING IN YOUR ROOM ALL THE TIME, MAKING LOUSY PRANK CALLS AND -
HEY, I DID SOME GREAT ONES. I JUST WAS, UM, HAVING AN OFF DAY.
NO, I'M SERIOUS. WHAT KIND OF PERSON DOES THAT?
OH, I DON'T KNOW. MAYBE, UH... DISGRUNTLED PHONE OPERATORS? FUCKED-UP PEOPLE WITH TOO MUCH FREE TIME?

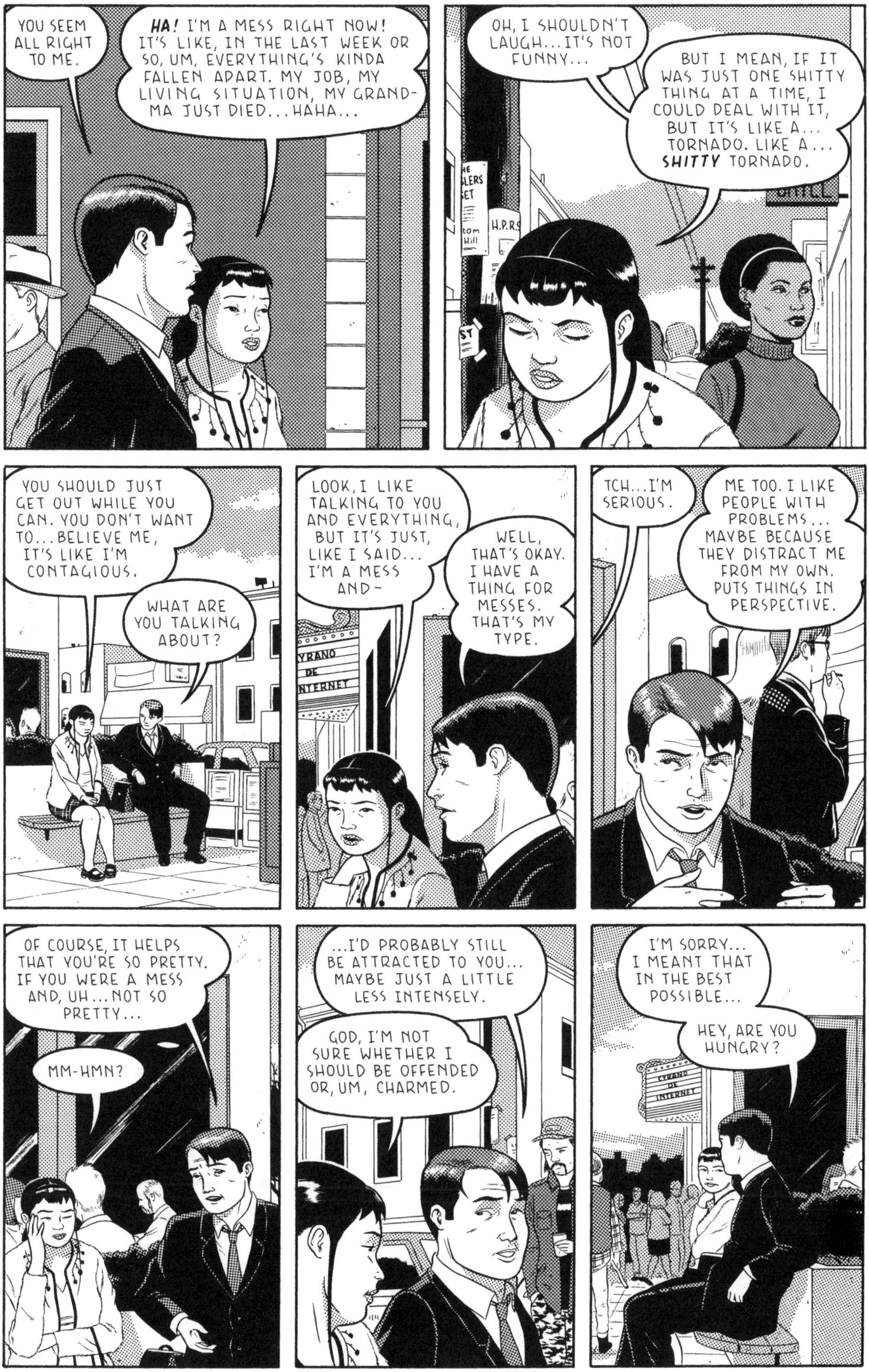

YOU SEEM ALL RIGHT TO ME.
HA! I'M A MESS RIGHT NOW! IT'S LIKE, IN THE LAST WEEK OR SO, UM, EVERYTHING'S KINDA FALLEN APART. MY JOB, MY LIVING SITUATION, MY GRAND-MA JUST DIED... HAHA...
OH, I SHOULDN'T LAUGH... IT'S NOT FUNNY...
BUT I MEAN, IF IT WAS JUST ONE SHITTY THING AT A TIME, I COULD DEAL WITH IT, BUT IT'S LIKE A... TORNADO. LIKE A... SHITTY TORNADO.
YOU SHOULD JUST GET OUT WHILE YOU CAN. YOU DON'T WANT TO... BELIEVE ME, IT'S LIKE I'M CONTAGIOUS.
WHAT ARE YOU TALKING ABOUT?
LOOK, I LIKE TALKING TO YOU AND EVERYTHING, BUT IT'S JUST, LIKE I SAID... I'M A MESS AND-
WELL, THAT'S OKAY. I HAVE A THING FOR MESSES. THAT'S MY TYPE.
TCH... I'M SERIOUS.
ME TOO. I LIKE PEOPLE WITH PROBLEMS... MAYBE BECAUSE THEY DISTRACT ME FROM MY OWN. PUTS THINGS IN PERSPECTIVE.
OF COURSE, IT HELPS THAT YOU'RE SO PRETTY. IF YOU WERE A MESS AND, UH... NOT SO PRETTY...
MM-HMN?
...I'D PROBABLY STILL BE ATTRACTED TO YOU... MAYBE JUST A LITTLE LESS INTENSELY.
GOD, I'M NOT SURE WHETHER I SHOULD BE OFFENDED OR, UM, CHARMED.
I'M SORRY... I MEANT THAT IN THE BEST POSSIBLE...
HEY, ARE YOU HUNGRY?

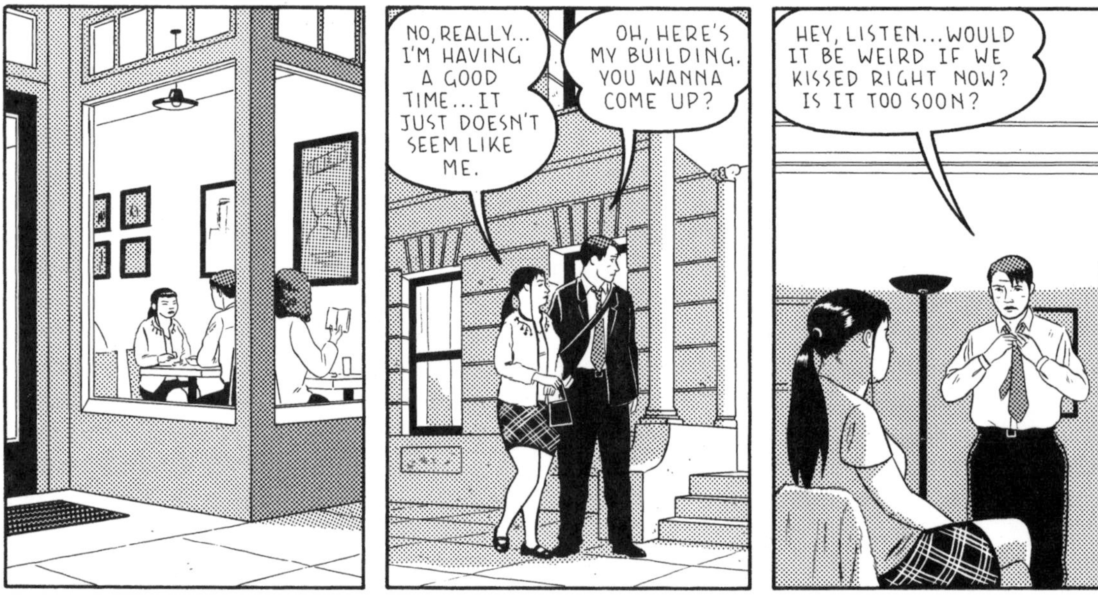
NO, REALLY... I'M HAVING A GOOD TIME... IT JUST DOESN'T SEEM LIKE ME.
OH, HERE'S MY BUILDING. YOU WANNA COME UP?
HEY, LISTEN... WOULD IT BE WEIRD IF WE KISSED RIGHT NOW? IS IT TOO SOON?

HE WAS PROBABLY RIGHT... IT **WAS** TOO SOON, BUT I WASN'T GOING TO SAY SO. MAYBE IT WAS ONE OF THOSE MYTHICAL LOVE-AT-FIRST-SIGHT THINGS (DOUBTFUL), OR MAYBE IT WAS JUST DEPRESSION-INDUCED SLUTTINESS (PROBABLY), BUT RIGHT THEN, THERE WAS NOTHING I WANTED MORE THAN THAT KIND OF PASSION AND ABANDON.

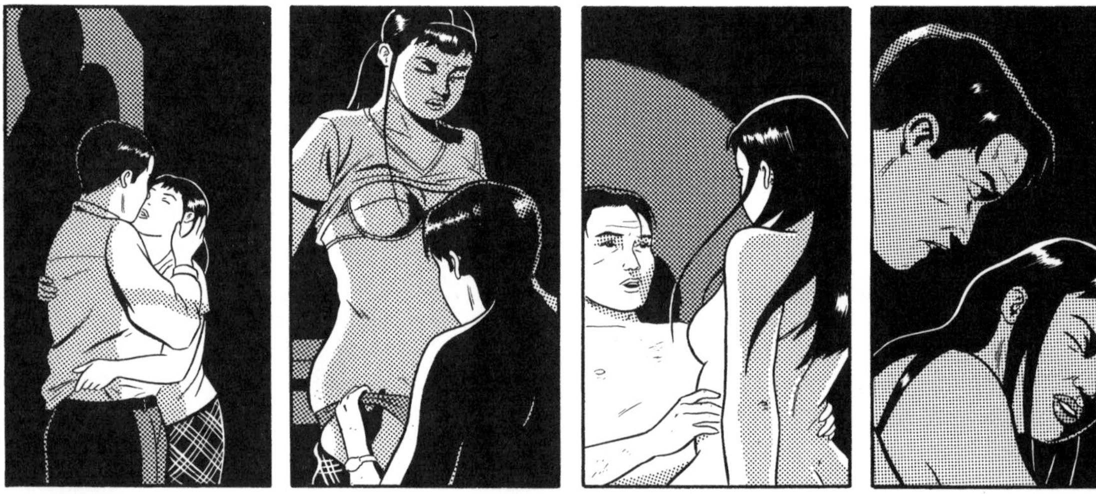

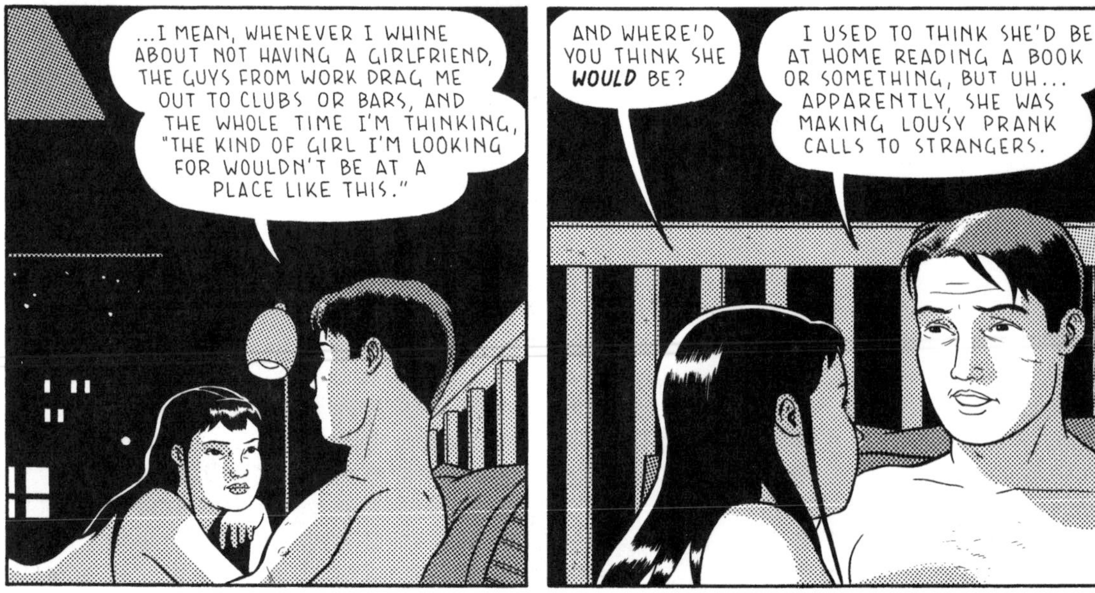
...I MEAN, WHENEVER I WHINE ABOUT NOT HAVING A GIRLFRIEND, THE GUYS FROM WORK DRAG ME OUT TO CLUBS OR BARS, AND THE WHOLE TIME I'M THINKING, "THE KIND OF GIRL I'M LOOKING FOR WOULDN'T BE AT A PLACE LIKE THIS."
AND WHERE'D YOU THINK SHE **WOULD** BE?
I USED TO THINK SHE'D BE AT HOME READING A BOOK OR SOMETHING, BUT UH... APPARENTLY, SHE WAS MAKING LOUSY PRANK CALLS TO STRANGERS.

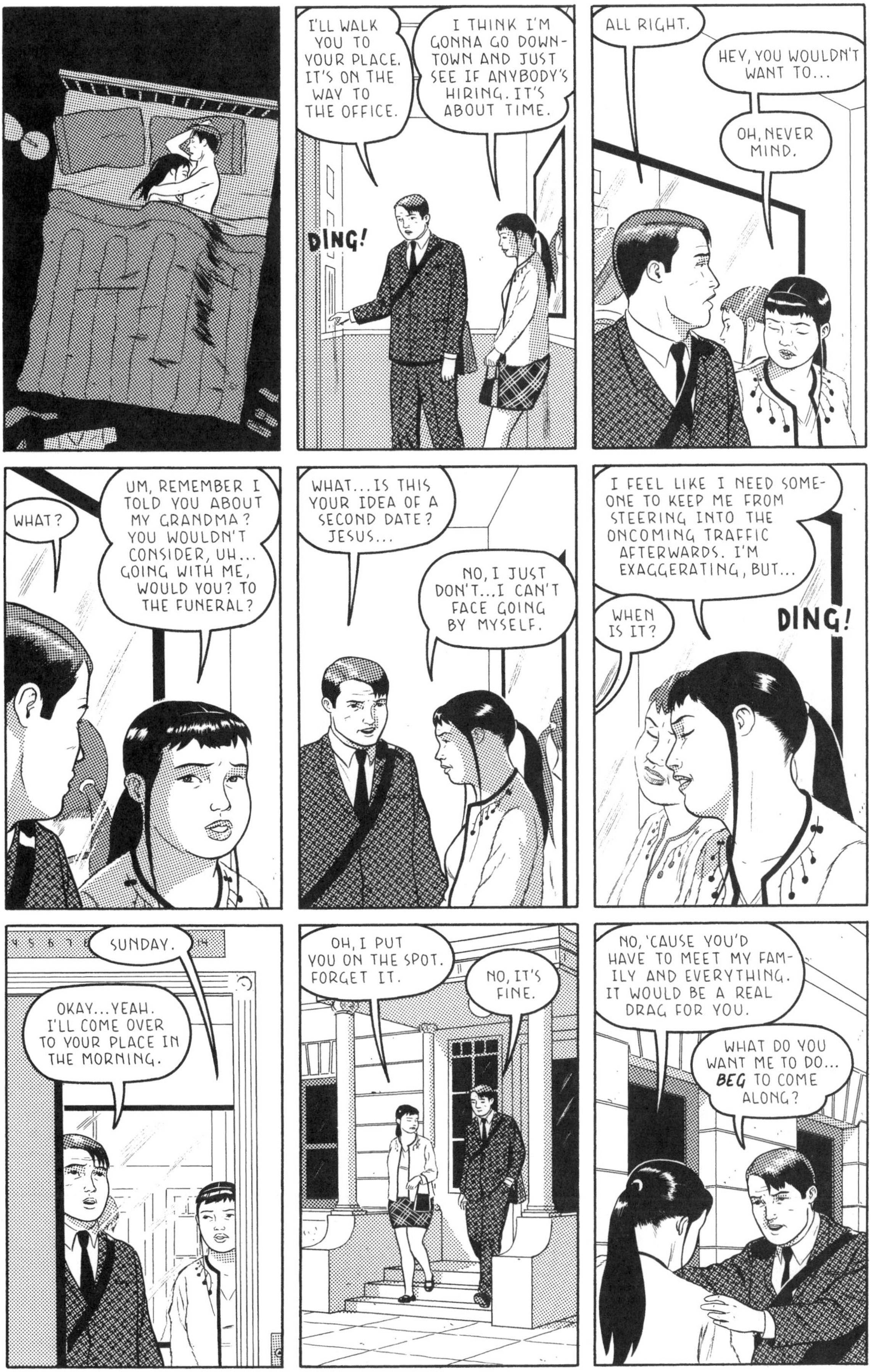
I'LL WALK YOU TO YOUR PLACE. IT'S ON THE WAY TO THE OFFICE.
I THINK I'M GONNA GO DOWN-TOWN AND JUST SEE IF ANYBODY'S HIRING. IT'S ABOUT TIME.
DING!
ALL RIGHT.
HEY, YOU WOULDN'T WANT TO...
OH, NEVER MIND.
WHAT?
UM, REMEMBER I TOLD YOU ABOUT MY GRANDMA? YOU WOULDN'T CONSIDER, UH... GOING WITH ME, WOULD YOU? TO THE FUNERAL?
WHAT... IS THIS YOUR IDEA OF A SECOND DATE? JESUS...
NO, I JUST DON'T... I CAN'T FACE GOING BY MYSELF.
I FEEL LIKE I NEED SOME-ONE TO KEEP ME FROM STEERING INTO THE ONCOMING TRAFFIC AFTERWARDS. I'M EXAGGERATING, BUT...
WHEN IS IT?
DING!
SUNDAY.
OKAY... YEAH. I'LL COME OVER TO YOUR PLACE IN THE MORNING.
OH, I PUT YOU ON THE SPOT. FORGET IT.
NO, IT'S FINE.
NO, 'CAUSE YOU'D HAVE TO MEET MY FAM-ILY AND EVERYTHING. IT WOULD BE A REAL DRAG FOR YOU.
WHAT DO YOU WANT ME TO DO... BEG TO COME ALONG?

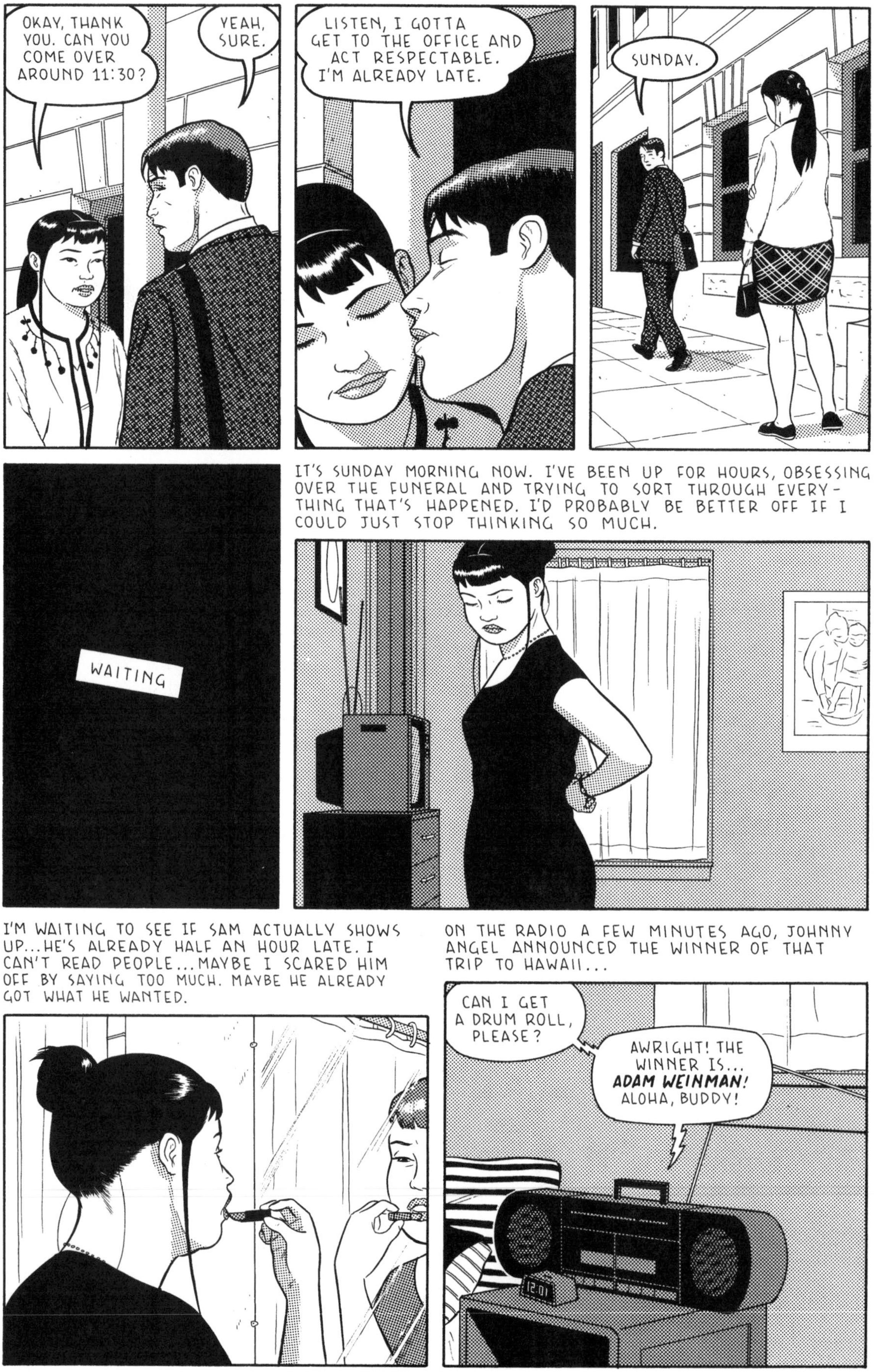
OKAY, THANK YOU. CAN YOU COME OVER AROUND 11:30?
YEAH, SURE.
LISTEN, I GOTTA GET TO THE OFFICE AND ACT RESPECTABLE. I'M ALREADY LATE.
SUNDAY.
WAITING
IT'S SUNDAY MORNING NOW. I'VE BEEN UP FOR HOURS, OBSESSING OVER THE FUNERAL AND TRYING TO SORT THROUGH EVERY-THING THAT'S HAPPENED. I'D PROBABLY BE BETTER OFF IF I COULD JUST STOP THINKING SO MUCH.
I'M WAITING TO SEE IF SAM ACTUALLY SHOWS UP...HE'S ALREADY HALF AN HOUR LATE. I CAN'T READ PEOPLE...MAYBE I SCARED HIM OFF BY SAYING TOO MUCH. MAYBE HE ALREADY GOT WHAT HE WANTED.
ON THE RADIO A FEW MINUTES AGO, JOHNNY ANGEL ANNOUNCED THE WINNER OF THAT TRIP TO HAWAII...
CAN I GET A DRUM ROLL, PLEASE?
AWRIGHT! THE WINNER IS... **ADAM WEINMAN!** ALOHA, BUDDY!
12:01

I KNEW IT WOULDN'T BE ME, BUT I STILL HAD TO LISTEN. AND FOR THE DURATION OF THAT ARTIFICIAL DRUM ROLL, I THOUGHT ABOUT WHEN I WAS A KID AND WE WENT TO MAUI ON A FAMILY VACATION.

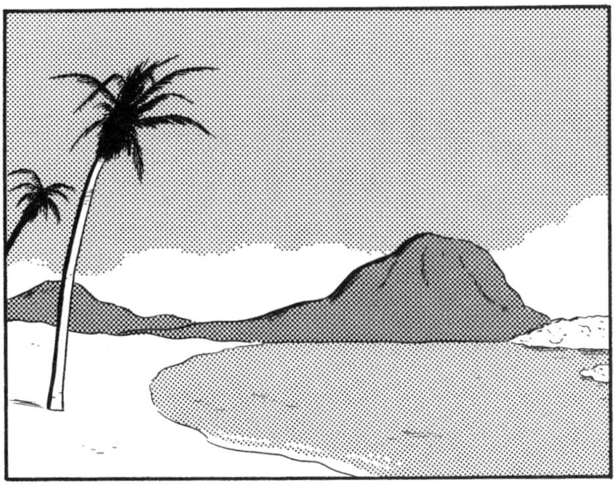

I'D JUST TURNED THIRTEEN, AND I WAS EMBARRASSED ABOUT EVERYTHING: WEARING A SWIMSUIT, BEING SEEN WITH MY PARENTS, ETC. JUST TO BE CONTRARY, I REFUSED TO PUT ON SUNSCREEN, AND BY THE SECOND DAY, MY SKIN HAD BURNED TO THE COLOR OF BRICK.

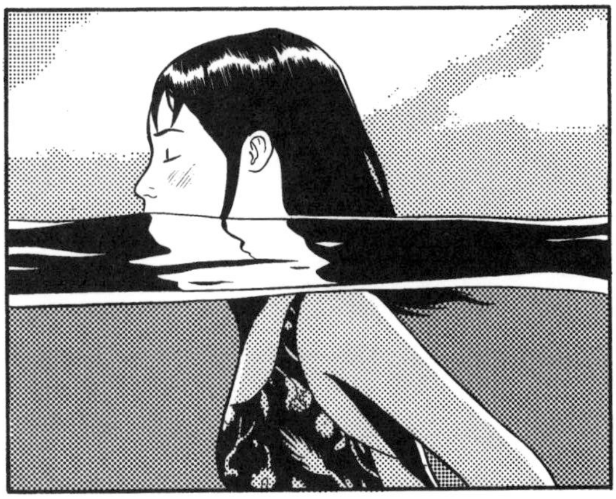

THE SUNBURN WAS SO BAD I COULDN'T EVEN LEAVE THE HOTEL ROOM (A FACT THAT SEEMED TO UPSET EVERYONE FAR MORE THAN ME). MY DAD SEEMED DISAPPOINTED, BUT MY MOM WAS LIVID.

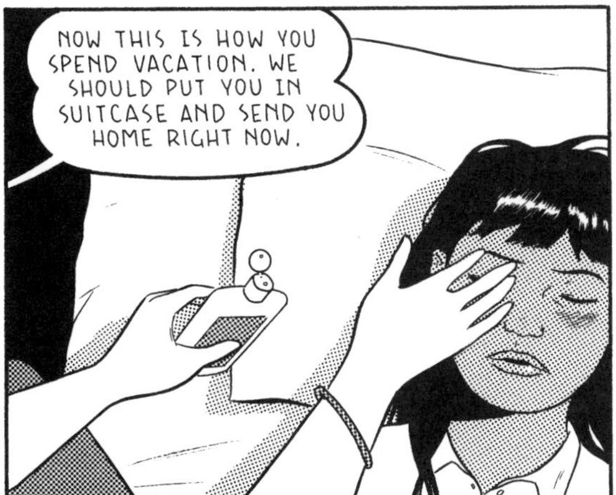
NOW THIS IS HOW YOU SPEND VACATION. WE SHOULD PUT YOU IN SUITCASE AND SEND YOU HOME RIGHT NOW.

THEY ALL LEFT TO GO BACK TO THE BEACH AND TO SEE SOME VOLCANO OR SOMETHING. I FELT FEVERISH AND PRICKLY ALL OVER, SO I CLOSED THE CURTAINS, STRIPPED DOWN TO MY UNDERWEAR, AND CRANKED UP THE AIR CONDITIONING.

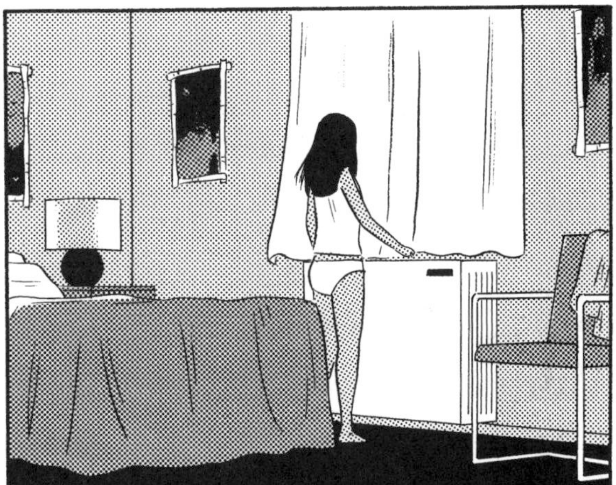

IMPULSIVELY, I TOOK OUT OUR BIGGEST SUITCASE AND OPENED IT ON THE FLOOR. I SAT ON THE EDGE OF THE BED, STARING AT THE SUITCASE, AND THEN CURLED UP INSIDE OF IT. I WAS SURPRISED HOW EASILY I FIT.

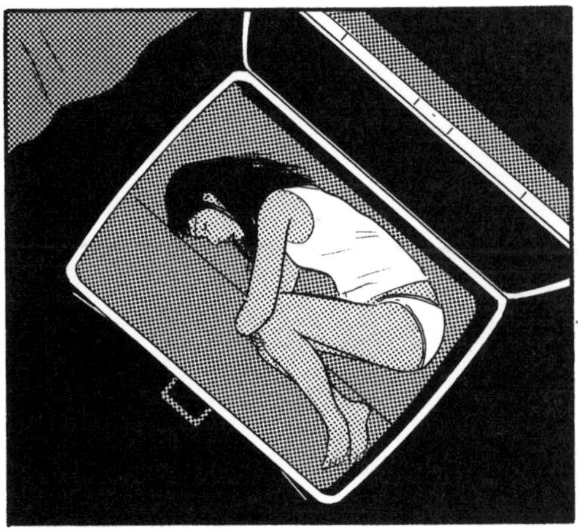

I REMEMBER LYING THERE AND EVENTUALLY FALLING ASLEEP LIKE THAT IN THE COOL, DARK HOTEL ROOM WHILE THE SKIN ALL ACROSS MY BODY BLISTERED AND PEELED. I CAN STILL FEEL IT NOW.

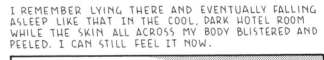

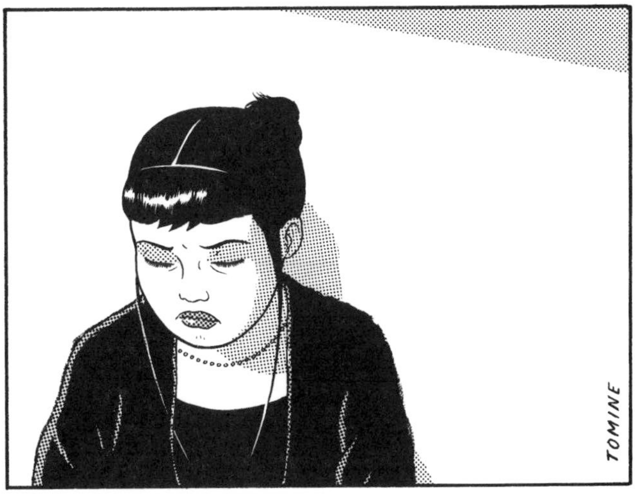
TOMINE

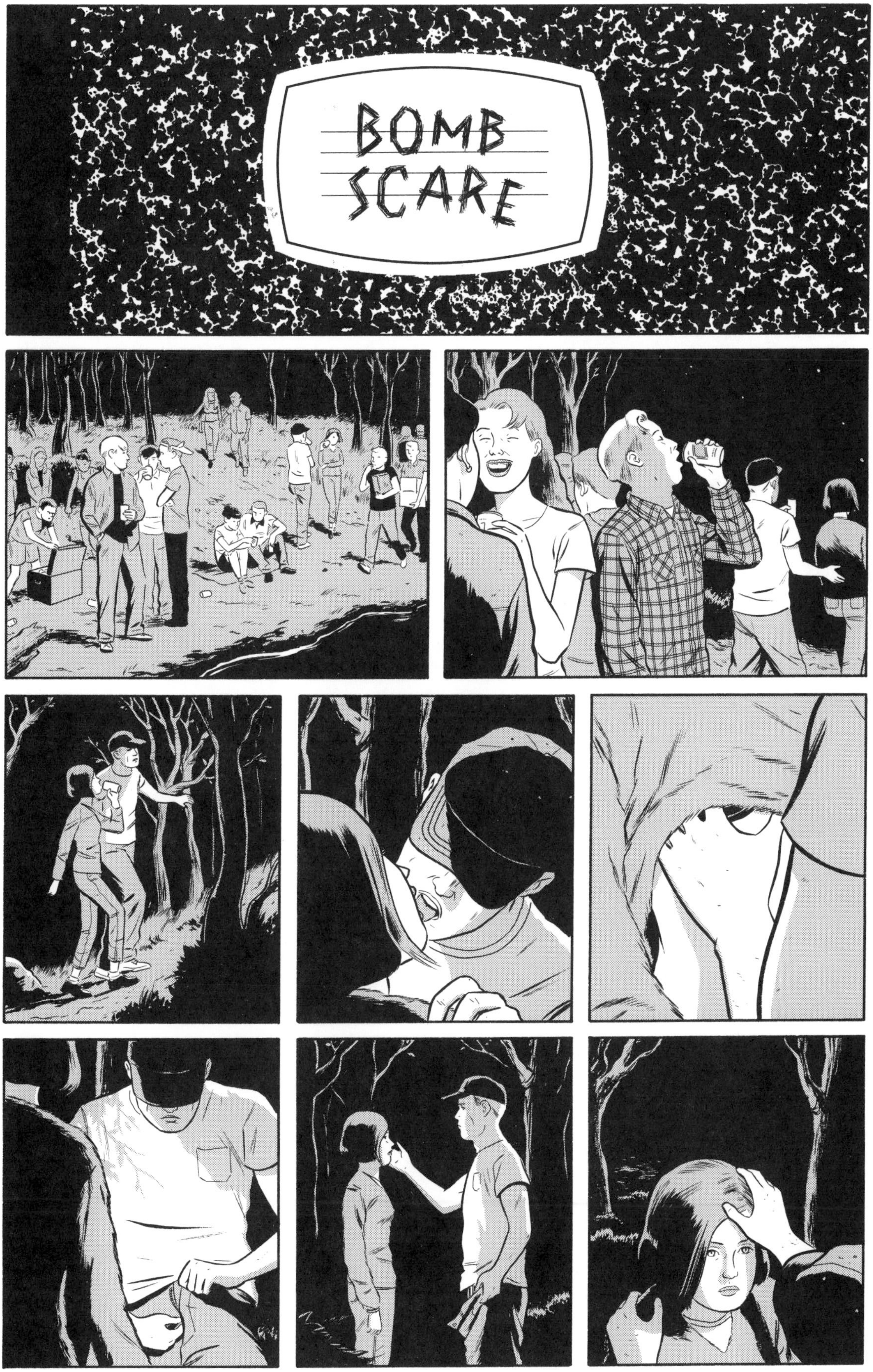
BOMB SCARE

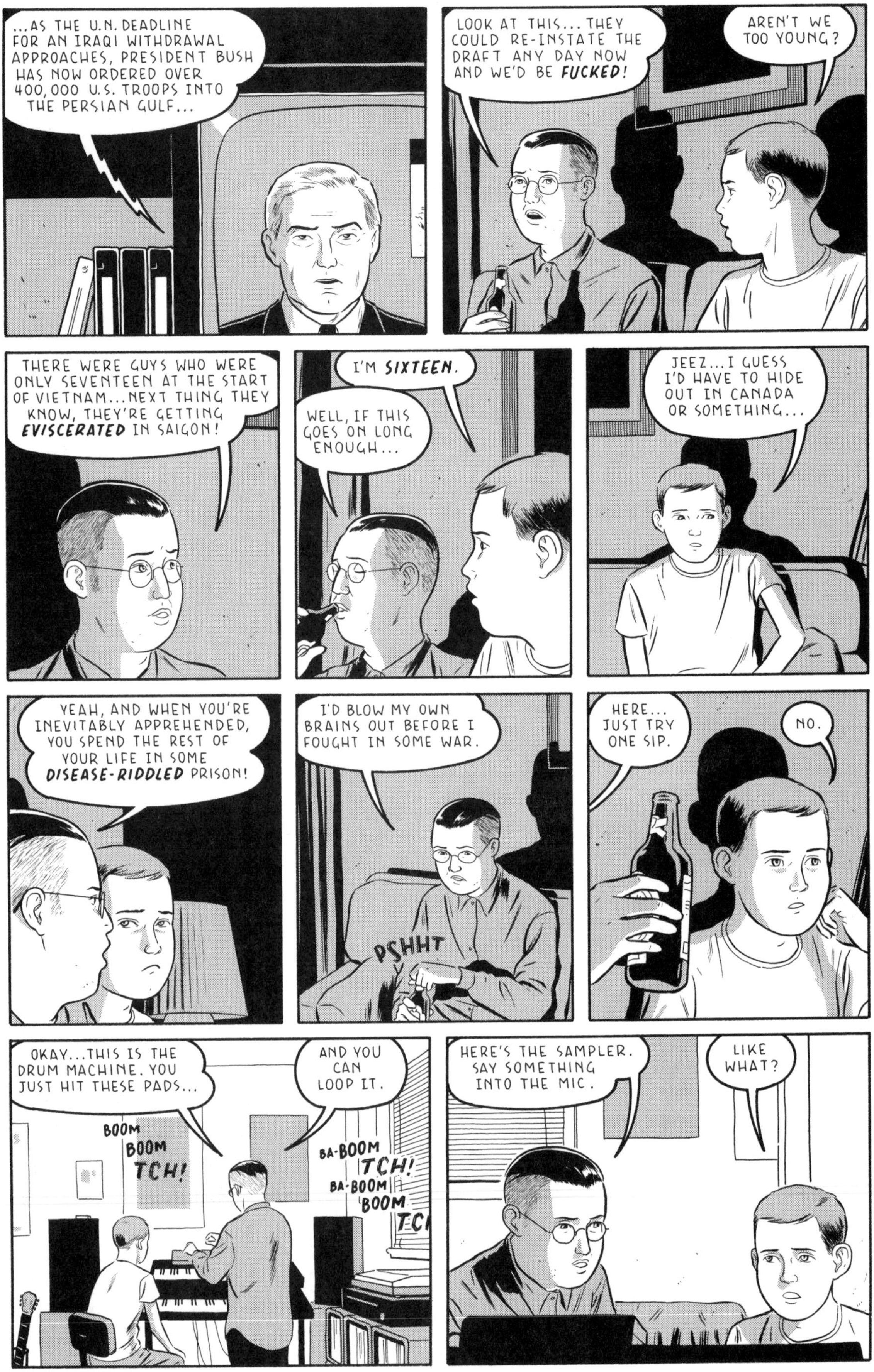
...AS THE U.N. DEADLINE FOR AN IRAQI WITHDRAWAL APPROACHES, PRESIDENT BUSH HAS NOW ORDERED OVER 400,000 U.S. TROOPS INTO THE PERSIAN GULF...
LOOK AT THIS... THEY COULD RE-INSTATE THE DRAFT ANY DAY NOW AND WE'D BE **FUCKED!**
AREN'T WE TOO YOUNG?
THERE WERE GUYS WHO WERE ONLY SEVENTEEN AT THE START OF VIETNAM... NEXT THING THEY KNOW, THEY'RE GETTING **EVISCERATED** IN SAIGON!
I'M **SIXTEEN.**
WELL, IF THIS GOES ON LONG ENOUGH...
JEEZ... I GUESS I'D HAVE TO HIDE OUT IN CANADA OR SOMETHING...
YEAH, AND WHEN YOU'RE INEVITABLY APPREHENDED, YOU SPEND THE REST OF YOUR LIFE IN SOME **DISEASE-RIDDLED** PRISON!
I'D BLOW MY OWN BRAINS OUT BEFORE I FOUGHT IN SOME WAR.
PSHHT
HERE... JUST TRY ONE SIP.
NO.
OKAY... THIS IS THE DRUM MACHINE. YOU JUST HIT THESE PADS...
AND YOU CAN LOOP IT.
BOOM BOOM TCH!
BA-BOOM TCH! BA-BOOM BOOM
HERE'S THE SAMPLER. SAY SOMETHING INTO THE MIC.
LIKE WHAT?

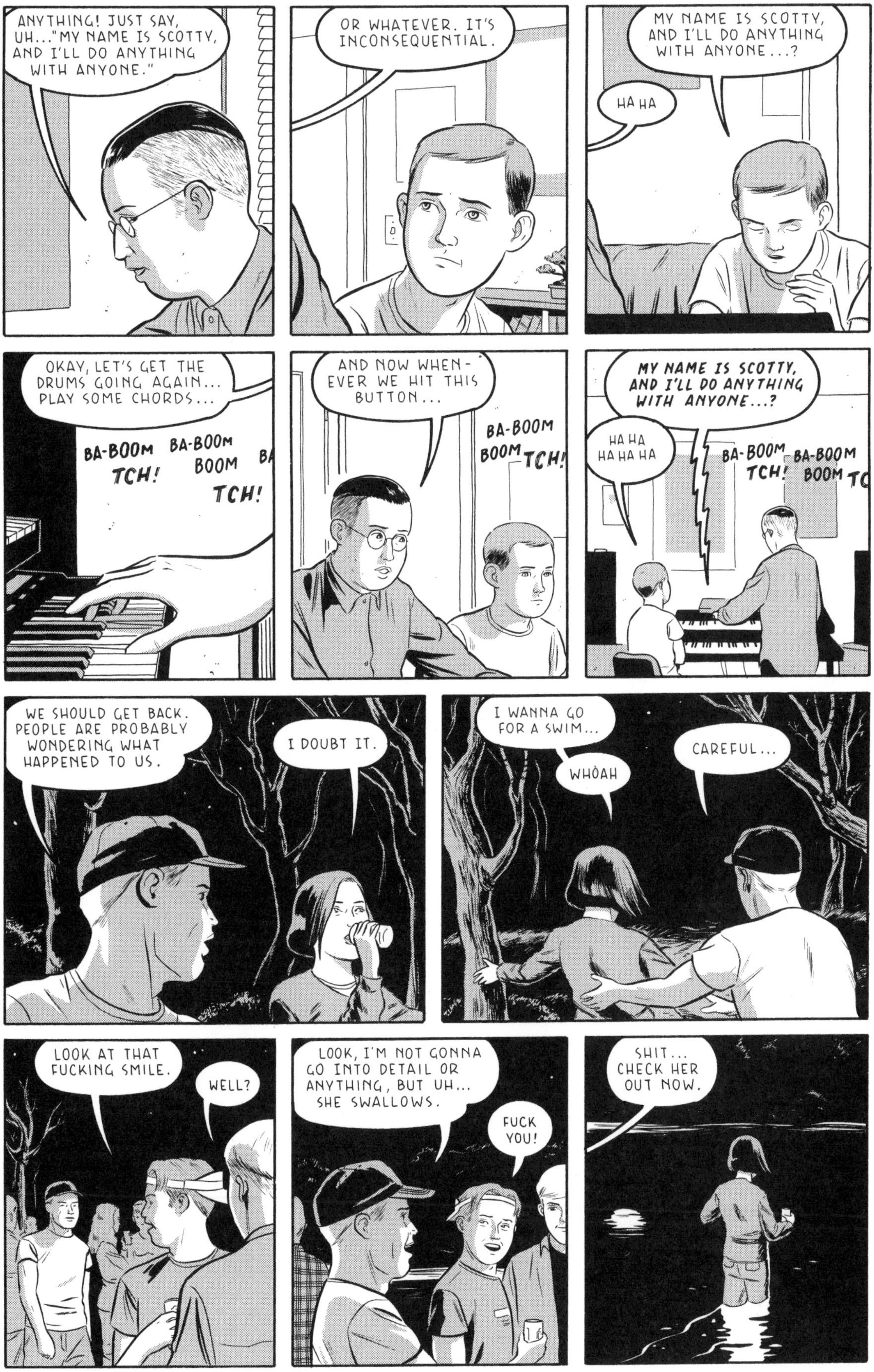
ANYTHING! JUST SAY, UH..."MY NAME IS SCOTTY, AND I'LL DO ANYTHING WITH ANYONE."
OR WHATEVER. IT'S INCONSEQUENTIAL.
MY NAME IS SCOTTY, AND I'LL DO ANYTHING WITH ANYONE...?
HA HA
OKAY, LET'S GET THE DRUMS GOING AGAIN... PLAY SOME CHORDS...
BA-BOOM BA-BOOM TCH! BOOM TCH!
AND NOW WHEN-EVER WE HIT THIS BUTTON...
BA-BOOM BOOM TCH!
MY NAME IS SCOTTY, AND I'LL DO ANYTHING WITH ANYONE...?
HA HA HA HA HA
BA-BOOM TCH! BA-BOOM BOOM
WE SHOULD GET BACK. PEOPLE ARE PROBABLY WONDERING WHAT HAPPENED TO US.
I DOUBT IT.
I WANNA GO FOR A SWIM...
WHOAH
CAREFUL...
LOOK AT THAT FUCKING SMILE.
WELL?
LOOK, I'M NOT GONNA GO INTO DETAIL OR ANYTHING, BUT UH... SHE SWALLOWS.
FUCK YOU!
SHIT... CHECK HER OUT NOW.

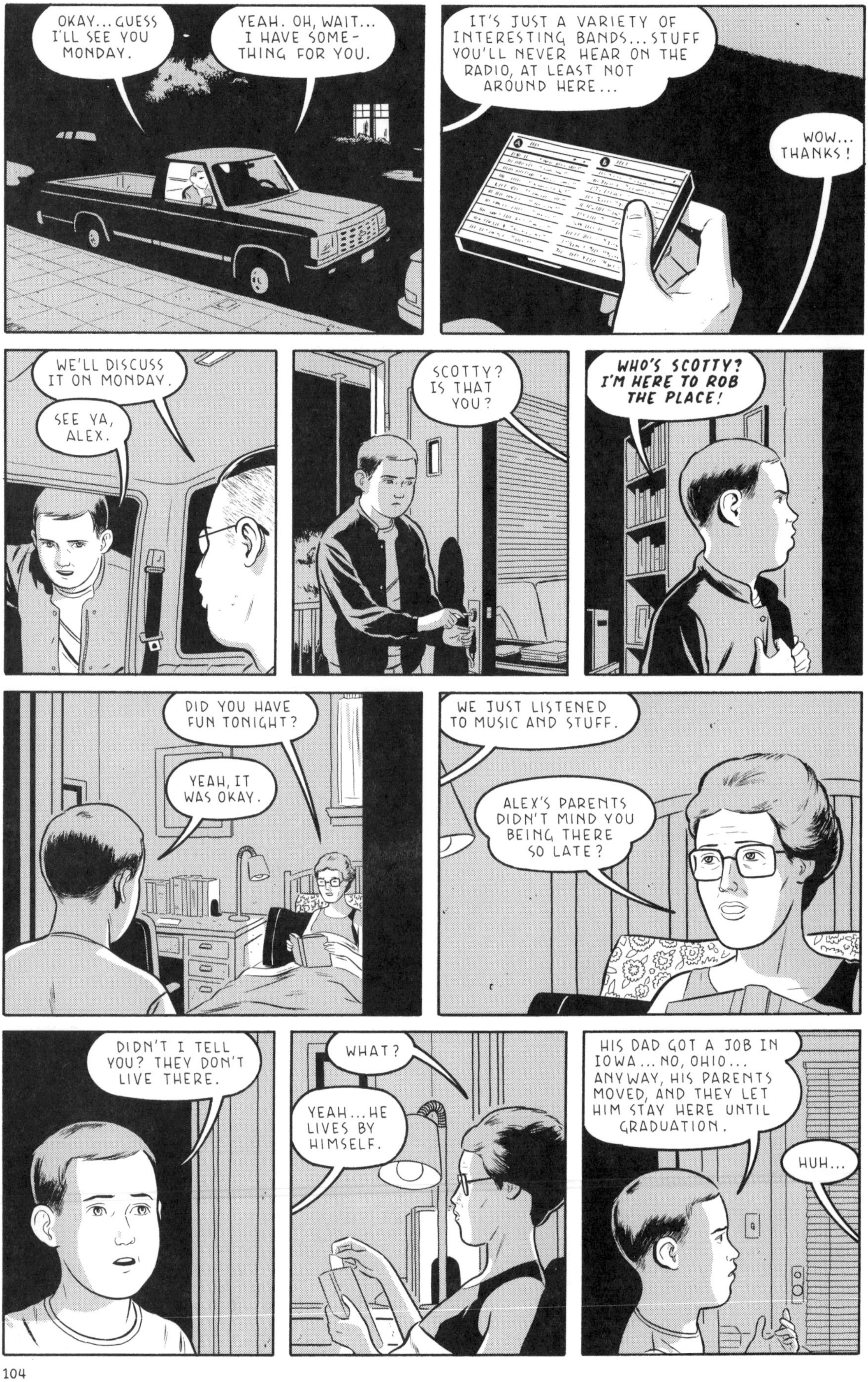

OKAY... GUESS I'LL SEE YOU MONDAY.
YEAH. OH, WAIT... I HAVE SOME-THING FOR YOU.
IT'S JUST A VARIETY OF INTERESTING BANDS... STUFF YOU'LL NEVER HEAR ON THE RADIO, AT LEAST NOT AROUND HERE...
WOW... THANKS!
WE'LL DISCUSS IT ON MONDAY.
SEE YA, ALEX.
SCOTTY? IS THAT YOU?
WHO'S SCOTTY? I'M HERE TO ROB THE PLACE!
DID YOU HAVE FUN TONIGHT?
YEAH, IT WAS OKAY.
WE JUST LISTENED TO MUSIC AND STUFF.
ALEX'S PARENTS DIDN'T MIND YOU BEING THERE SO LATE?
DIDN'T I TELL YOU? THEY DON'T LIVE THERE.
WHAT?
YEAH... HE LIVES BY HIMSELF.
HIS DAD GOT A JOB IN IOWA... NO, OHIO... ANYWAY, HIS PARENTS MOVED, AND THEY LET HIM STAY HERE UNTIL GRADUATION.
HUH...

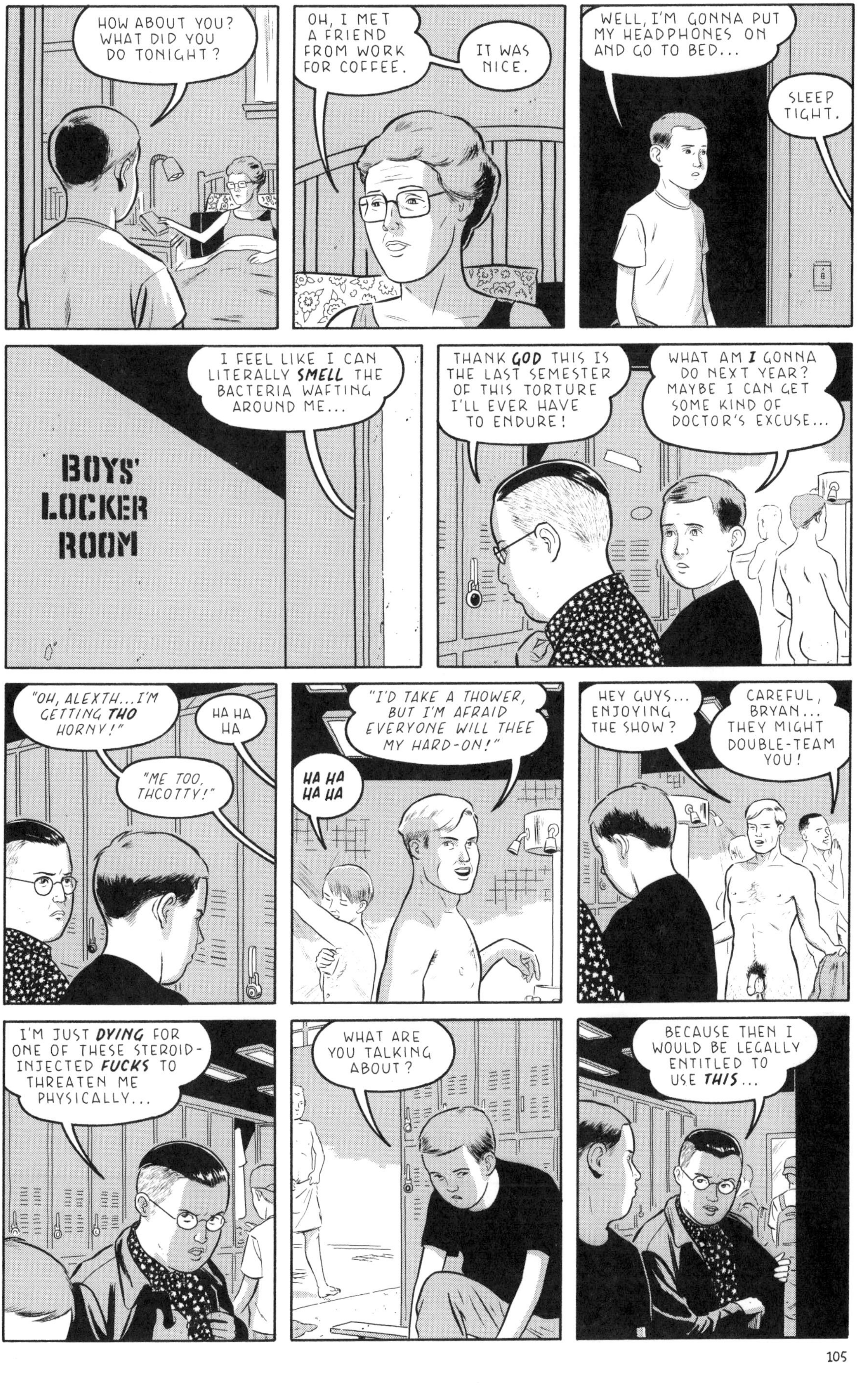
HOW ABOUT YOU? WHAT DID YOU DO TONIGHT?
OH, I MET A FRIEND FROM WORK FOR COFFEE.
IT WAS NICE.
WELL, I'M GONNA PUT MY HEADPHONES ON AND GO TO BED...
SLEEP TIGHT.
BOYS' LOCKER ROOM
I FEEL LIKE I CAN LITERALLY SMELL THE BACTERIA WAFTING AROUND ME...
THANK GOD THIS IS THE LAST SEMESTER OF THIS TORTURE I'LL EVER HAVE TO ENDURE!
WHAT AM I GONNA DO NEXT YEAR? MAYBE I CAN GET SOME KIND OF DOCTOR'S EXCUSE...
"OH, ALEXTH...I'M GETTING THO HORNY!"
HA HA HA
"ME TOO, THCOTTY!"
"I'D TAKE A THOWER, BUT I'M AFRAID EVERYONE WILL THEE MY HARD-ON!"
HA HA HA HA
HEY GUYS... ENJOYING THE SHOW?
CAREFUL, BRYAN... THEY MIGHT DOUBLE-TEAM YOU!
I'M JUST DYING FOR ONE OF THESE STEROID-INJECTED FUCKS TO THREATEN ME PHYSICALLY...
WHAT ARE YOU TALKING ABOUT?
BECAUSE THEN I WOULD BE LEGALLY ENTITLED TO USE THIS...

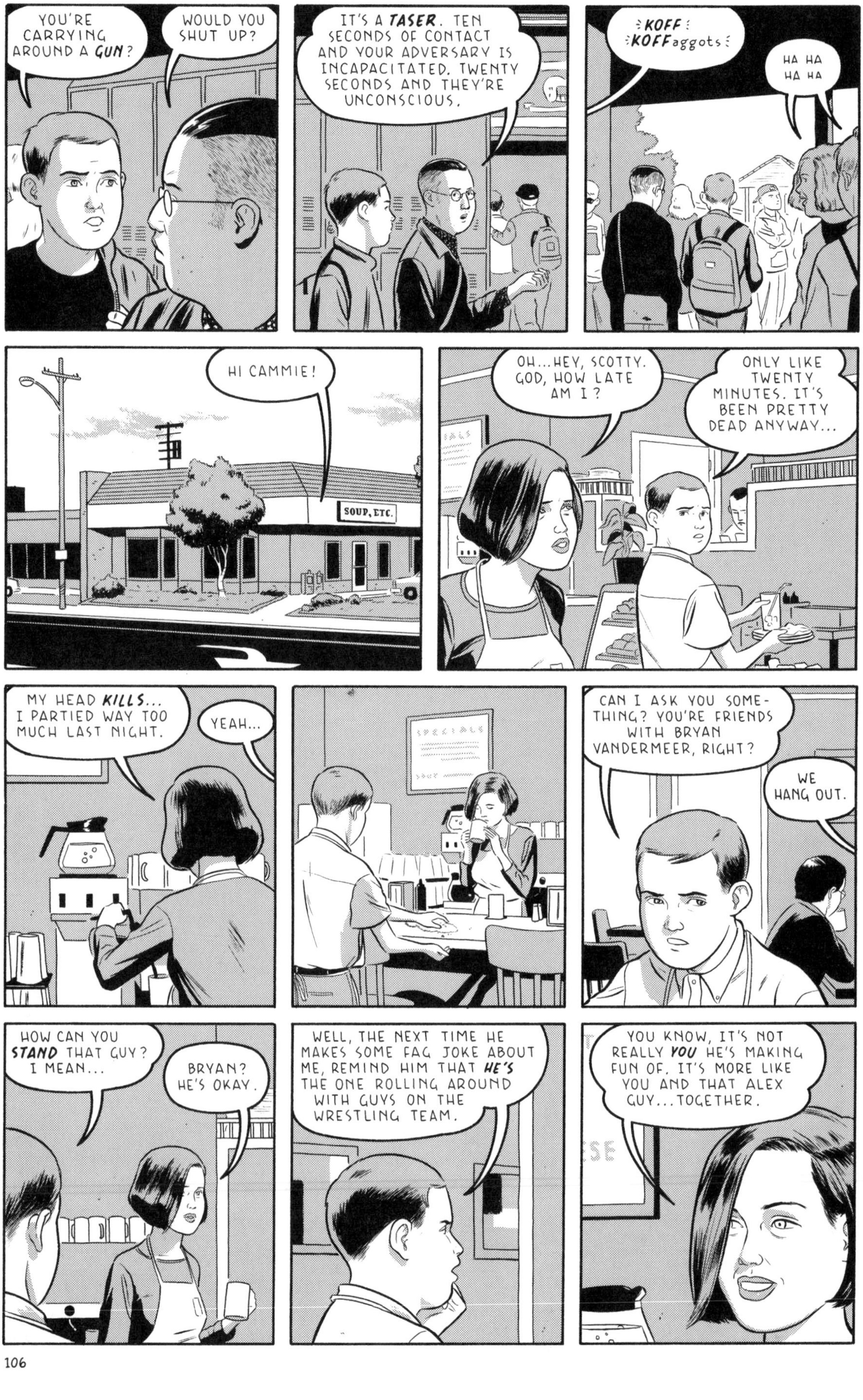
YOU'RE CARRYING AROUND A GUN?
WOULD YOU SHUT UP?
IT'S A TASER. TEN SECONDS OF CONTACT AND YOUR ADVERSARY IS INCAPACITATED. TWENTY SECONDS AND THEY'RE UNCONSCIOUS.
KOFF KOFFaggots
HA HA HA HA
HI CAMMIE!
SOUP, ETC.
OH... HEY, SCOTTY. GOD, HOW LATE AM I?
ONLY LIKE TWENTY MINUTES. IT'S BEEN PRETTY DEAD ANYWAY...
MY HEAD KILLS... I PARTIED WAY TOO MUCH LAST NIGHT.
YEAH...
CAN I ASK YOU SOMETHING? YOU'RE FRIENDS WITH BRYAN VANDERMEER, RIGHT?
WE HANG OUT.
HOW CAN YOU STAND THAT GUY? I MEAN...
BRYAN? HE'S OKAY.
WELL, THE NEXT TIME HE MAKES SOME FAG JOKE ABOUT ME, REMIND HIM THAT HE'S THE ONE ROLLING AROUND WITH GUYS ON THE WRESTLING TEAM.
YOU KNOW, IT'S NOT REALLY YOU HE'S MAKING FUN OF. IT'S MORE LIKE YOU AND THAT ALEX GUY... TOGETHER.

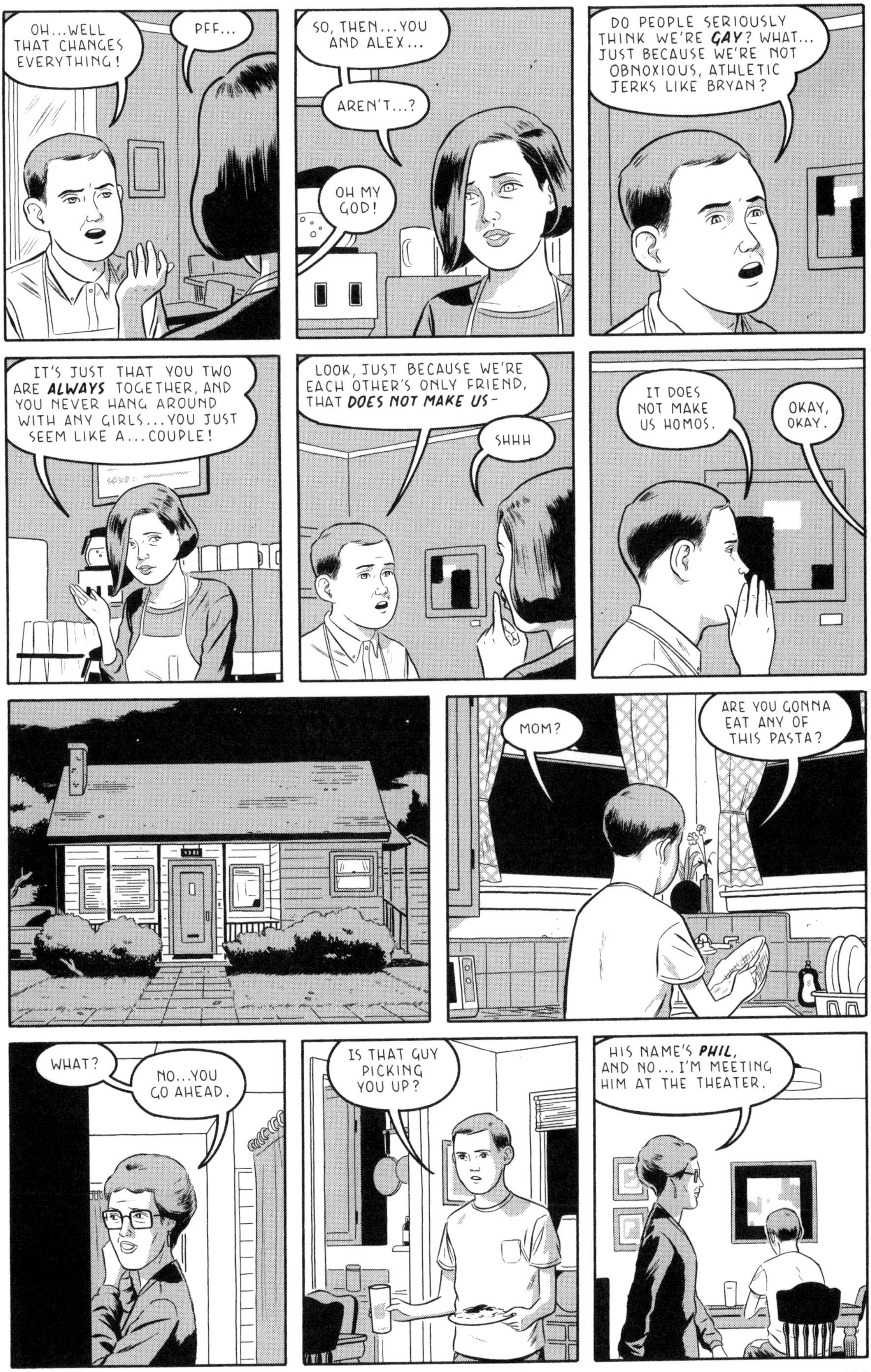
OH...WELL THAT CHANGES EVERYTHING!
PFF...
SO, THEN... YOU AND ALEX...
AREN'T...?
OH MY GOD!
DO PEOPLE SERIOUSLY THINK WE'RE GAY? WHAT... JUST BECAUSE WE'RE NOT OBNOXIOUS, ATHLETIC JERKS LIKE BRYAN?
IT'S JUST THAT YOU TWO ARE ALWAYS TOGETHER, AND YOU NEVER HANG AROUND WITH ANY GIRLS... YOU JUST SEEM LIKE A... COUPLE!
LOOK, JUST BECAUSE WE'RE EACH OTHER'S ONLY FRIEND, THAT DOES NOT MAKE US-
SHHH
IT DOES NOT MAKE US HOMOS.
OKAY, OKAY.
MOM?
ARE YOU GONNA EAT ANY OF THIS PASTA?
WHAT?
NO... YOU GO AHEAD.
IS THAT GUY PICKING YOU UP?
HIS NAME'S PHIL, AND NO... I'M MEETING HIM AT THE THEATER.

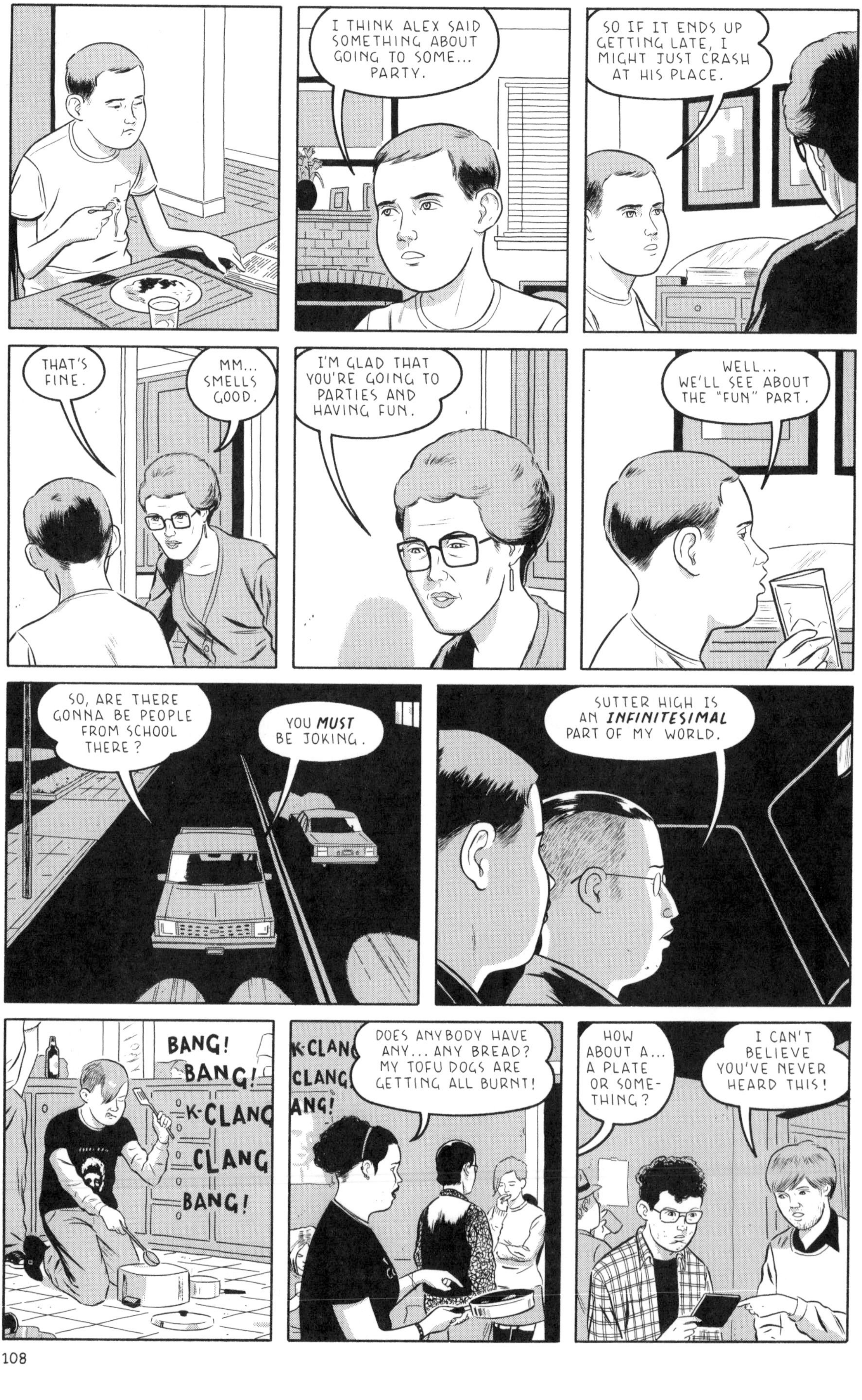

I THINK ALEX SAID SOMETHING ABOUT GOING TO SOME... PARTY.
SO IF IT ENDS UP GETTING LATE, I MIGHT JUST CRASH AT HIS PLACE.
THAT'S FINE.
MM... SMELLS GOOD.
I'M GLAD THAT YOU'RE GOING TO PARTIES AND HAVING FUN.
WELL... WE'LL SEE ABOUT THE "FUN" PART.
SO, ARE THERE GONNA BE PEOPLE FROM SCHOOL THERE?
YOU MUST BE JOKING.
SUTTER HIGH IS AN INFINITESIMAL PART OF MY WORLD.
BANG!
BANG!
K-CLANG
CLANG
BANG!
K-CLANG
CLANG
ANG!
DOES ANYBODY HAVE ANY... ANY BREAD? MY TOFU DOGS ARE GETTING ALL BURNT!
HOW ABOUT A... A PLATE OR SOME-THING?
I CAN'T BELIEVE YOU'VE NEVER HEARD THIS!

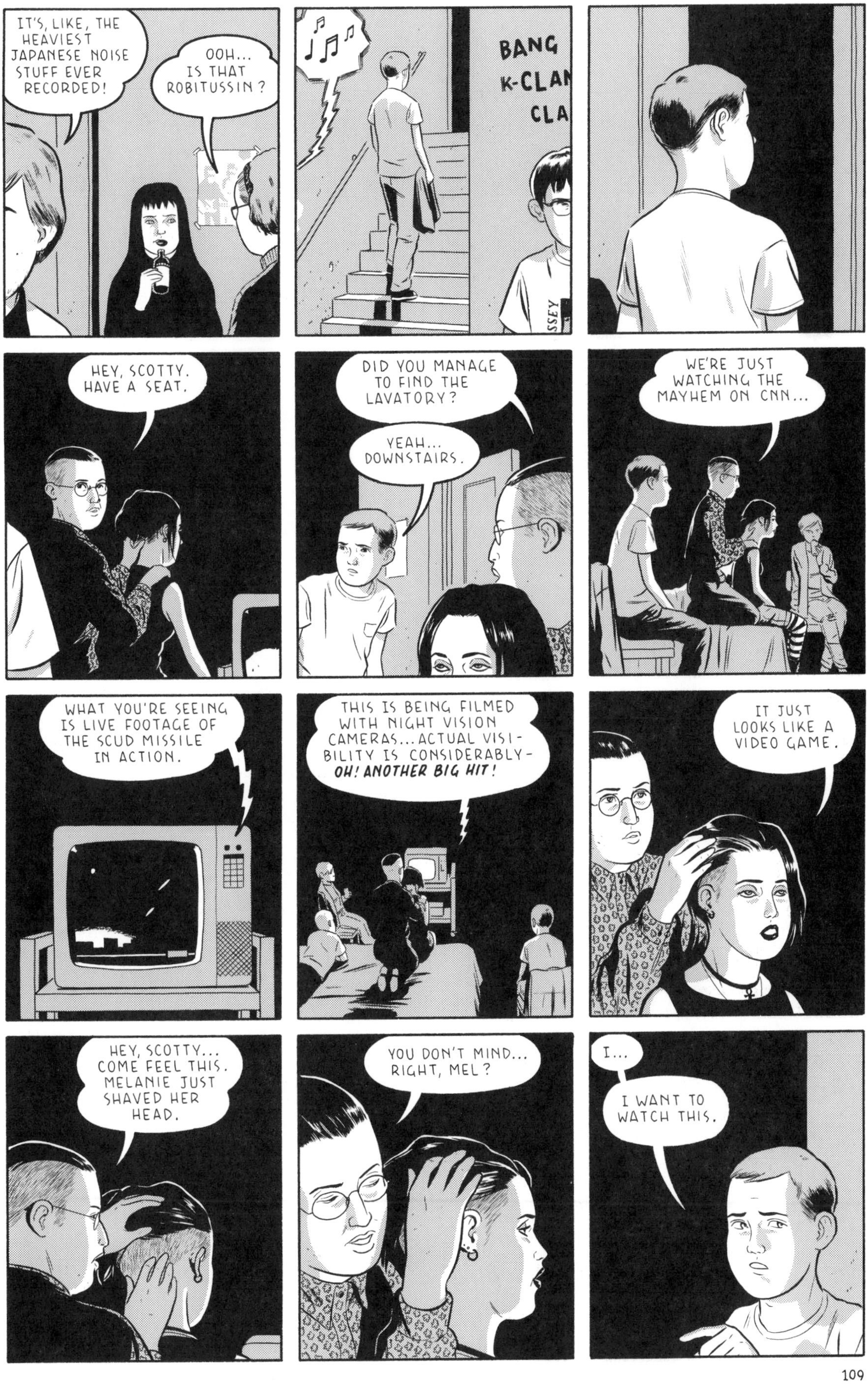
IT'S, LIKE, THE HEAVIEST JAPANESE NOISE STUFF EVER RECORDED!
OOH... IS THAT ROBITUSSIN?
BANG
K-CLAN
CLA
HEY, SCOTTY. HAVE A SEAT.
DID YOU MANAGE TO FIND THE LAVATORY?
YEAH... DOWNSTAIRS.
WE'RE JUST WATCHING THE MAYHEM ON CNN...
WHAT YOU'RE SEEING IS LIVE FOOTAGE OF THE SCUD MISSILE IN ACTION.
THIS IS BEING FILMED WITH NIGHT VISION CAMERAS... ACTUAL VISIBILITY IS CONSIDERABLY- OH! ANOTHER BIG HIT!
IT JUST LOOKS LIKE A VIDEO GAME.
HEY, SCOTTY... COME FEEL THIS. MELANIE JUST SHAVED HER HEAD.
YOU DON'T MIND... RIGHT, MEL?
I...
I WANT TO WATCH THIS.

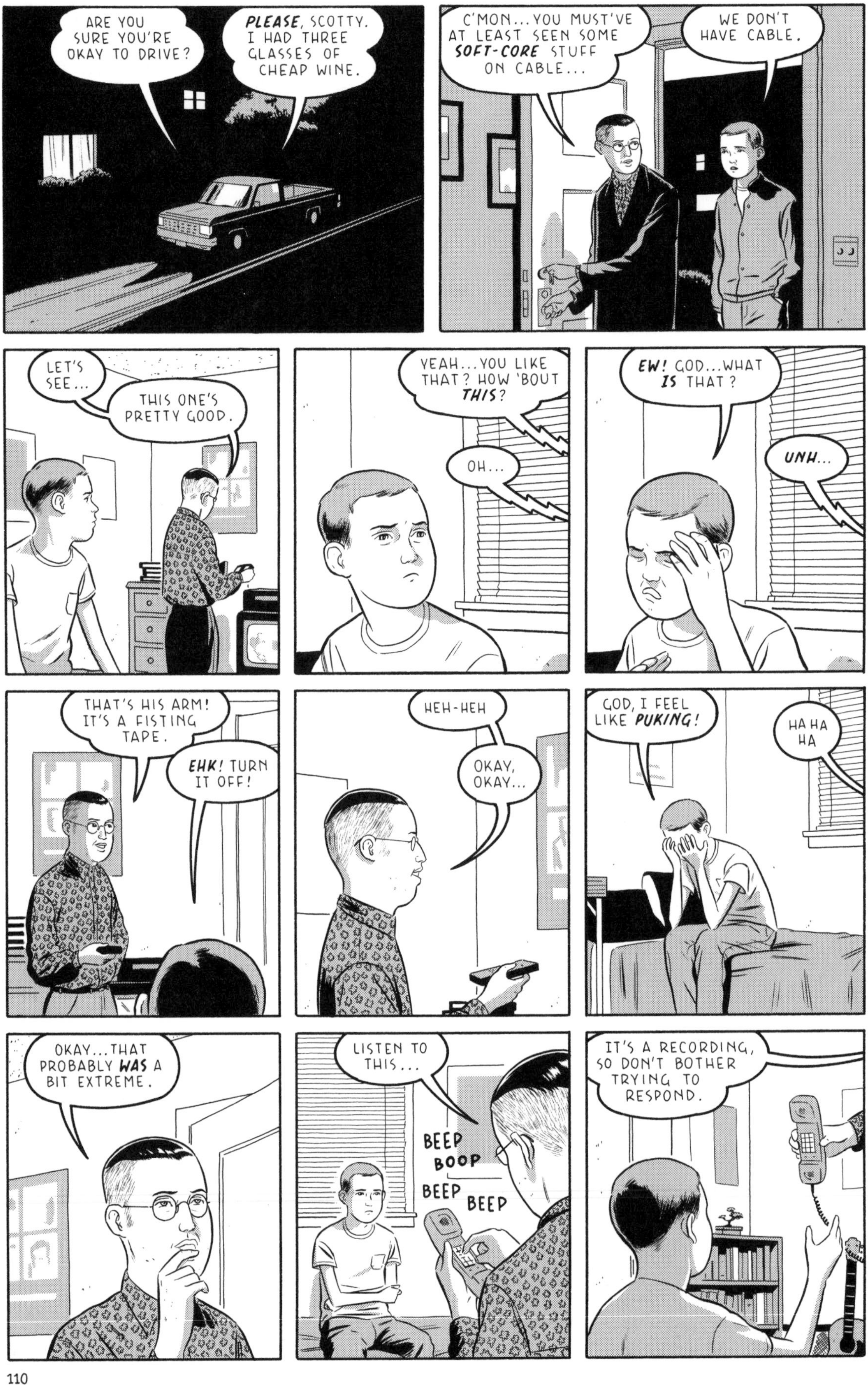
ARE YOU SURE YOU'RE OKAY TO DRIVE?
PLEASE, SCOTTY. I HAD THREE GLASSES OF CHEAP WINE.
C'MON... YOU MUST'VE AT LEAST SEEN SOME SOFT-CORE STUFF ON CABLE...
WE DON'T HAVE CABLE.
LET'S SEE...
THIS ONE'S PRETTY GOOD.
YEAH... YOU LIKE THAT? HOW 'BOUT THIS?
OH...
EW! GOD... WHAT IS THAT?
UNH...
THAT'S HIS ARM! IT'S A FISTING TAPE.
EHK! TURN IT OFF!
HEH-HEH
OKAY, OKAY...
GOD, I FEEL LIKE PUKING!
HA HA HA
OKAY... THAT PROBABLY WAS A BIT EXTREME.
LISTEN TO THIS...
BEEP
BOOP
BEEP
BEEP
IT'S A RECORDING, SO DON'T BOTHER TRYING TO RESPOND.

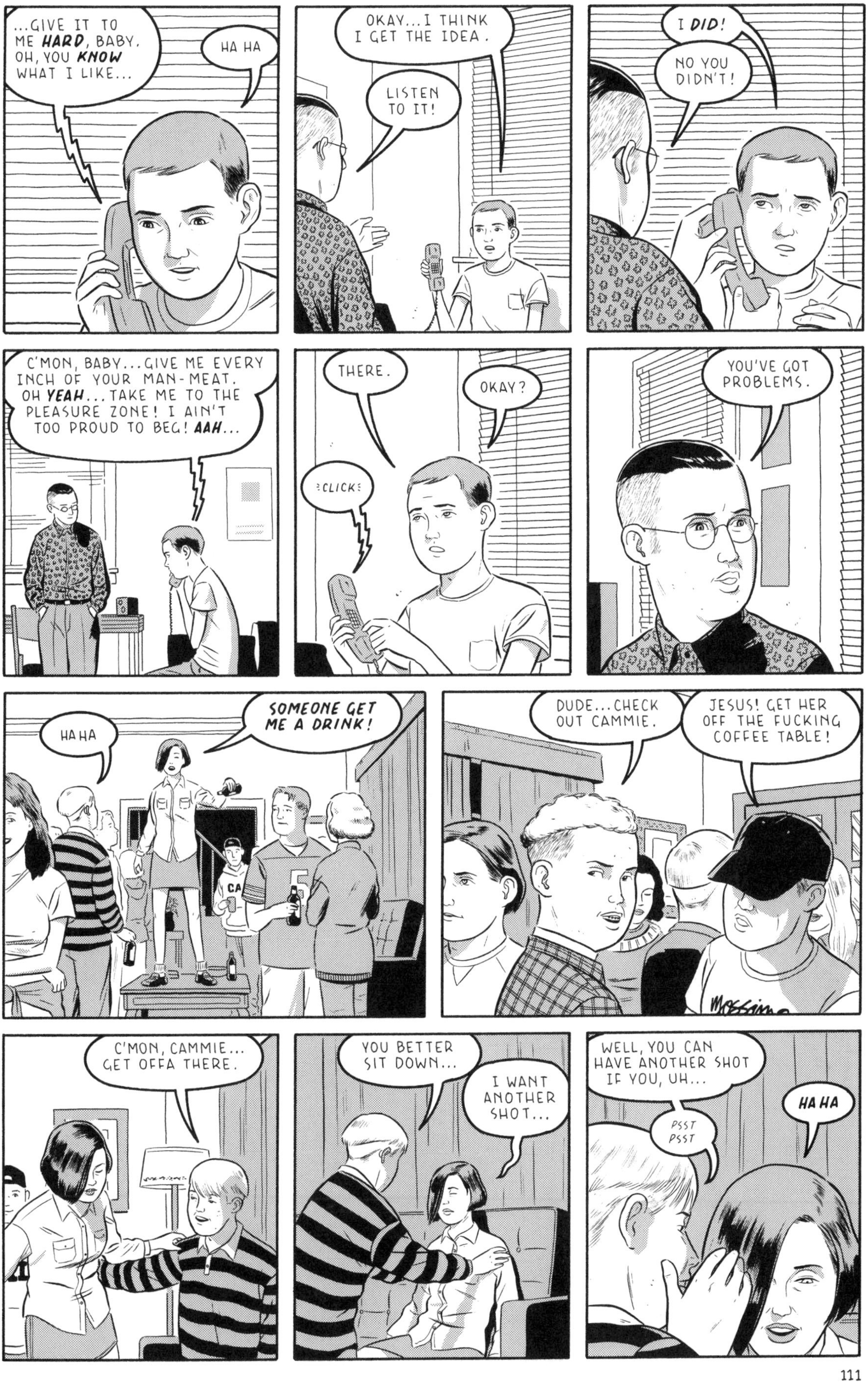
...GIVE IT TO ME **HARD**, BABY. OH, YOU **KNOW** WHAT I LIKE...
HA HA
OKAY...I THINK I GET THE IDEA.
LISTEN TO IT!
I **DID**!
NO YOU DIDN'T!
C'MON, BABY...GIVE ME EVERY INCH OF YOUR MAN-MEAT. OH **YEAH**...TAKE ME TO THE PLEASURE ZONE! I AIN'T TOO PROUD TO BEG! **AAH**...
THERE.
OKAY?
CLICK
YOU'VE GOT PROBLEMS.
HA HA
SOMEONE GET ME A DRINK!
DUDE...CHECK OUT CAMMIE.
JESUS! GET HER OFF THE FUCKING COFFEE TABLE!
C'MON, CAMMIE... GET OFFA THERE.
YOU BETTER SIT DOWN...
I WANT ANOTHER SHOT...
WELL, YOU CAN HAVE ANOTHER SHOT IF YOU, UH...
PSST PSST
HA HA

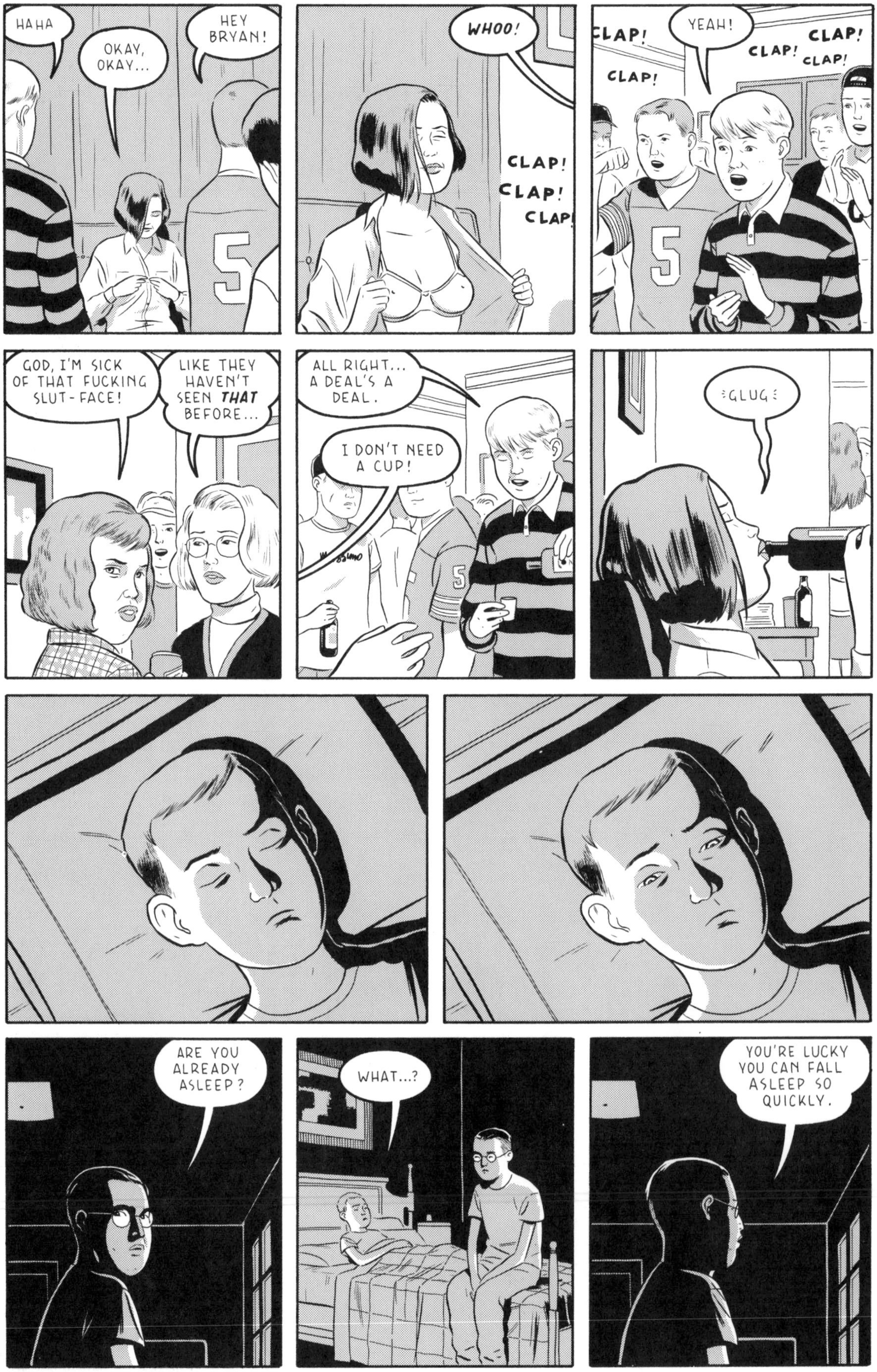
HAHA
OKAY, OKAY...
HEY BRYAN!
WHOO!
CLAP! CLAP! CLAP!
CLAP!
YEAH!
CLAP! CLAP! CLAP! CLAP!
GOD, I'M SICK OF THAT FUCKING SLUT-FACE!
LIKE THEY HAVEN'T SEEN THAT BEFORE...
ALL RIGHT... A DEAL'S A DEAL.
I DON'T NEED A CUP!
GLUG
ARE YOU ALREADY ASLEEP?
WHAT...?
YOU'RE LUCKY YOU CAN FALL ASLEEP SO QUICKLY.

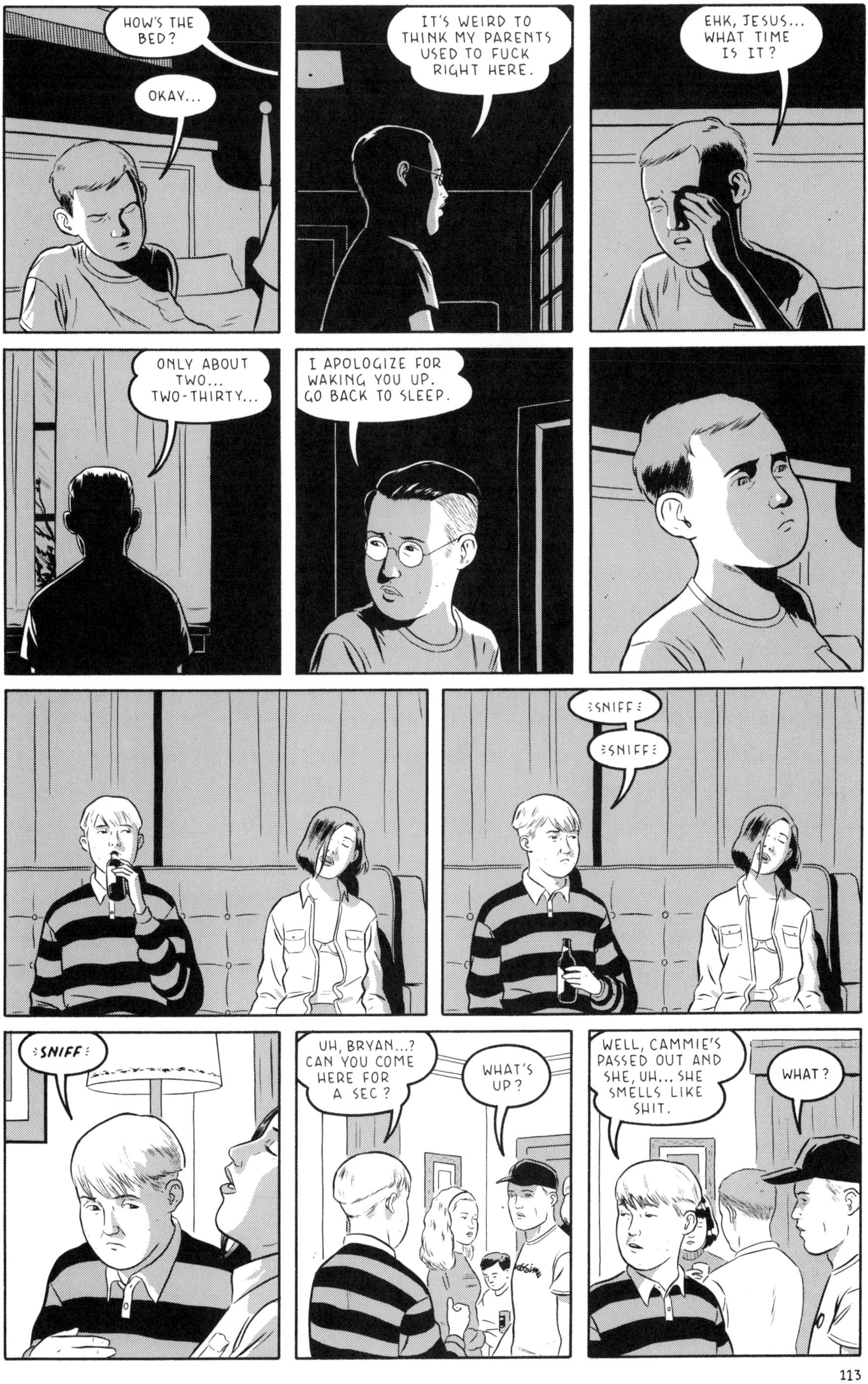

HOW'S THE BED?
OKAY...
IT'S WEIRD TO THINK MY PARENTS USED TO FUCK RIGHT HERE.
EHK, JESUS... WHAT TIME IS IT?
ONLY ABOUT TWO... TWO-THIRTY...
I APOLOGIZE FOR WAKING YOU UP. GO BACK TO SLEEP.
SNIFF
SNIFF
SNIFF
UH, BRYAN...? CAN YOU COME HERE FOR A SEC?
WHAT'S UP?
WELL, CAMMIE'S PASSED OUT AND SHE, UH... SHE SMELLS LIKE SHIT.
WHAT?

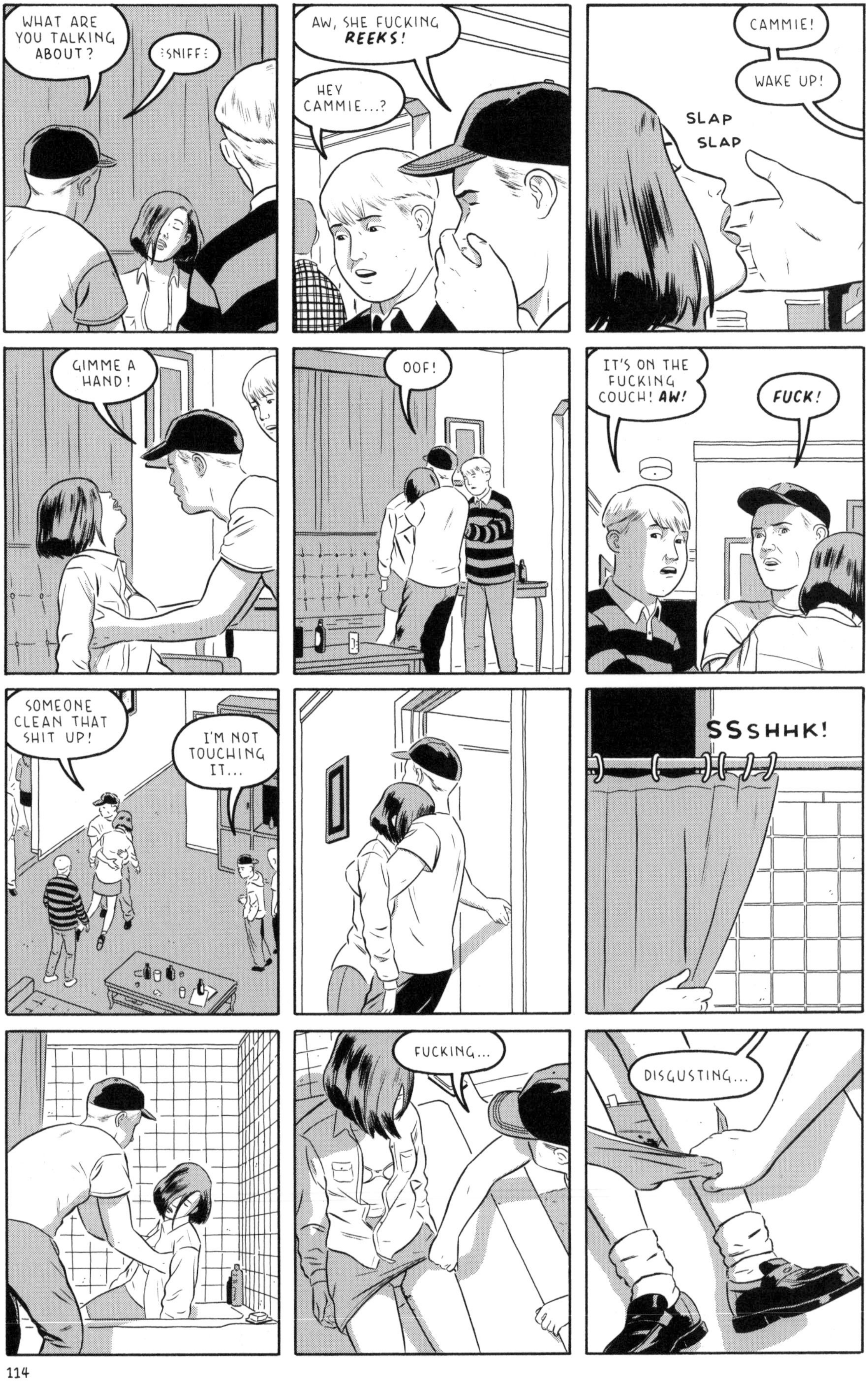
WHAT ARE YOU TALKING ABOUT?
SNIFF
AW, SHE FUCKING REEKS!
HEY CAMMIE...?
CAMMIE!
WAKE UP!
SLAP
SLAP
GIMME A HAND!
OOF!
IT'S ON THE FUCKING COUCH! AW!
FUCK!
SOMEONE CLEAN THAT SHIT UP!
I'M NOT TOUCHING IT...
SSSHHK!
FUCKING...
DISGUSTING...

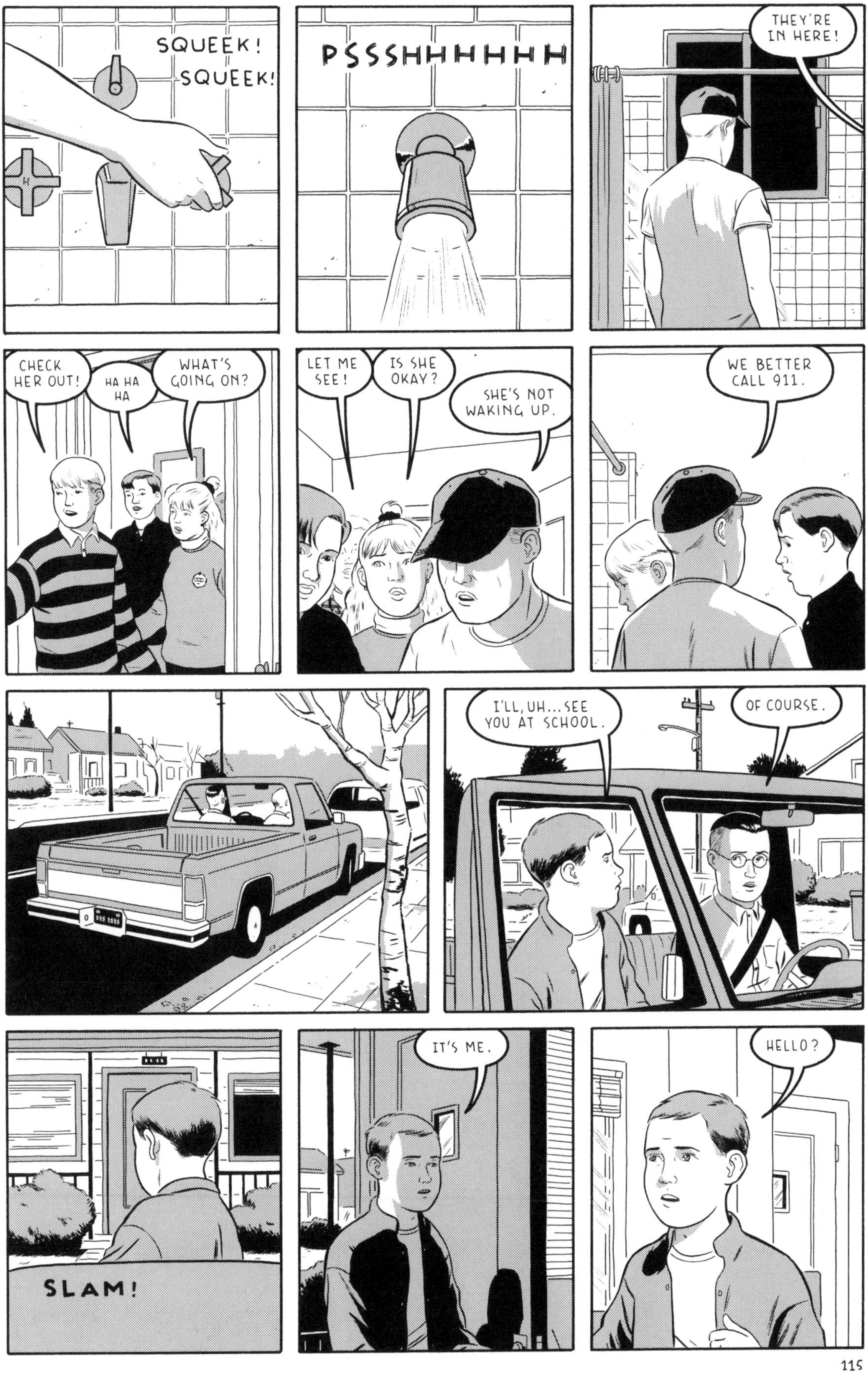
SQUEEK!
SQUEEK!
PSSSHHHHHH
THEY'RE IN HERE!
CHECK HER OUT!
HA HA HA
WHAT'S GOING ON?
LET ME SEE!
IS SHE OKAY?
SHE'S NOT WAKING UP.
WE BETTER CALL 911.
I'LL, UH... SEE YOU AT SCHOOL.
OF COURSE.
SLAM!
IT'S ME.
HELLO?

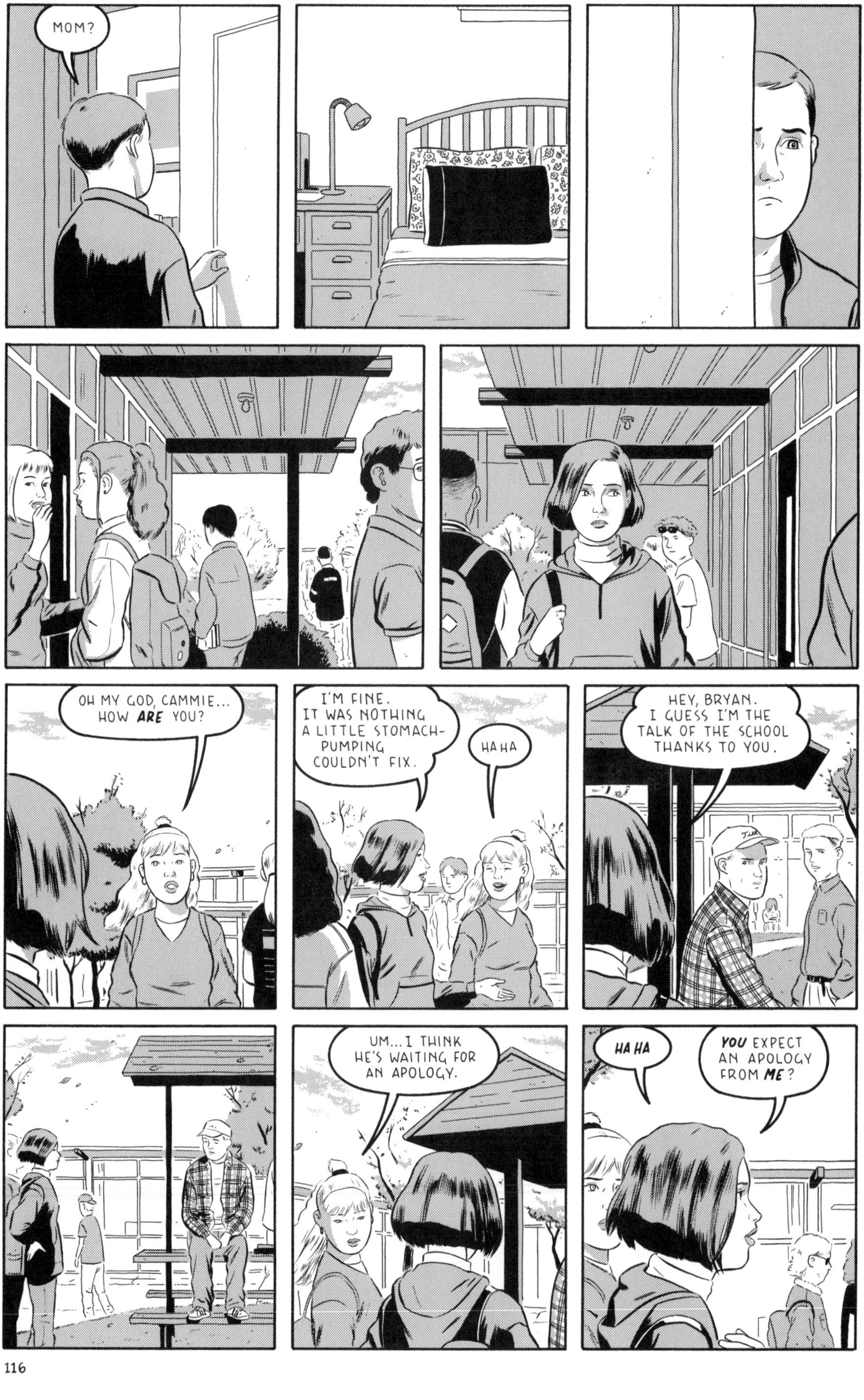
MOM?
OH MY GOD, CAMMIE... HOW ARE YOU?
I'M FINE. IT WAS NOTHING A LITTLE STOMACH-PUMPING COULDN'T FIX.
HA HA
HEY, BRYAN. I GUESS I'M THE TALK OF THE SCHOOL THANKS TO YOU.
UM... I THINK HE'S WAITING FOR AN APOLOGY.
HA HA
YOU EXPECT AN APOLOGY FROM ME?

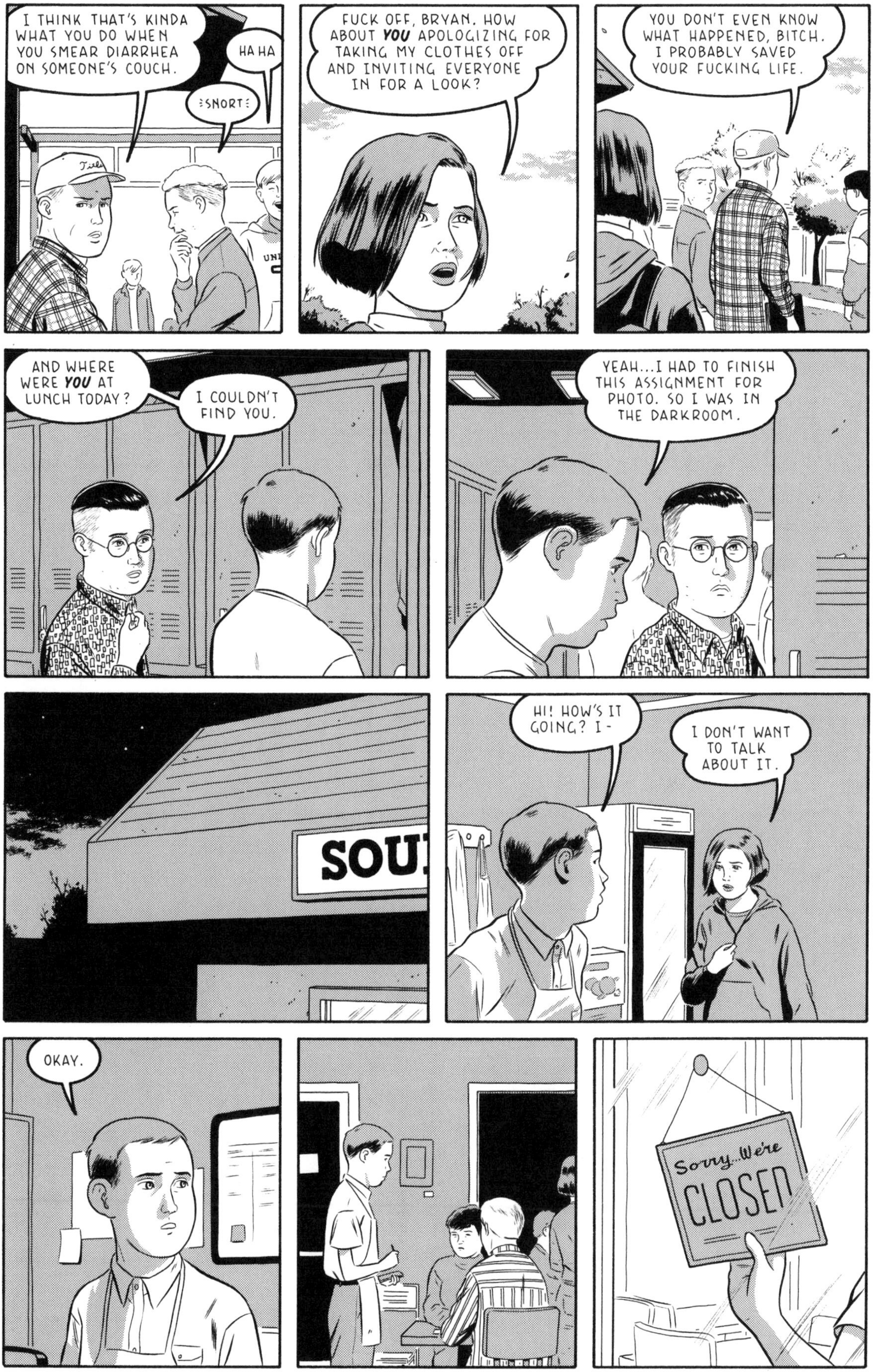
I THINK THAT'S KINDA WHAT YOU DO WHEN YOU SMEAR DIARRHEA ON SOMEONE'S COUCH.
HA HA
SNORT
FUCK OFF, BRYAN. HOW ABOUT YOU APOLOGIZING FOR TAKING MY CLOTHES OFF AND INVITING EVERYONE IN FOR A LOOK?
YOU DON'T EVEN KNOW WHAT HAPPENED, BITCH. I PROBABLY SAVED YOUR FUCKING LIFE.
AND WHERE WERE YOU AT LUNCH TODAY?
I COULDN'T FIND YOU.
YEAH...I HAD TO FINISH THIS ASSIGNMENT FOR PHOTO. SO I WAS IN THE DARKROOM.
SOU
HI! HOW'S IT GOING? I-
I DON'T WANT TO TALK ABOUT IT.
OKAY.
Sorry...We're CLOSED

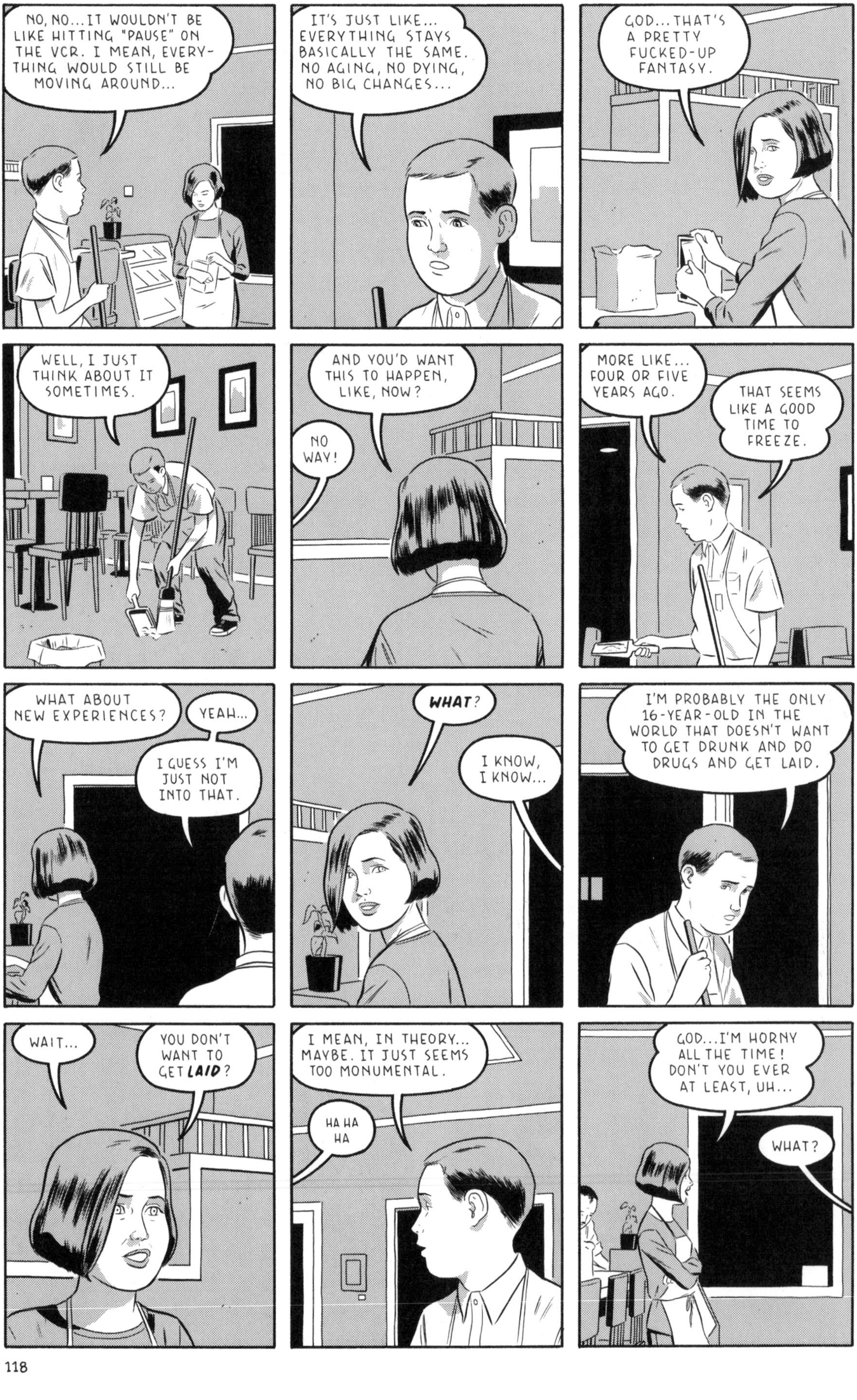
NO, NO...IT WOULDN'T BE LIKE HITTING "PAUSE" ON THE VCR. I MEAN, EVERYTHING WOULD STILL BE MOVING AROUND...
IT'S JUST LIKE... EVERYTHING STAYS BASICALLY THE SAME. NO AGING, NO DYING, NO BIG CHANGES...
GOD...THAT'S A PRETTY FUCKED-UP FANTASY.
WELL, I JUST THINK ABOUT IT SOMETIMES.
AND YOU'D WANT THIS TO HAPPEN, LIKE, NOW?
NO WAY!
MORE LIKE... FOUR OR FIVE YEARS AGO.
THAT SEEMS LIKE A GOOD TIME TO FREEZE.
WHAT ABOUT NEW EXPERIENCES?
YEAH...
I GUESS I'M JUST NOT INTO THAT.
WHAT?
I KNOW, I KNOW...
I'M PROBABLY THE ONLY 16-YEAR-OLD IN THE WORLD THAT DOESN'T WANT TO GET DRUNK AND DO DRUGS AND GET LAID.
WAIT...
YOU DON'T WANT TO GET LAID?
I MEAN, IN THEORY... MAYBE. IT JUST SEEMS TOO MONUMENTAL.
HA HA HA
GOD...I'M HORNY ALL THE TIME! DON'T YOU EVER AT LEAST, UH...
WHAT?

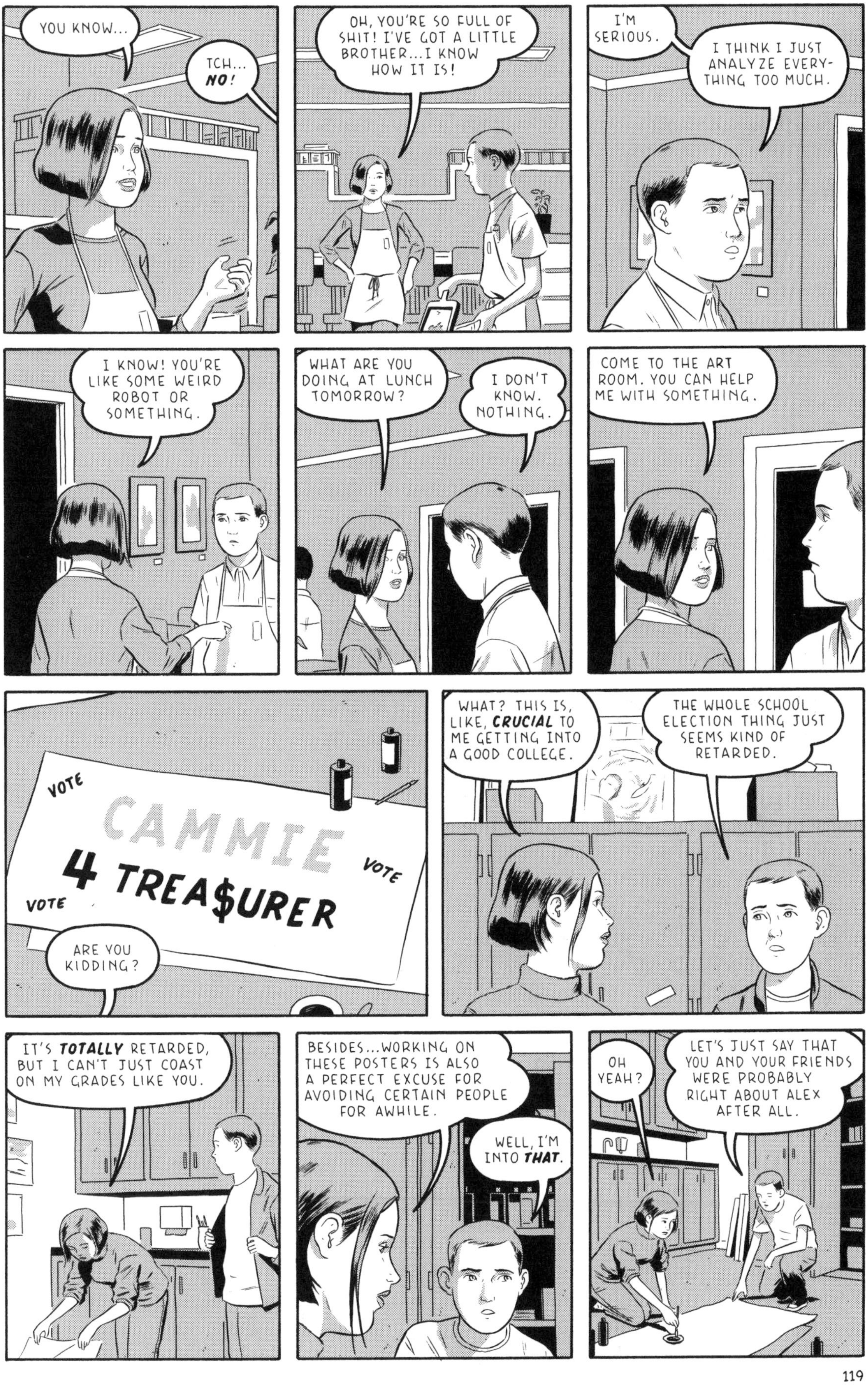

YOU KNOW...
TCH... NO!
OH, YOU'RE SO FULL OF SHIT! I'VE GOT A LITTLE BROTHER... I KNOW HOW IT IS!
I'M SERIOUS.
I THINK I JUST ANALYZE EVERYTHING TOO MUCH.
I KNOW! YOU'RE LIKE SOME WEIRD ROBOT OR SOMETHING.
WHAT ARE YOU DOING AT LUNCH TOMORROW?
I DON'T KNOW. NOTHING.
COME TO THE ART ROOM. YOU CAN HELP ME WITH SOMETHING.
VOTE
CAMMIE
4 TREA$URER
VOTE
VOTE
ARE YOU KIDDING?
WHAT? THIS IS, LIKE, CRUCIAL TO ME GETTING INTO A GOOD COLLEGE.
THE WHOLE SCHOOL ELECTION THING JUST SEEMS KIND OF RETARDED.
IT'S TOTALLY RETARDED, BUT I CAN'T JUST COAST ON MY GRADES LIKE YOU.
BESIDES... WORKING ON THESE POSTERS IS ALSO A PERFECT EXCUSE FOR AVOIDING CERTAIN PEOPLE FOR AWHILE.
WELL, I'M INTO THAT.
OH YEAH?
LET'S JUST SAY THAT YOU AND YOUR FRIENDS WERE PROBABLY RIGHT ABOUT ALEX AFTER ALL.

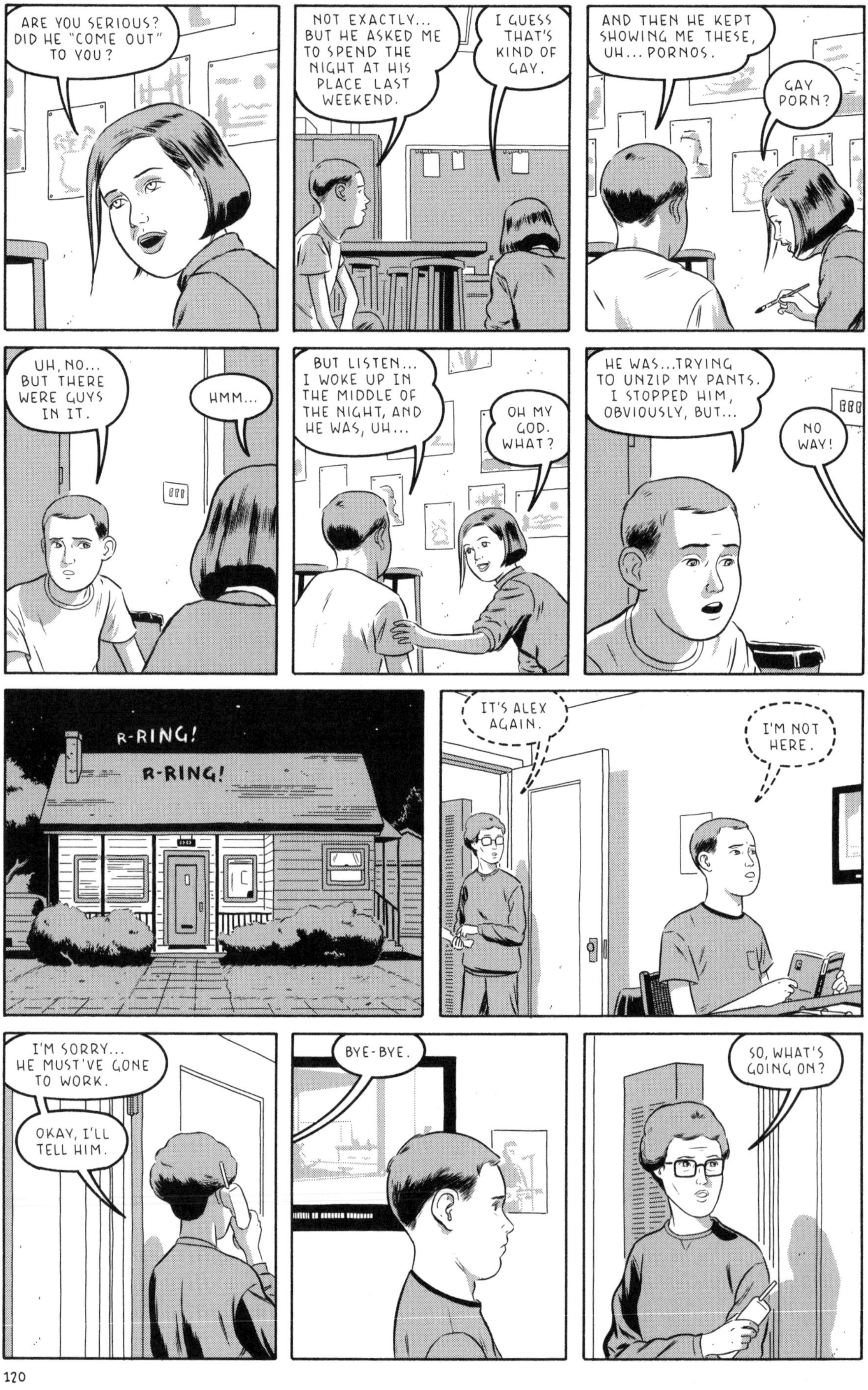
ARE YOU SERIOUS? DID HE "COME OUT" TO YOU?
NOT EXACTLY... BUT HE ASKED ME TO SPEND THE NIGHT AT HIS PLACE LAST WEEKEND.
I GUESS THAT'S KIND OF GAY.
AND THEN HE KEPT SHOWING ME THESE, UH... PORNOS.
GAY PORN?
UH, NO... BUT THERE WERE GUYS IN IT.
HMM...
BUT LISTEN... I WOKE UP IN THE MIDDLE OF THE NIGHT, AND HE WAS, UH...
OH MY GOD. WHAT?
HE WAS...TRYING TO UNZIP MY PANTS. I STOPPED HIM, OBVIOUSLY, BUT...
NO WAY!
R-RING!
R-RING!
IT'S ALEX AGAIN.
I'M NOT HERE.
I'M SORRY... HE MUST'VE GONE TO WORK.
OKAY, I'LL TELL HIM.
BYE-BYE.
SO, WHAT'S GOING ON?

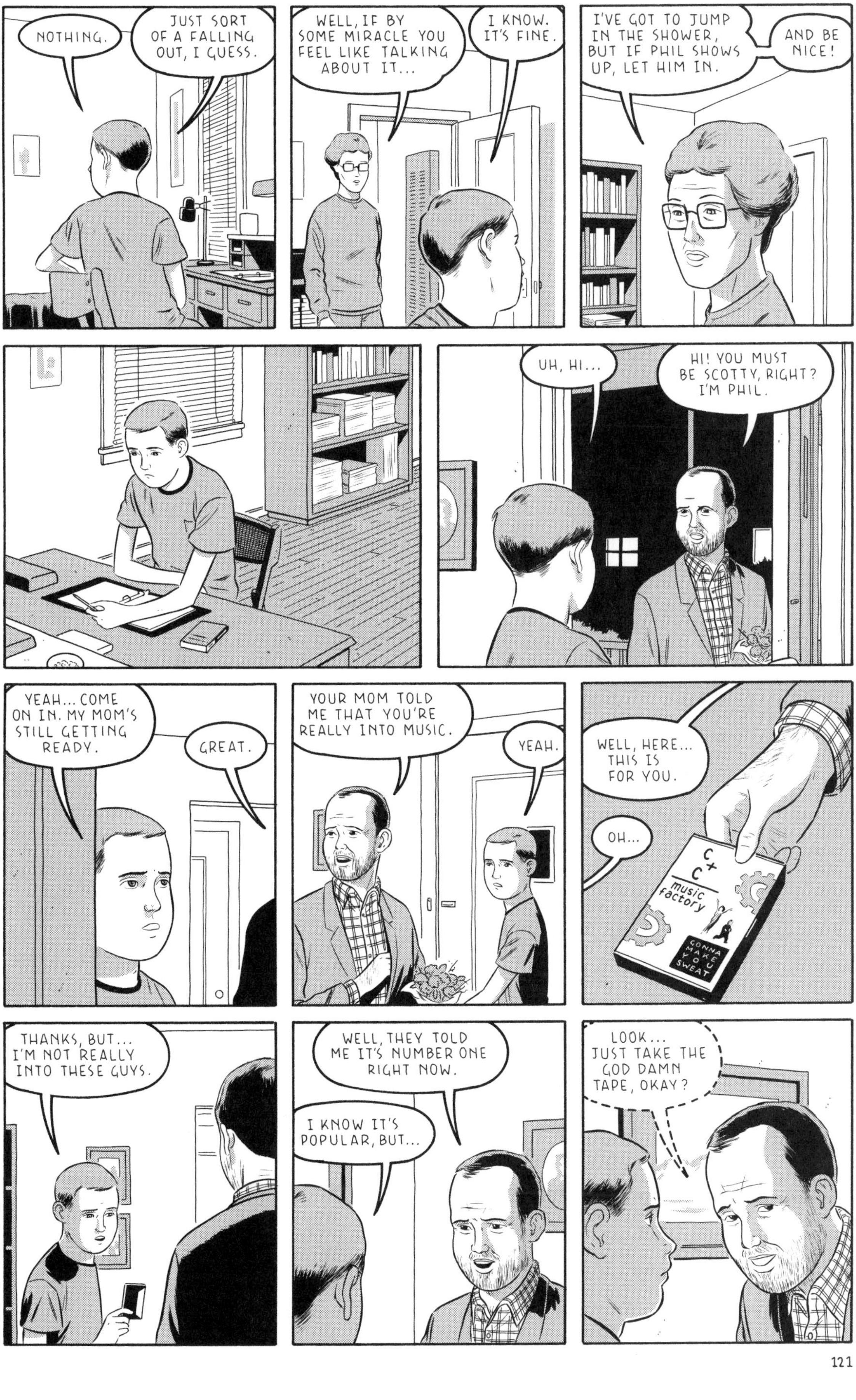
NOTHING.
JUST SORT OF A FALLING OUT, I GUESS.
WELL, IF BY SOME MIRACLE YOU FEEL LIKE TALKING ABOUT IT...
I KNOW. IT'S FINE.
I'VE GOT TO JUMP IN THE SHOWER, BUT IF PHIL SHOWS UP, LET HIM IN.
AND BE NICE!
UH, HI...
HI! YOU MUST BE SCOTTY, RIGHT? I'M PHIL.
YEAH... COME ON IN. MY MOM'S STILL GETTING READY.
GREAT.
YOUR MOM TOLD ME THAT YOU'RE REALLY INTO MUSIC.
YEAH.
WELL, HERE... THIS IS FOR YOU.
OH...
C+C music factory
GONNA MAKE YOU SWEAT
THANKS, BUT... I'M NOT REALLY INTO THESE GUYS.
WELL, THEY TOLD ME IT'S NUMBER ONE RIGHT NOW.
I KNOW IT'S POPULAR, BUT...
LOOK... JUST TAKE THE GOD DAMN TAPE, OKAY?

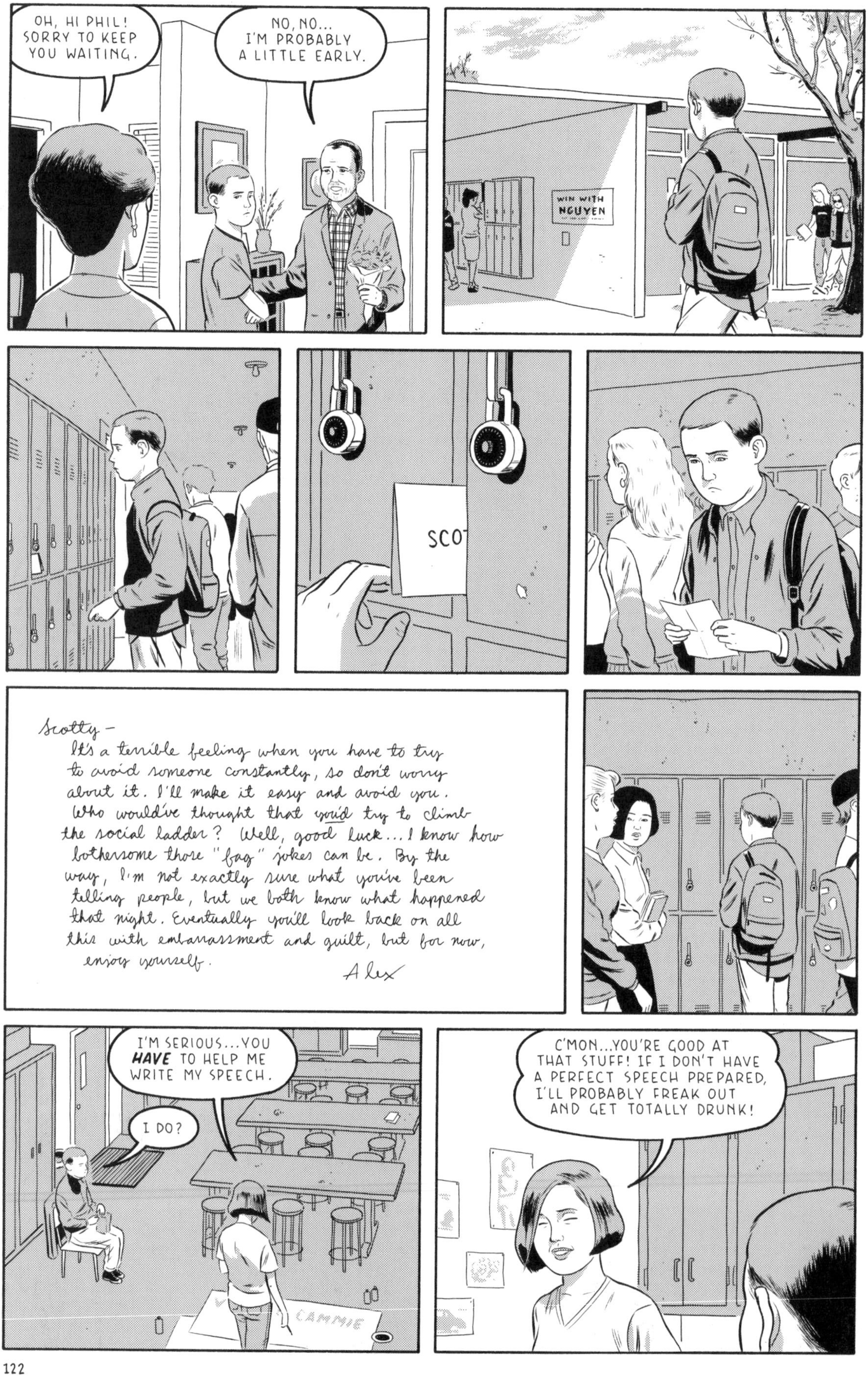
OH, HI PHIL! SORRY TO KEEP YOU WAITING.
NO, NO... I'M PROBABLY A LITTLE EARLY.
WIN WITH NGUYEN
SCOT
Scotty -
It's a terrible feeling when you have to try
to avoid someone constantly, so don't worry
about it. I'll make it easy and avoid you.
Who would've thought that you'd try to climb
the social ladder? Well, good luck... I know how
bothersome those "fag" jokes can be. By the
way, I'm not exactly sure what you've been
telling people, but we both know what happened
that night. Eventually you'll look back on all
this with embarrassment and guilt, but for now,
enjoy yourself.
Alex
I'M SERIOUS... YOU **HAVE** TO HELP ME WRITE MY SPEECH.
I DO?
CAMMIE
C'MON... YOU'RE GOOD AT THAT STUFF! IF I DON'T HAVE A PERFECT SPEECH PREPARED, I'LL PROBABLY FREAK OUT AND GET TOTALLY DRUNK!

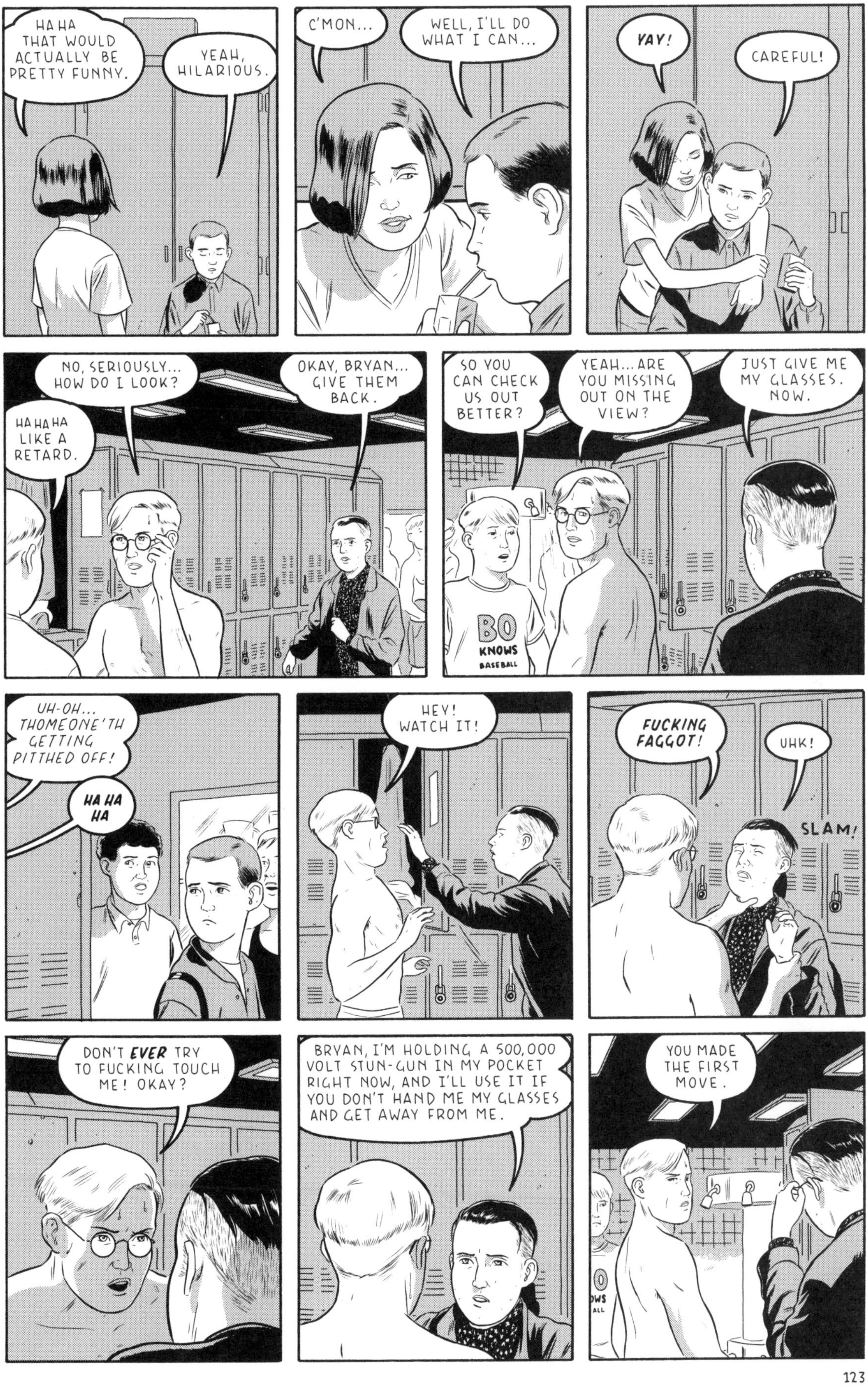
HA HA THAT WOULD ACTUALLY BE PRETTY FUNNY.
YEAH, HILARIOUS.
C'MON...
WELL, I'LL DO WHAT I CAN...
YAY!
CAREFUL!
NO, SERIOUSLY... HOW DO I LOOK?
HA HA HA LIKE A RETARD.
OKAY, BRYAN... GIVE THEM BACK.
SO YOU CAN CHECK US OUT BETTER?
YEAH... ARE YOU MISSING OUT ON THE VIEW?
JUST GIVE ME MY GLASSES. NOW.
BO KNOWS BASEBALL
UH-OH... THOMEONE'TH GETTING PITTHED OFF!
HA HA HA
HEY! WATCH IT!
FUCKING FAGGOT!
UHK!
SLAM!
DON'T EVER TRY TO FUCKING TOUCH ME! OKAY?
BRYAN, I'M HOLDING A 500,000 VOLT STUN-GUN IN MY POCKET RIGHT NOW, AND I'LL USE IT IF YOU DON'T HAND ME MY GLASSES AND GET AWAY FROM ME.
YOU MADE THE FIRST MOVE.

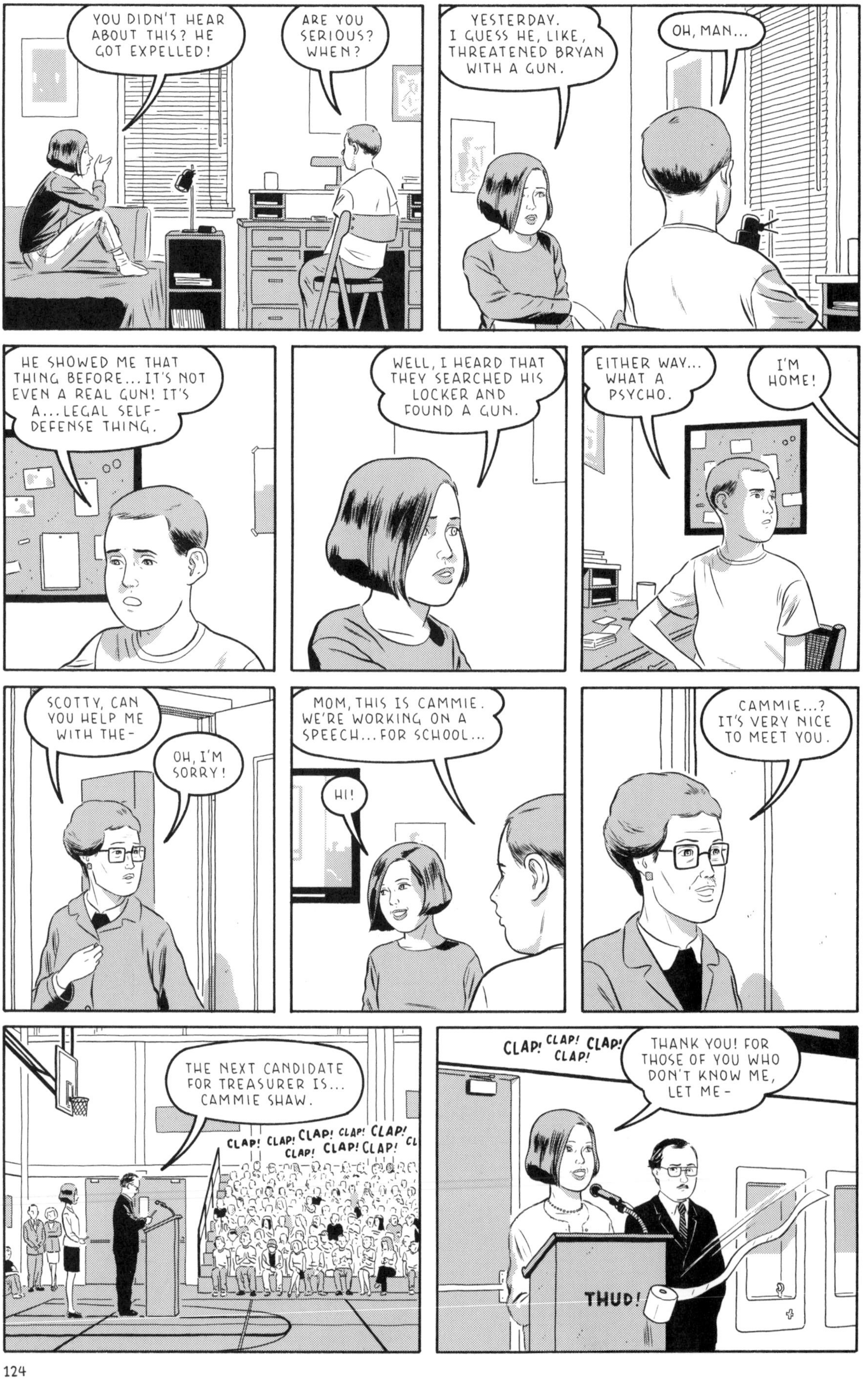
YOU DIDN'T HEAR ABOUT THIS? HE GOT EXPELLED!
ARE YOU SERIOUS? WHEN?
YESTERDAY. I GUESS HE, LIKE, THREATENED BRYAN WITH A GUN.
OH, MAN...
HE SHOWED ME THAT THING BEFORE... IT'S NOT EVEN A REAL GUN! IT'S A... LEGAL SELF-DEFENSE THING.
WELL, I HEARD THAT THEY SEARCHED HIS LOCKER AND FOUND A GUN.
EITHER WAY... WHAT A PSYCHO.
I'M HOME!
SCOTTY, CAN YOU HELP ME WITH THE-
OH, I'M SORRY!
MOM, THIS IS CAMMIE. WE'RE WORKING ON A SPEECH... FOR SCHOOL...
HI!
CAMMIE...? IT'S VERY NICE TO MEET YOU.
THE NEXT CANDIDATE FOR TREASURER IS... CAMMIE SHAW.
CLAP! CLAP! CLAP! CLAP! CLAP! CLAP! CLAP! CLAP!
CLAP! CLAP! CLAP! CLAP!
THANK YOU! FOR THOSE OF YOU WHO DON'T KNOW ME, LET ME-
THUD!

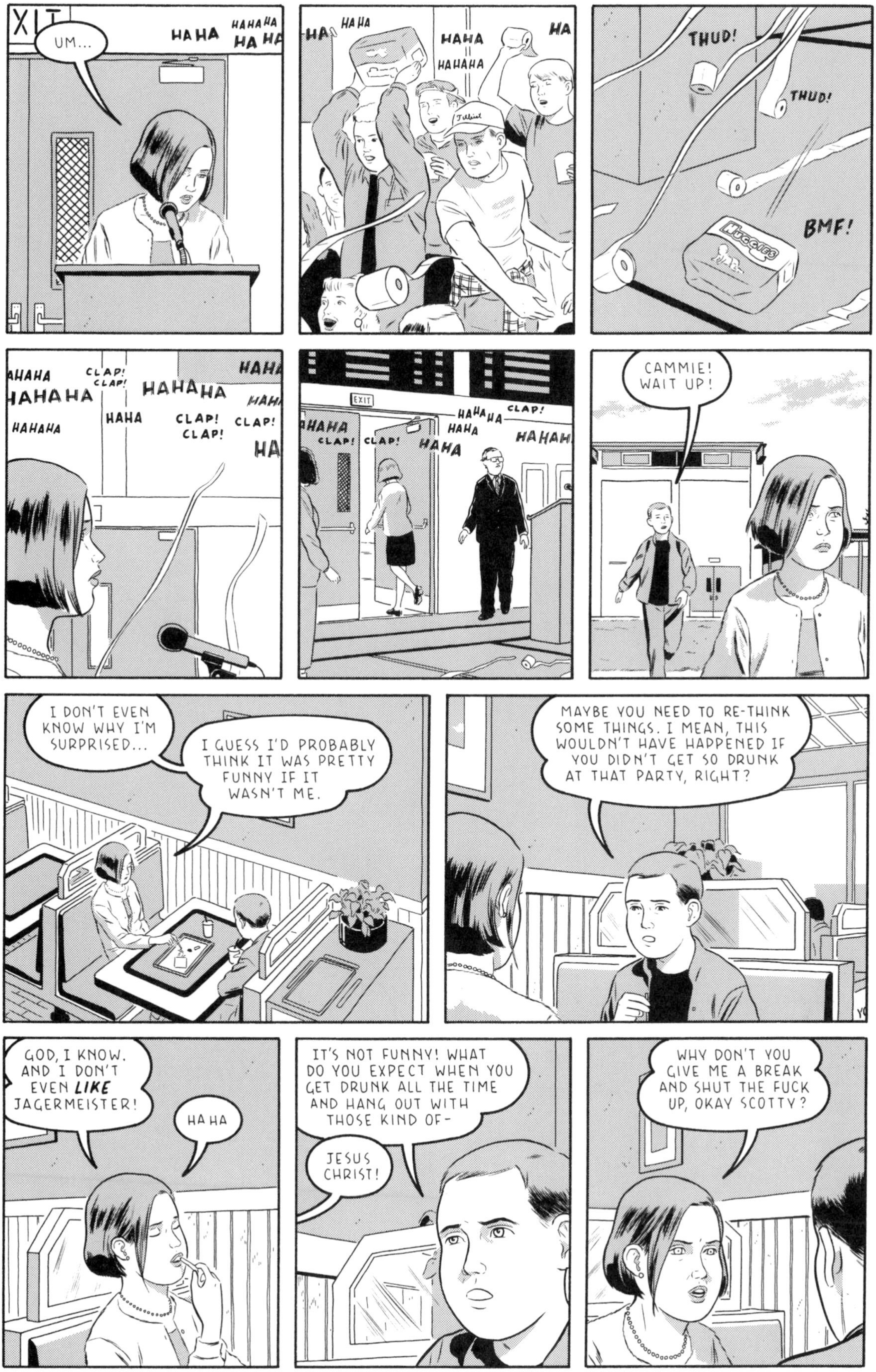
UM...
HAHA
HAHAHA
HAHA
HAHA
HAHA
HAHAHA
HA
THUD!
THUD!
BMF!
HAHAHA
CLAP! CLAP!
HAHAHA
HAHAHA
HAHA
CLAP! CLAP!
CLAP!
HAHAHA
HAHA
HAHA
CLAP!
CLAP!
HAHA
HAHAHA
HAHA
CLAP!
HAHAH
CAMMIE! WAIT UP!
I DON'T EVEN KNOW WHY I'M SURPRISED...
I GUESS I'D PROBABLY THINK IT WAS PRETTY FUNNY IF IT WASN'T ME.
MAYBE YOU NEED TO RE-THINK SOME THINGS. I MEAN, THIS WOULDN'T HAVE HAPPENED IF YOU DIDN'T GET SO DRUNK AT THAT PARTY, RIGHT?
GOD, I KNOW. AND I DON'T EVEN LIKE JAGERMEISTER!
HA HA
IT'S NOT FUNNY! WHAT DO YOU EXPECT WHEN YOU GET DRUNK ALL THE TIME AND HANG OUT WITH THOSE KIND OF-
JESUS CHRIST!
WHY DON'T YOU GIVE ME A BREAK AND SHUT THE FUCK UP, OKAY SCOTTY?

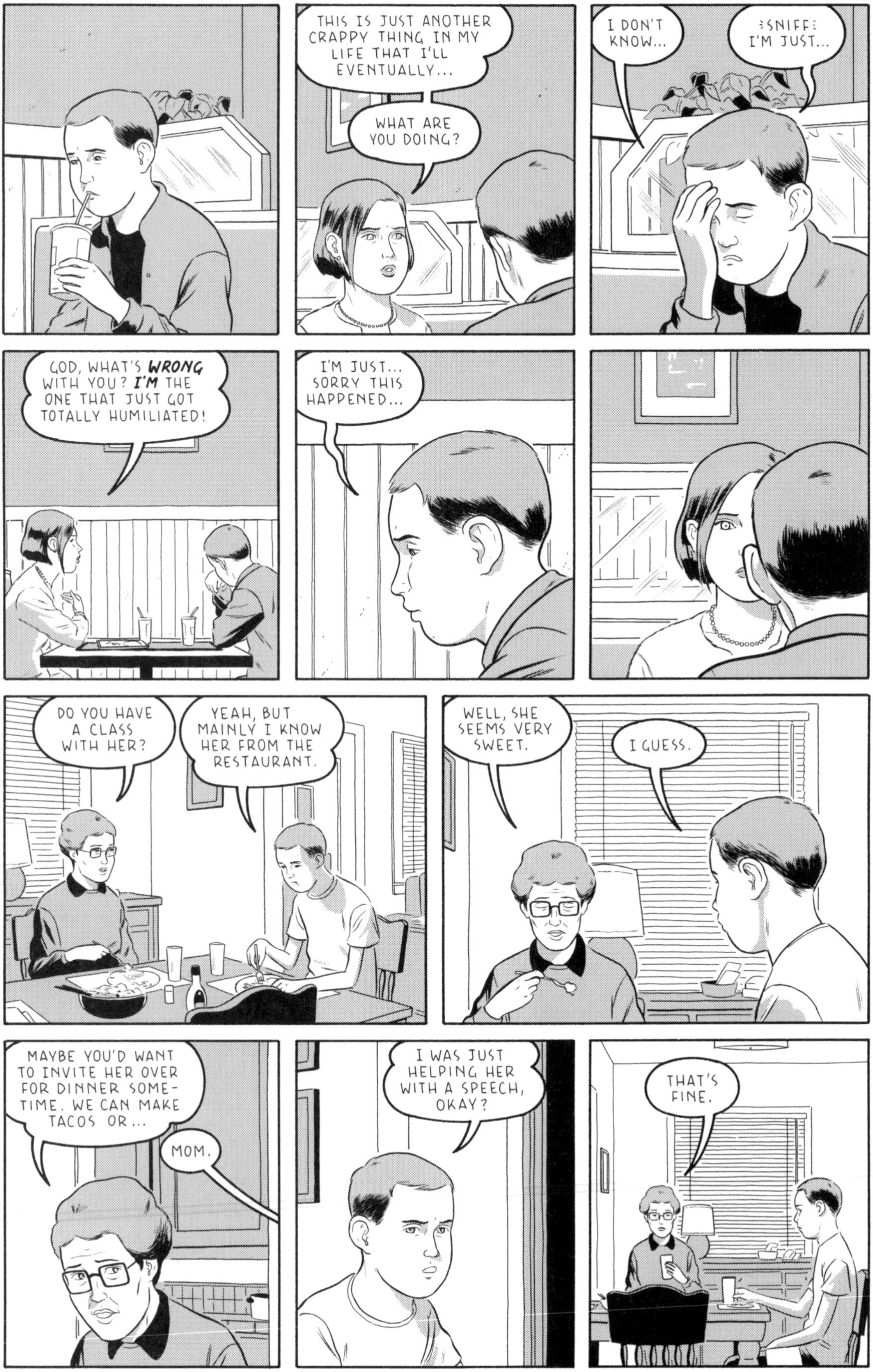
THIS IS JUST ANOTHER CRAPPY THING IN MY LIFE THAT I'LL EVENTUALLY...
WHAT ARE YOU DOING?
I DON'T KNOW...
SNIFF I'M JUST...
GOD, WHAT'S **WRONG** WITH YOU? ***I'M*** THE ONE THAT JUST GOT TOTALLY HUMILIATED!
I'M JUST... SORRY THIS HAPPENED...
DO YOU HAVE A CLASS WITH HER?
YEAH, BUT MAINLY I KNOW HER FROM THE RESTAURANT.
WELL, SHE SEEMS VERY SWEET.
I GUESS.
MAYBE YOU'D WANT TO INVITE HER OVER FOR DINNER SOME-TIME. WE CAN MAKE TACOS OR...
MOM.
I WAS JUST HELPING HER WITH A SPEECH, OKAY?
THAT'S FINE.

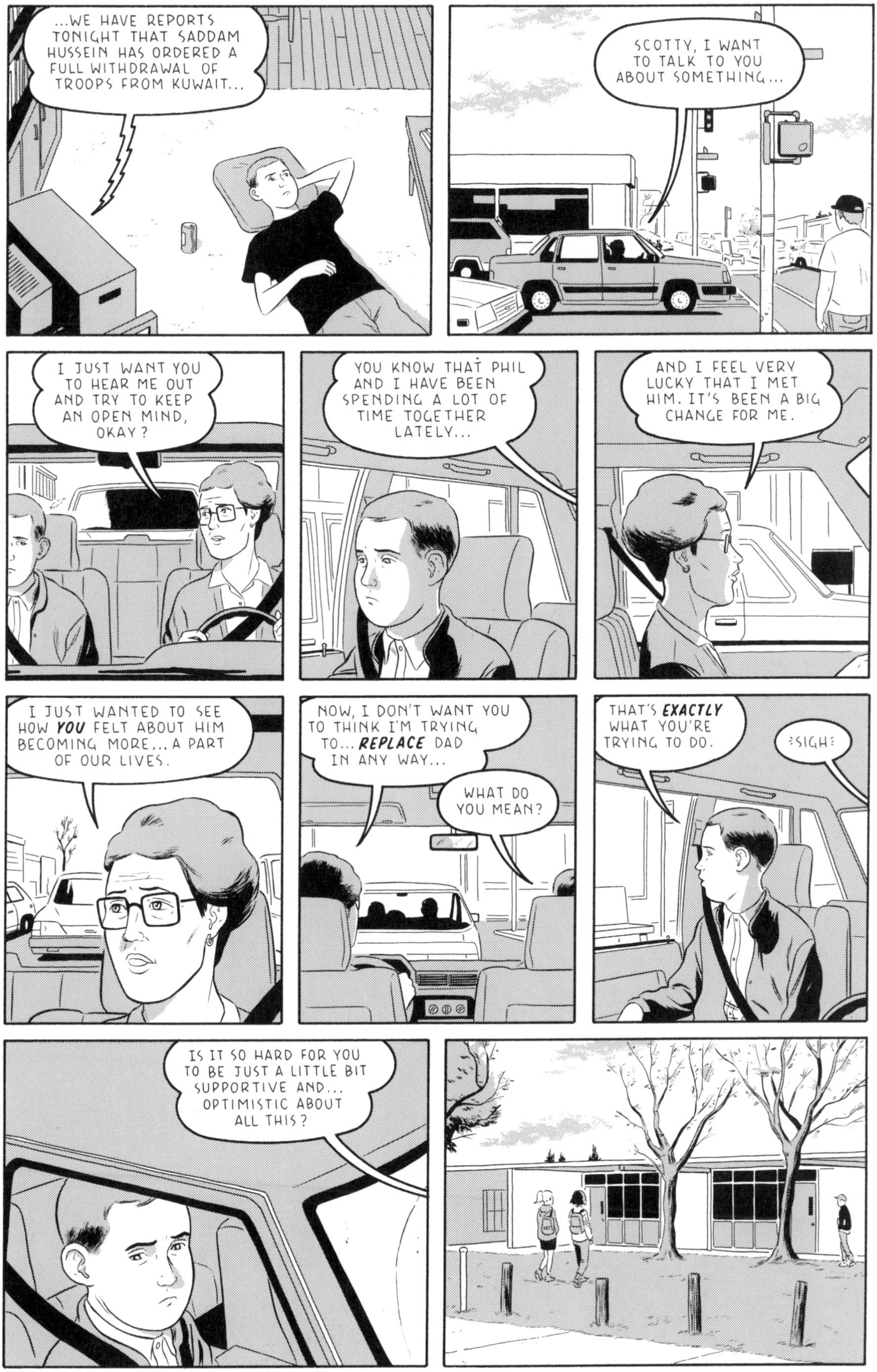
...WE HAVE REPORTS TONIGHT THAT SADDAM HUSSEIN HAS ORDERED A FULL WITHDRAWAL OF TROOPS FROM KUWAIT...
SCOTTY, I WANT TO TALK TO YOU ABOUT SOMETHING...
I JUST WANT YOU TO HEAR ME OUT AND TRY TO KEEP AN OPEN MIND, OKAY?
YOU KNOW THAT PHIL AND I HAVE BEEN SPENDING A LOT OF TIME TOGETHER LATELY...
AND I FEEL VERY LUCKY THAT I MET HIM. IT'S BEEN A BIG CHANGE FOR ME.
I JUST WANTED TO SEE HOW YOU FELT ABOUT HIM BECOMING MORE... A PART OF OUR LIVES.
NOW, I DON'T WANT YOU TO THINK I'M TRYING TO... REPLACE DAD IN ANY WAY...
WHAT DO YOU MEAN?
THAT'S EXACTLY WHAT YOU'RE TRYING TO DO.
SIGH
IS IT SO HARD FOR YOU TO BE JUST A LITTLE BIT SUPPORTIVE AND... OPTIMISTIC ABOUT ALL THIS?

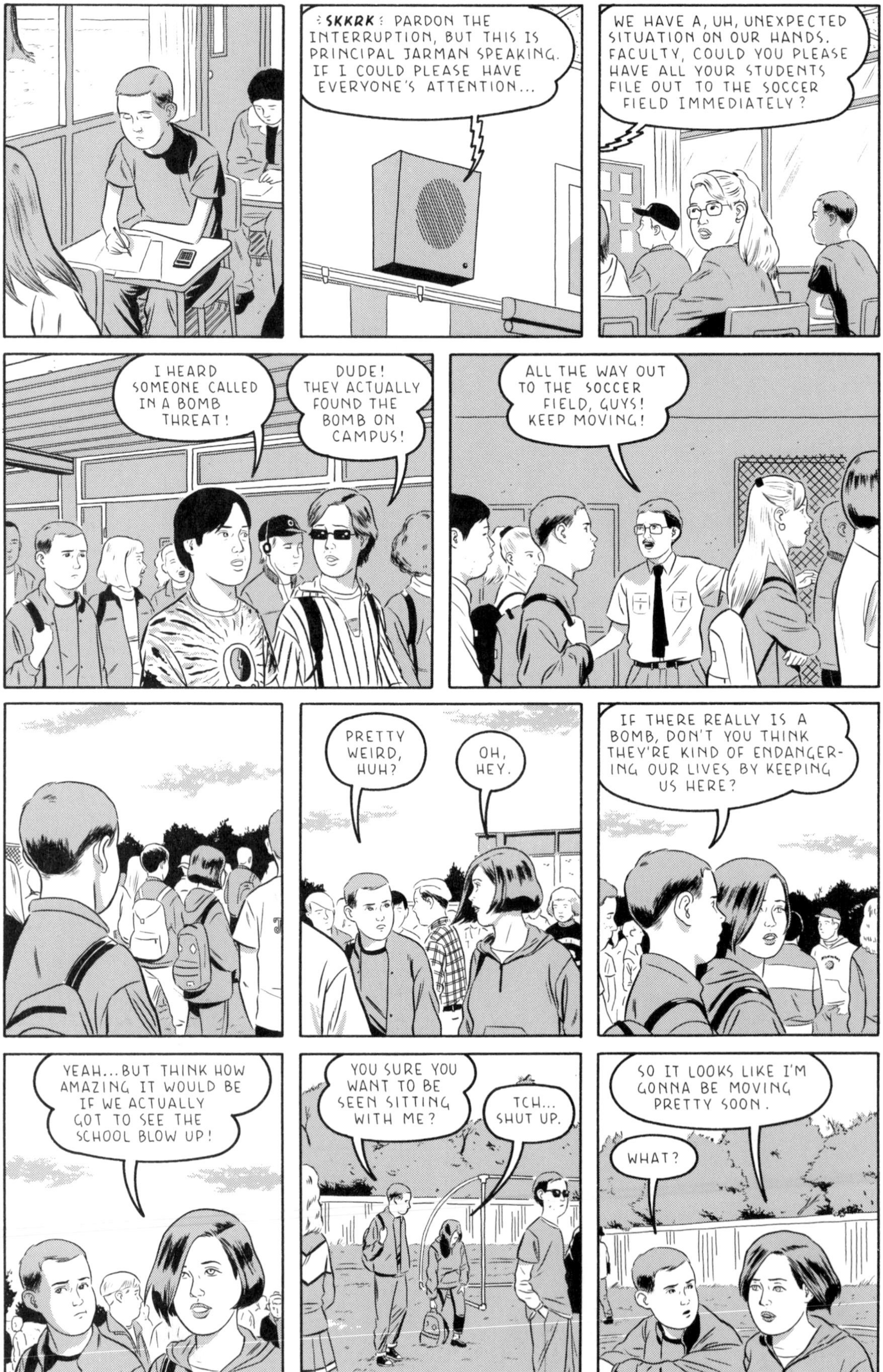
SKKRK PARDON THE INTERRUPTION, BUT THIS IS PRINCIPAL JARMAN SPEAKING. IF I COULD PLEASE HAVE EVERYONE'S ATTENTION...
WE HAVE A, UH, UNEXPECTED SITUATION ON OUR HANDS. FACULTY, COULD YOU PLEASE HAVE ALL YOUR STUDENTS FILE OUT TO THE SOCCER FIELD IMMEDIATELY?
I HEARD SOMEONE CALLED IN A BOMB THREAT!
DUDE! THEY ACTUALLY FOUND THE BOMB ON CAMPUS!
ALL THE WAY OUT TO THE SOCCER FIELD, GUYS! KEEP MOVING!
PRETTY WEIRD, HUH?
OH, HEY.
IF THERE REALLY IS A BOMB, DON'T YOU THINK THEY'RE KIND OF ENDANGERING OUR LIVES BY KEEPING US HERE?
YEAH... BUT THINK HOW AMAZING IT WOULD BE IF WE ACTUALLY GOT TO SEE THE SCHOOL BLOW UP!
YOU SURE YOU WANT TO BE SEEN SITTING WITH ME?
TCH... SHUT UP.
SO IT LOOKS LIKE I'M GONNA BE MOVING PRETTY SOON.
WHAT?

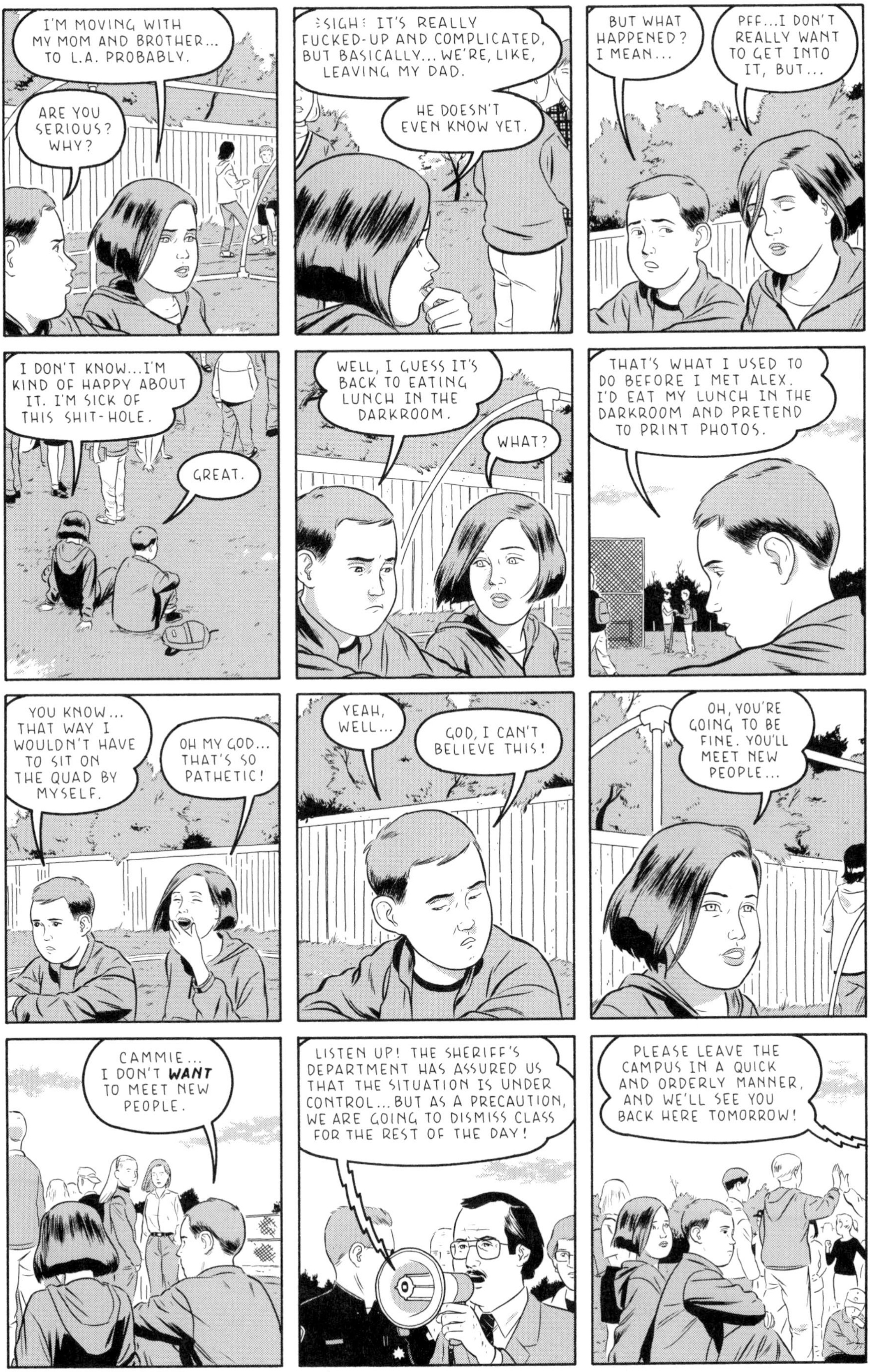

I'M MOVING WITH MY MOM AND BROTHER... TO L.A. PROBABLY.
ARE YOU SERIOUS? WHY?
⁝SIGH⁝ IT'S REALLY FUCKED-UP AND COMPLICATED, BUT BASICALLY... WE'RE, LIKE, LEAVING MY DAD.
HE DOESN'T EVEN KNOW YET.
BUT WHAT HAPPENED? I MEAN...
PFF...I DON'T REALLY WANT TO GET INTO IT, BUT...
I DON'T KNOW...I'M KIND OF HAPPY ABOUT IT. I'M SICK OF THIS SHIT-HOLE.
GREAT.
WELL, I GUESS IT'S BACK TO EATING LUNCH IN THE DARKROOM.
WHAT?
THAT'S WHAT I USED TO DO BEFORE I MET ALEX. I'D EAT MY LUNCH IN THE DARKROOM AND PRETEND TO PRINT PHOTOS.
YOU KNOW... THAT WAY I WOULDN'T HAVE TO SIT ON THE QUAD BY MYSELF.
OH MY GOD... THAT'S SO PATHETIC!
YEAH, WELL...
GOD, I CAN'T BELIEVE THIS!
OH, YOU'RE GOING TO BE FINE. YOU'LL MEET NEW PEOPLE...
CAMMIE... I DON'T **WANT** TO MEET NEW PEOPLE.
LISTEN UP! THE SHERIFF'S DEPARTMENT HAS ASSURED US THAT THE SITUATION IS UNDER CONTROL... BUT AS A PRECAUTION, WE ARE GOING TO DISMISS CLASS FOR THE REST OF THE DAY!
PLEASE LEAVE THE CAMPUS IN A QUICK AND ORDERLY MANNER, AND WE'LL SEE YOU BACK HERE TOMORROW!

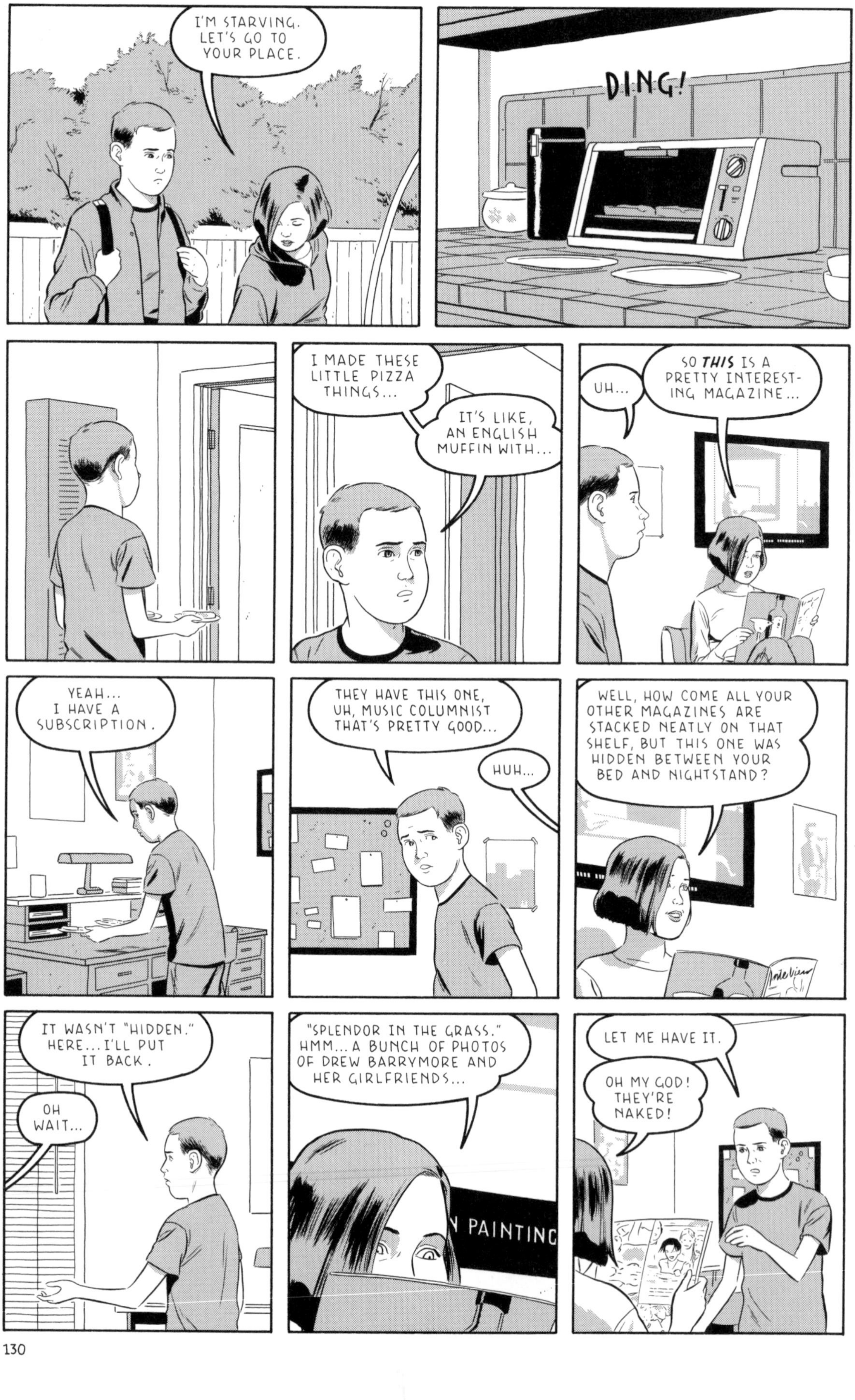

I'M STARVING. LET'S GO TO YOUR PLACE.
DING!
I MADE THESE LITTLE PIZZA THINGS...
IT'S LIKE, AN ENGLISH MUFFIN WITH...
UH...
SO THIS IS A PRETTY INTERESTING MAGAZINE...
YEAH... I HAVE A SUBSCRIPTION.
THEY HAVE THIS ONE, UH, MUSIC COLUMNIST THAT'S PRETTY GOOD...
HUH...
WELL, HOW COME ALL YOUR OTHER MAGAZINES ARE STACKED NEATLY ON THAT SHELF, BUT THIS ONE WAS HIDDEN BETWEEN YOUR BED AND NIGHTSTAND?
IT WASN'T "HIDDEN." HERE... I'LL PUT IT BACK.
OH WAIT...
"SPLENDOR IN THE GRASS." HMM... A BUNCH OF PHOTOS OF DREW BARRYMORE AND HER GIRLFRIENDS...
N PAINTING
LET ME HAVE IT.
OH MY GOD! THEY'RE NAKED!

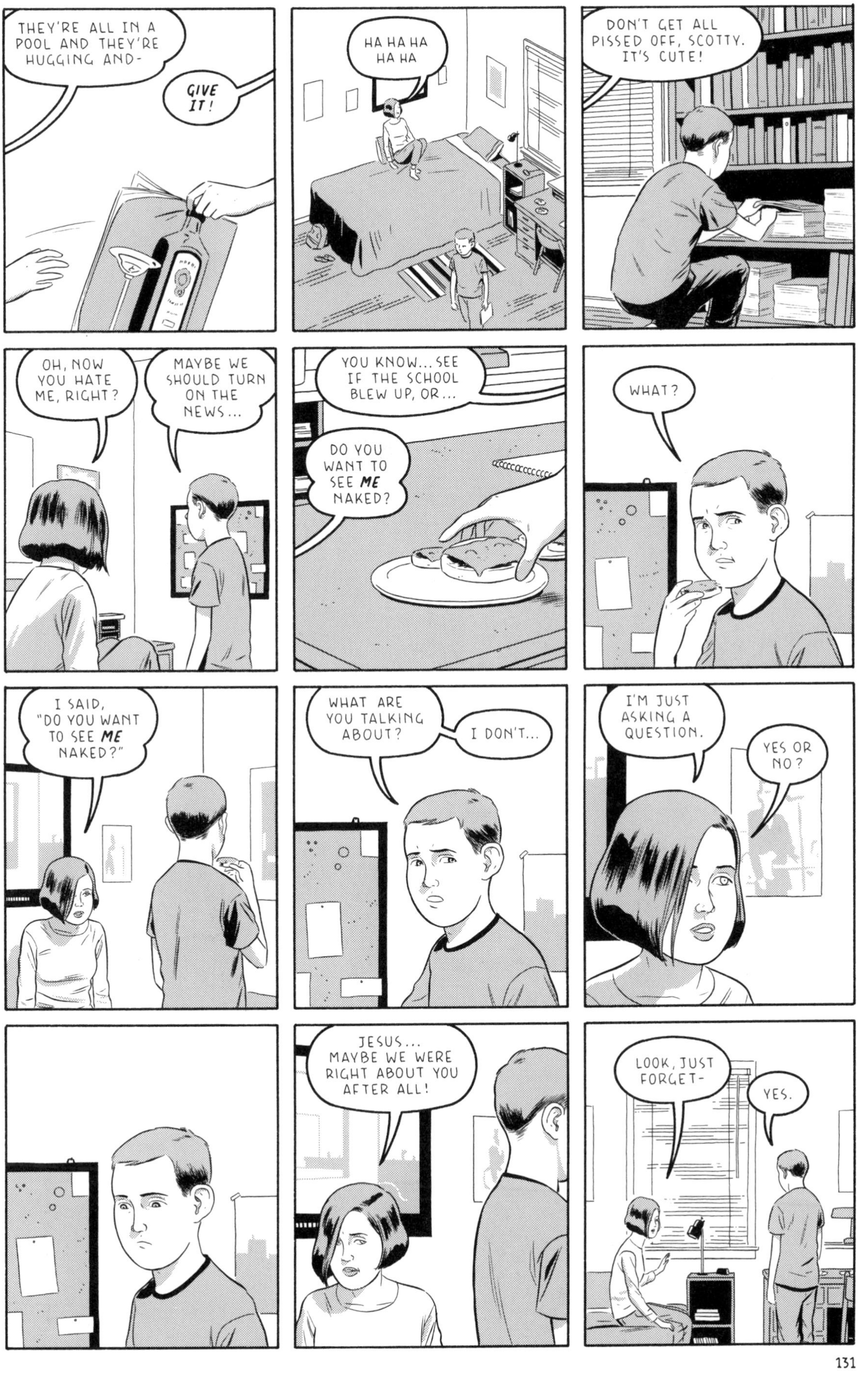
THEY'RE ALL IN A POOL AND THEY'RE HUGGING AND-
GIVE IT!
HA HA HA HA HA
DON'T GET ALL PISSED OFF, SCOTTY. IT'S CUTE!
OH, NOW YOU HATE ME, RIGHT?
MAYBE WE SHOULD TURN ON THE NEWS...
YOU KNOW... SEE IF THE SCHOOL BLEW UP, OR...
DO YOU WANT TO SEE ME NAKED?
WHAT?
I SAID, "DO YOU WANT TO SEE ME NAKED?"
WHAT ARE YOU TALKING ABOUT?
I DON'T...
I'M JUST ASKING A QUESTION.
YES OR NO?
JESUS... MAYBE WE WERE RIGHT ABOUT YOU AFTER ALL!
LOOK, JUST FORGET-
YES.

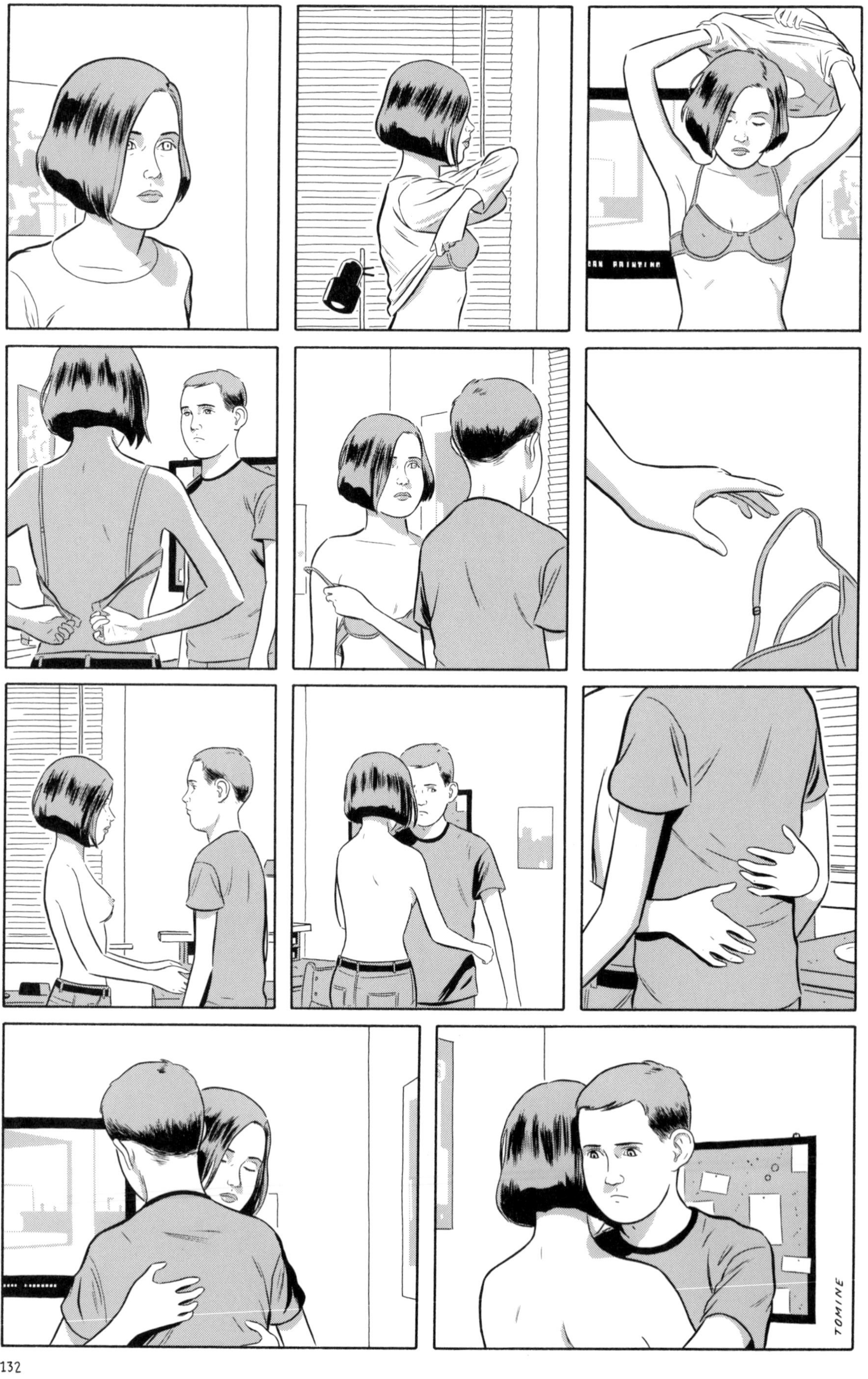
TOMINE

ACKNOWLEDGMENTS

Thank you to Chris Oliveros, John Kuramoto, Dan Raeburn, Jeff Voris, Amy Favreau, Carson Hall, Claudine Ko, Mark Everett, cartoonist pals, and, most of all, the inestimable Wendy Jung.